Yes,
We Did

The Southern Argument
for Progressive Change

Linda Hansen

PROGRESSIVE JOURNAL PUBLISHING

The Pageland Progressive Journal
Pageland, S.C.

Acclaim for **Linda Hansen**

Yes, We Did

"Readers unfamiliar with Hansen's writing will very quickly come to enjoy the whip-smart insights she serves up in her very own southern-fried crackling prose. What they will come to savor, however, especially today, in the era of a billion blogs, is the genuine reflection and rich life experience that guides the writing. Hansen's well-informed convictions have made her a stand-out progressive political columnist in South Carolina, but they have also made her something even more rare: an exceptional writer."

— John Tomasic,
managing editor of The Huffington Post, OffTheBus

"This writer — at the peak of her powers — is a woman of incredibly rich experiences, both good and bad. Superb intelligence, humor and deep compassion, along with the ability to write movingly and logically, moves the reader to accept her conclusions. An avid reader all her life, she can remember it all and call upon this for the apt quote or illustrative anecdote. As a writer, and as a human being, she stands far above almost everyone else."

— Betty M. Sowell,
former editor of The Pageland Journal

"In the war of the words during Election '08 — when Americans faced a choice between real change or fears as old as our republic — Linda Hansen's convictions and rapid-fire insights burned straight to our hearts and souls. Southern progressives have worn a special badge of courage in the battle for social and political change, and Hansen upholds that tradition beautifully. In Yes, We Did: The Southern Argument for Progressive Change, Hansen shows us why the pen is mightier than the sword."

— Tananarive Due, American Book Award winner, co-author of Freedom in the Family: A Mother-Daughter Memoir of the Fight for Civil Rights *(with Patricia Stephens Due)*

Acclaim for **Linda Hansen**

"On the subject of writing, sportswriter Red Smith once said, 'Writing is easy. All you do is sit down ... and open a vein.' All wordsmiths understand the trepidation and exhilaration of opening that vein in our work, but few writers know what Linda Hansen knows; that to see her words in print is to commit an act of political courage, to open herself not just to potential rejection or criticism, but to face rage, ridicule, and personal attacks simply for writing the truth. Her words are brave, funny, insightful, wise, and always, always true. Just like Linda is, herself."

— *Deanie Mills, author of* Faces of Evil *and* Ordeal

"This rabble-rouser with a heart of gold thoughtfully and fearlessly probes Southern understandings of gender, race, family, and history, and their impact on the region's political discourse.

"Alternately witty and moving, without ever descending into cynicism, Linda Hansen has drawn on an observant eye, lived geographical and historical knowledge, and her rapport with those she writes about to create a body of work that insightfully chronicles the anxieties and hopes of the New South."

— *Neil Nagraj, producer, The Huffington Post, OffTheBus*

"I've known this remarkable writer for a very short time, but it doesn't take a long time to recognize her talent. Her keen insight teamed with her ability to express herself, and her sense of humor, are apparent in her outstanding columns."

— *Eddie Sweatt,*
former editor and publisher of The Cheraw Chronicle

*For Betty Sowell and Eddie Sweatt, two retired
Southern journalists whose work serves as examples
of the highest journalistic standards. Both editors
of South Carolina newspapers in the mid-twentieth
century, Betty and Eddie had the courage to speak
the truth to power, arguing for the dignity, equality
and freedom of all Americans during the Civil
Rights Era. It was no easy task in the Deep South.*

*You have been, and remain,
my constant inspiration.*

Introduction

Yes, we can.

That simple declarative, early on, became the mantra of the Obama Campaign. If ever an unembellished, three word sentence carried multiple meanings for multiple people, this was the one.

For the candidate, his staff and core supporters, it meant "Yes, we can rise above the pseudo-issues of race, age, religion, naiveté and 'Got experience?'; yes, we can rise above the naysayers, pollsters and pundits, who tell us the numbers are not on our side now and never will be."

For minority Americans it meant "Yes, we can, in today's America, elect a president based upon the content of his character rather than the color of his skin."

For millions of frustrated liberals, disillusioned independents and conservatives, who were committed to other candidates seeking the Democratic nomination, the words "Yes, we can" resonated nonetheless. "Yes, we can rise above poisonous, petty, personal politics and take our country back from the far-right brink."

Here, in the Deep South, there were believers, too. Progressives and independents who desperately wanted change. Positive, progressive change. We were willing to do whatever we could to end the era of the Bush Doctrine; of senseless, endless war; of corporate greed and cronyism; of Bush tax cuts, shamelessly weighted on the wrong end of the economic scale; of the sullying of the American brand of democracy worldwide.

But we enjoyed no sure declarative. In this bona fide Red Zone we progressives are a true minority. This calcified Southern Bloc wholly rejected the word "liberal" on March 15, 1965 — the day President Lyndon Baines Johnson signed the Voting Rights Act into law. Nothing has changed since. The best we Southern seekers of progressive change could muster sounded mighty like a question:

Yes, we can?

Oh, we worked for change here. Each of us offered up what time and talent we had during Campaign 2008. The South hadn't seen so much flaming liberal writing, rallying, canvassing and phone-banking in decades. In generations. *Ever.*

There was a national momentum building for progressive change. That was fact. That was clear. But we Southerners harbor the notion that, like the weather, social change fronts begin in some far-off, nether-zone like California and move East. And we know there's something funky about the Southeastern cultural/political jet stream: the damn thing always rears up at the wrong time — and all that sunny socio-political weather we've been hankering for goes right over our heads and moves up the coast to the Northeast.

Southern liberals have grown accustomed to bad political weather. We've grown accustomed to losing. Those of us who write political commentary from the progressive point of view have been arguing for change for years, despite the apparent futility of such an endeavor. Despite the fact that our collective point of view makes us about as popular as a passel of skunks at a picnic. It has been, at best, an exercise in frustration. At its worst, it's been right irritating when we met an implacable wall of deafness or denial or outright denunciation.

George W. Bush & Co. ushered in a new (and narrow) era in more ways than one. The political climate, no matter where a writer worked and lived, turned toxic. The push-back from the White House was shameful — and shamefully effective. Question public policy? Criticize George W.'s war? His tax cuts? His love affair with a greedy, unregulated corporate America? The moral validity of an administration pandering to the wealthy? Extraordinary rendition? Black sites? Violating FISA? In a Republican era of absolute neoconservative good vs. absolute liberal evil, any hard question, any direct criticism, got us labeled. We were un-patriotic, unAmerican, Godless heathens who loved al Qaeda and hated our troops. The South was particularly vulnerable to the right-wing-name-game vilification of journalists who challenged the GOParty line. It was enough to make us pick up our rhetorical marbles and go home.

Almost.

Election 2004 made us angry. By 2006 we were furious and even here, in the Deep South, the progressive press were pushing back. Hard.

The first, tentative whiff of Change was in the air. The public, it seemed, was as fed up with the D.C./GOP status quo as was the liberal media. Dubya's house of cards began to collapse. Conventional wisdom: A Democrat would likely win the White House in 2008.

Which one?

Enter a young, dynamic Senator Barack Obama. A visionary. An eloquent, inspiring intellectual candidate who, it appeared, had not lost (or sold) his soul. He was the anti-Bush. But so were a field of Democratic hopefuls vying for the nomination. Obama was, I thought, highly unlikely to win his party's nomination. But maybe, just maybe, this was the candidate who could accomplish the near-impossible. Maybe he could elevate political discourse in this country; haul our reigning Atwater/Rove hate-speech politics out of the gutter. And maybe he'd become the vice-president to Hillary's or John's presidency.

Got hope? Oh, yeah.

I chose to follow Senator Obama's candidacy, to write some of his campaign story. Not because I thought he'd win, but because I knew what we all knew in February 2007: His campaign would be the most important, the most historic one in our lifetimes. For those of us who came of age in the Jim Crow South, Barack Obama's ascendance as a leading candidate for president was something we never thought we'd live to see.

Summer, 2007. A small army of Obama for President staffers moved into the South. They were young, well-educated, energetic and idealistic. Field organizers moved into Southern cities and small towns. They came well-trained, with a collective community organizer mindset. This campaign, they told us, would be organized — and won — from the ground up.

The momentum for change, Barack Obama style, swept the nation. Millions of ordinary Americans hooked up online, joining My.BarackObama.com in support of their candidate. The grassroots movement of all time was emerging as a powerful voice for change.

Even here. In the South.

But still, Southern pragmatism trumped the national "Yes, we can" declarative.

I'd been writing liberal commentary for South Carolina's Progressive Journal since 2005. In September 2007 I began writing for the Huffington Post, OffTheBus as well. And, by that September, I was a believer in Barack Obama's candidacy and in his vision for America. In the main, I still doubted he could win either the Democratic nod or the presidency. While I had my moments, on the page, of absolute faith in the success of Obama's quest for the White House, "Yes, we can?" remained my mantra. Everyone knew the Solid South would remain solidly GOP.

There did come a moment, however, when I felt sure Senator Obama really could become the 44th president of the United States. Someone asked me, not long ago, when and where that defining moment happened. I didn't hesitate in responding: December 9, 2007, the balmy South Carolina day I stood in the press section at Williams-Brice Stadium in Columbia for the Obama/Oprah event. An astonishing 30,000 South Carolinians (and other Southerners) came together for that rally. It was a huge, multi-cultural crowd; an eager, enthusiastic powerhouse of Southern voters whose "Yes, we can" had no question mark at the end. To lift a phrase from the hymn "Amazing Grace," it was the hour I first believed.

In the general election the Southern Bloc cracked wide open. The South was no longer red; it was a healthy purple. Virginia, Florida and North Carolina broke ranks, voted Obama. In all, 18.6 million Southerners voted for Barack Obama. He won at least 40% of the vote in every Southern state except for Alabama and Arkansas, where he took 39% of the vote.

My home state, South Carolina, went McCain — but not by the 20% margin predicted in pre-election polls. The gap here, by election day, had narrowed to 9%. A comfortable GOP margin to be sure, but indicative of a Palmetto State no longer shackled to uber-conservative politics. In 2000, George W. beat Al Gore here by a 15.9% margin. In 2004? Bush over Kerry by 17.08%. In November 2008 a single-digit percentage point loss had never felt so much like a moral victory.

Southern progressives have long argued for change. I did my share of pleading and sniping. This book is an anthology of columns for The Pageland Progressive Journal and Huffington Post, written over several years, arguing against the policies of the far-right and for progressive change. I like to think we writers made some measurable impact on the vote down here; that we helped change the political conversation.

"Yes, we can?"

"Yes, we can."

Did we Southerners respond to the message of change and change a little ourselves? Did we South Carolinians, with a convincing 2-1 Democratic primary victory for Obama in January 2008, help turn the tide for his campaign? Did we make a difference? Yes. Yes. And yes.

Yes, we did.

Linda Hansen
Pageland, South Carolina
January, 2009

YES,
WE DID

**The Southern Argument
for Progressive Change**

Uncle Sam Wants You!
Well, Some of You, Anyway...

"We're transforming the military. The things I look for are the following: morale, retention and recruitment. And retention is high, recruitment is meeting goals and people are feeling strong about the mission." — George W. Bush

Right. "The things I look for..." Sounds like the president is getting all hands-on about the military. And, the way he tells it, he really doesn't have to — everything's just hunky-dory. He's only being conscientious. Or a wee bit deceptive. "We're transforming the military," alright. Thanks to journalists, Salon.com and the Freedom of Information Act, we know how it's being done.

Take "retention is high," for example. It's a fair statement when you consider as many as 50,000 soldiers/reservists have remained on extended active duty. That's a lot of troops. Morale? Maybe no so good. The Pentagon calls it "Stop-Loss," others call it the "Back-Door-Draft." You're in it, buddy — we need the numbers and no matter how badly you want to, you can't get out.

"Recruitment is meeting goals." Well, yeah, you might say that. Sort of. According to the Assistant Secretary of Defense for Public Affairs, 17 percent of 2005 recruits got into the military under waivers. That's a 42% increase since 2000. Or maybe not. It may be higher than that. Sources say the numbers might have been prettied up a bit. So what?

Waivers, pre-Iraq, meant something like, say, a ticket for jaywalking or opting not to feed the meter when you parked your car outside the bank. You broke some minor little traffic law but, other than that, you're clean. A good citizen. Besides, you scored in the upper 50 percent on the Military Aptitude Test. They gave you a waiver and sang a rousing chorus of "You're in the Army Now!" Fair enough. But that's not what's happening here and now. Waivers are flying like bullets outside the Green Zone. Convicted of DUI? No problem. Convicted of domestic abuse? No problem. How about possession of marijuana, drug paraphernalia and a stolen license plate? How about being on probation for breaking and entering? No sweat. No lie: Uncle Sam wants YOU.

He even wants you if you're a high school dropout without a GED — even if you score so near the bottom of the Military Aptitude Test your new nickname is "Low-crawl Louie" and you think "Baghdad" is the brown paper sack your pappy's six-pack came in.

All we have to do to meet recruitment goals and boost morale is dig a hole so deep lowering the standards for military service you can get authentic Chinese take-out from there. Handing loaded weapons to folks with drug, alcohol and anger management issues ought to keep everybody happy — and safe. Test scores? You don't have to be Einstein to be IED fodder in Iraq.

BUT. If you're an Arab/Farsi speaking Phi Beta Kappa with an advanced degree in thermonuclear physics, a double minor in ballistics technology and Middle Eastern psychology, with no criminal record...and you're gay...there ain't a back door big enough for you to serve your country, honey. Morale and all. Who knows what you might do with a gun?

We have to draw the damned line somewhere.

American Idle:
The Case for Administrative R&R

April 18, 2006

How can the Bush White House make one bungled move after another? They've cruised from "Harriet Miers is qualified — really she is..." to the Dubai Ports debacle, losing support, even from their own party, on every leg of the trip. This administration has been called everything from inept and corrupt to having a tin ear for policy matters. The latest? We have too much federal debt to borrow more money? Raise the debt ceiling to $8.99 trillion and think like any used car salesman would: Don't say $9 trillion when $8.99 trillion sounds so much better.

What's going on here?

Bush & Co. are tired. All that stress. Running the country aground, spending the surplus, fighting two wars, scaring the pants off the public, keeping secrets, stifling scandals, fumbling around before (during and after) Katrina, spinning news like a cheap washer, raising GOP cash and racing to keep your job/ power base intact. It's exhausting. Really. When your Veep is so tired he can't tell a hunting buddy from a bird, you've got problems. And that's the new spin out of D.C.: This administration has worked so hard they can't think straight. Maybe there's some truth to it.

This president has told us he doesn't read newspapers. He depends on his inner circle, those same cronies he's surrounded himself with for years and years, to tell him what's going on in the world. So the same old handful of folks get stuck doing everything — and then they have to explain it all to the Boss. Maybe they never get a day off. Maybe their brains have been

Bushwhacked.

This Commander-in-Chief, however, needs his rest. He doesn't work weekends. He goes to bed with the Capitol Hill chickens. He takes off a couple of hours most every day to work out. And, in the first four years of his presidency, Dubya took about 335 vacation days (365 days, remember, is a full year). As of August 2005, this president had spent roughly 25% of his time at his Crawford, Texas ranch. That's where he was spending the month of August before 9/11, when he got the PDB warning him that al Qaeda was determined to strike the U.S. — and would likely use airplanes to do it.

That's where he was when he was warned about Katrina, that the levees might well be compromised; where he said not to worry. We're ready! And folks, it doesn't matter one whit to the people of New Orleans whether the levees were breached or over-topped. A cataclysmic flood is a cataclysmic flood. To those who died, to those who lost family, friends and everything they owned, the lame defense that Bush's warning said "over-topped" rather than "breached" is as ridiculous as it sounds. Unless you're on vacation. And your mind's on other things. Like riding your bike or golf or clearing your damned brush.

Maybe Dubya's staff is bushed. Maybe they're worn slap out. And maybe it's time for some fresh blood up there. One thing's certain: We've had about enough of the gang who couldn't shoot — or think — straight.

Splendor in the Gas:
Living in the Golden Age of Big Oil

May 16, 2006

Exxon CEO Lee Raymond is retiring. He's headed his company for about 12 years now and he's been well paid to do it. His paycheck for post 9/11, post-Katrina 2005? $51.5 million. That's about $141,000 a day. $6,000 per hour.

His retirement package? $400 million. Safe to say Mr. Raymond won't be too concerned over the plight of Social Security or Medicare or the impact of prescription drug prices on a fixed income.

They say he's worth it. Under his management Exxon made a $36 billion profit in 2005; the largest of any corporation in history. And they're right on target to do it again in 2006. In fact, all the American oil companies and their top execs are enjoying the same prosperity. They say they have it coming. They work hard for their money and this is what a free market economy is all about. What's more American than success?

Try greed. In the face of spiraling federal debt, soaring health care costs for working Americans who can't afford them, millions with no health insurance at all, a war costing taxpayers hundreds of billions with no end in sight, outsourcing of jobs and lay-offs, that kind of profit, salary and benefits are obscene. Inflating gas prices to line your own pockets by the billion is not profit. It's profiteering.

The Bush administration says we can expect no real relief for three years. Josh Bolton, the new White House chief of staff, says, "There's no magic bullet." The president declares, "There's no magic wand." Congress bickers over who's at fault while they tool around Washington in their SUVs and Town Cars. They'd have us believe there's nothing they can do about big oil companies.

Why not Iraq 'em? These bullies are terrorizing us at the pump. And this president, this congress, don't put up with that kind of thing — right? "They're either with us, or they're with the terrorists!" Sound familiar? And that's who else makes a major profit on all this imported oil. The cash goes to Middle Eastern countries who don't much like Americans.

So…we start with sanctions: Freeze oil company assets like we did al Qaeda's and Iraq's. Then we send in the troops. Overthrow their axis-of-evil leadership. Tell them we're not there to occupy oil companies, but to liberate them from cruel, corrupt dictatorships which oppress the public. All those hundreds of billions of profit and benefits dollars could be seized, used to shore up Social Security, reform the ailing health care system and poured into a serious effort to find alternative sources of energy. Free us from our sick addiction to oil.

Then we tax gas-guzzling behemoths right off the market. Force auto makers to build and sell smaller, fuel efficient cars. We make hybrids practical, available and affordable; give tax breaks — big ones — to folks who buy them. We win hearts and minds, make conservation attractive and mandatory.

Make it all patriotic, for Pete's sake! If this bunch running government isn't good at much else, they're masters at defining what's unAmerican and what isn't. They need to get on the terrorist offensive. Now. And start with Lee Raymond and Exxon.

The Madness of King George: Making Up the Rules As He Goes

May 23, 2006

"It takes a lot of degeneration before a country falls into dictatorship, but we should avoid these ends by avoiding these beginnings." — Former Supreme Court Justice Sandra Day O'Connor, Georgetown University, March 2006

Ms. O'Connor was referring to the gathering dangers she saw in current "...judicial reforms driven by nakedly partisan reasoning...those who would strong-arm the judiciary into adopting their preferred policies." The same warning applies to an administration which ignores the judiciary — and the law — altogether.

Only months ago the White House was taken to task for illegal domestic wiretapping, for side-stepping the FISA court and the warrants required by law for electronic spying. Constitutional experts cried foul. Bush got a pass. Why? His party controls both houses of Congress...he's only protecting America...he's doing this for our own good...he's President-In-Wartime and that gives him the power to do as he sees fit. Why is warrantless wiretapping suddenly legal? Because George W. Bush says it is. Besides, this was a very narrow operation which targeted only known terrorists.

"In other words," George W. told us, "one end of the communication must be outside the United States." So, you had to be a foreigner — or talking to one — to get caught up in the catch-a-terrorist net. That's what he said. Real Americans, who didn't fool around with suspicious strangers, didn't have to worry about lists or invasion of privacy.

It wasn't true. Now we find out the NSA has been secretly

collecting information about the telephone calls of millions and millions of us, keeping records of every call we make — across town or across the country. They've been doing it since 2001. BellSouth, AT&T and Verizon have all cooperated, turning over every scrap of information the NSA demanded.

Qwest balked. Their lawyers weren't sure all this "sharing" was entirely legal. The NSA turned up the heat. They told Qwest they were the only holdout; they told them their refusal to do their part in building the database might compromise national security. And then the NSA suggested that failure to cooperate might just mean Qwest would have a little trouble getting future government contracts...

So Qwest's legal staff asked the NSA to take the request to the FISA court. No deal. The NSA said they didn't want to do that. The court might not go along with the program. Qwest, concerned about their own liability, then asked for a letter of authorization from the U.S. Attorney General's office. The NSA refused that, too.

George Washington University constitutional law expert, Jonathan Turley, says of President Bush, "He believes he has the inherent right to violate the law." Turley wonders what Bush was thinking when he took the Oath of Office, pledging to "...support and defend the Constitution..."

This pattern of governance does not serve to protect America. When the laws which ensure democracy are twisted, mangled and broken, when power is usurped by a single branch of government, we no longer have a democratically elected president. We have a dictator. Or a king.

The Land of Milk and Money:
The Promised Land is a Gated Community

May 30, 2006

Yippee! Mid-term elections are only six months away, voters are unhappy with Congress, the president's approval rating hits 31% and that's below freezing...what to do?

Give the masses another tax cut. They just love it when we do that! Everybody's happy when they've got a little extra cash to spend!

And that's exactly what it is for the vast majority of Americans. A little extra cash. Very little. Miniscule.

We're getting a $70 billion tax cut. A big break for the capital gains crowd. A break for families who might have to pay the Alternate Minimum Tax. There's something for everyone. Sort of. Most of us don't have enough money in our investment portfolios to see relief through capital gains breaks. The Alternate Minimum Tax, in the main, targets upper-middle income families. The rest of us? If your annual income is between $20-30 thousand, you'll net about $9. If you're bringing in upwards of $50 thousand you can look for, maybe, somewhere between $46 and $100.

So what's so great about this tax cut? Well, if you're raking in a million dollars or more a year, honey, you'll average upwards of $42,000.

Let's not look the proverbial gift horse in the mouth. Look at it this way: On the income scale, if you fall in the $20-30,000 category, you can afford to buy one and one-half pairs of rubber flip-flops at Walmart. You make more like $50,000? You can afford between nine and eighteen pounds of fresh

T-bone steaks at Bi-Lo — but it only works if you go right now and have your BonusCard with you for the $5-off-per-lb sale.

You're a millionaire? You can buy two new Pontiac G-6 Vibes at Lawrence Chevrolet for $46,000. It's a neat little car, too. Handles well, gets around 36-40 mpg. You cannot, however, afford the new red Corvette in the showroom. Sorry. But we all have to suffer a little when the federal debt is reaching critical mass.

What a country! The more you make, the more you make. Whether you need it or not. Just say the magic words "tax cut" and folks get all misty-eyed and grateful. Most of us don't bother to ask where the money's going. And, if someone does ask — like last time — George W. (millionaire category) will tell us, once again, that the bulk of his tax cuts go to working- and middle-class Americans.

The first time he made that claim I accused him of lying. But I've had time to think about it; to do the math, if you will. Here's how I think he figures it: Don't count the cash! Count the number of folks who get cash back! It's ingenious. You can give, say, 85% of $70 billion to those who make a million or more a year and 15% to everybody else. It looks like somebody's pandering to the wealthy, right? Yeah. But if we say, for the sake of argument, that out of a U.S. population of three hundred million, there are 9.3 million millionaires and about 290 million working- and middle-class Americans, then it doesn't really matter who's really getting most of the money. It's obvious that far more average Americans than rich ones are getting tax cuts. See?

Feel better?

Shock and Aw-w-w!
The Bush Meltdown at G8

July 25, 2006

He's THE DECIDER. He said so himself. It's safe to assume then, that when the leaders of the Big 8 industrialized nations met in Russia, our leader decided — all by himself — what he'd say. Decided how he'd behave with the world watching. And listening.

Here's how the United States looked and sounded on the world stage:

Bush made it clear he intended to take Vladimir Putin to task for backsliding in fostering real democracy in Russia. During a joint press conference with Putin, after being asked by a journalist how that planned lecture went, George W. hemmed and hawed and rambled and, finally, said America just wants Russia to enjoy the same democracy we're affording Iraq. A free press, freedom of religion. All that good stuff. He couldn't have set himself up better for a snappy, sarcastic comeback if he'd hired Jon Stewart to write for him.

Putin's response? He did a classic double-take and said the last thing Russia wants is the kind of democracy we're seeing in Iraq. Bush looked stunned. The whole room erupted in laughter. Then we heard a petulant voice over the crowd: "Just wait!" It was our president speaking; the politics of the playground, the semantics of the sand box. At least he didn't holler "Nanny-nanny-boo-boo, you old poopy-pants!"

Before we have a chance to stop blushing, Bush has his little "open mic moment" with Britain's Tony Blair, and the world hears the Born Again President of the United States saying, "Hezbollah needs to stop doing this shit!" Jeez, Louise! Frat boy potty-mouth — and only a year after he signed the Broadcast Decency Act to protect America's children (and the rest of us, I suppose) from foul language on TV. The BDA imposes a $325 thousand fine for cursing on the airwaves. So pony up, Mr. President. Wash your mouth out with soap.

And ask your mother how crude it looks when you talk dirty with your mouth full. You said (expletive deleted) around a huge, gross hunk of your supper.

Then, while the Middle East blows sky-high, due, in part, to this administration's "hands-off" policy about the perpetual Israeli-Palestinian crisis, The Decider gets hands-on. With German Chancellor Angela Merkel. This bit of video is stunning. Really. Bush strides into the room, heads straight for Merkel and starts giving her a two-handed neck and shoulder massage. Her reaction said it all: A jolt, a look of disbelief and distaste, and a no-nonsense pulling away, a hands-in-the-air rebuff. Dadgum, Dubya! This woman is the duly elected leader of one of the G8 nations — not some pom-pom girl at a football banquet! You get a ten yard penalty for inappropriate touching.

Some of us are pretty sure this president isn't the sharpest stinger on a bee's bottom. We no longer look to him for eloquence or profound thought. Or even the ability to string a few words together without a gaffe. But we do expect a little common sense, clean language and decent manners when he's in public. When he's representing American ideals.

When he's representing us.

Pampers, Huggies and Baby Wipes:
The real reason America can't get out of Iraq

June 27, 2006

Disposable diapers, I've whined for years, have ruined this country.

I was joking — sort of — and referring, primarily, to an accelerating divorce rate. The issue, however, is broader in scope. Bear with me, here.

My first child was born in 1970. Pampers were fairly new while he was a baby. Huggies hadn't even come along yet. The whole idea of disposable diapers was as liberating for young mothers as the notion of overthrowing a ham-fisted tyrant (one with a mean streak and a yen for WMD).

Imagine how we felt. The baby poops and in three easy steps you're done with the doo-doo. Take off the Pampers, wipe the kid's butt and toss the whole nasty wad in the trash. Not the baby, of course. You kept him; freshly diapered, smiling and smelling like Johnson & Johnson... And you went back to your Harlequin Romance.

The allure of disposability had never been so evident, so attractive.

The whole thing snowballed. I still believe the toss-it-when-soiled mindset impacted badly on marriage, but there was worse to come. After Pampers, we were sure, if something got stinky, we could always throw it out and get a fresh one.

Being a born-again liberal in 1970 meant that, while I coveted both disposability and freedom from responsibility, I worried about it. Liberals, by nature, feel guilty about every-thing. And something about wrapping my baby in plastic all the time — then adding that plastic to the chemical stew in the local landfill — really bothered me. So I had four dozen cloth diapers for my son. I used cloth during the day, Pampers only at night. It was a nifty compromise. I did a little for the environment and, ever the fiscal conservative, I saved money.

That compromise meant daytime diapering wasn't of the three-easy-steps-and-you're-free variety. I did, however, learn a valuable lesson:

If you want the baby, sometimes you have to get your hands dirty. Cloth diapers clogged with urine and baby poop have to be cleaned up before you toss them on the laundry pile and get on with your day. This means you're up to your elbows in the toilet, scraping the ka-ka, flushing, scraping and rinsing again, flushing again. And you can't let go of that diaper. No way. No matter how slimy it is or how bad it smells. If you do, it'll go down the toilet, clog up your pipes, stink up your house and get you a plumbing bill you hadn't counted on and can't afford.

What does all this have to do with Iraq? Under Dubya's leadership, we invaded with a Pampers, Huggies and Baby Wipes war plan. Three quick steps and we'd be out of there. Yank Saddam, wipe and toss. The baby would be clean and happy. Easy.

But we've ended up with a screaming brat we can't control and don't want — and an enormous, slimy, stinking cloth dia-per-full. We're up to our elbows in the crapper and if we let go now…well, the back-up of all that sewage isn't an option we're quite prepared to deal with, is it? Turns out there was nothing disposable about invading Iraq. George W. Bush and his neocon buddies wanted that baby. In the worst way. They got it.

Now we're all left holding the dirty diaper. We have to keep scraping and flushing and hanging on, no matter how we feel about it, until the kid smells good and smiles.

Another Election Year's Usual Fun & Games: Playing Trivial Pursuit

August 8, 2006

And here we are: The Middle East in meltdown mode. A nuclear North Korea making threats, firing off missiles. Iraq's "civil-war-that-isn't-really" bloodier by the day. Iran growling at the West, going nuclear. Afghanistan suffering the resurgence of the Taliban. Somalia in the hands of radical Islamists. Relations with Russia going sour as Bush finds out he couldn't "see into Putin's soul" after all. Popular elections, worldwide, going to whichever candidate is most vehemently anti-American. The cost of war in the hundreds of billions with no way out. Spiraling debt here at home. Gas prices soaring. Climate change wreaking havoc.

Scandals, about everything from the selling of America to lobbyists to a secretive White House skirting the law for power under the guise of keeping us safe, break so often we can't keep them straight.

Even some hard-core neocons are worried about the direction American foreign policy has taken.

Chairman of the House Intelligence Committee, Peter

Hoekstra (R-Mich.), blasts the administration for failing to brief his committee on "significant" intelligence programs as required by law. "Some people within the intelligence community brought to my attention some programs they believed we had not been briefed on. They were right," Hoekstra said. "We have [only] now been briefed..." he went on. "I wanted to reinforce to the president and to the executive branch and the intelligence community how important, and by law, the requirement [is] that they keep the legislative branch informed of what they are doing." No president, Hoekstra declared, has the right to ignore that law.

Serious stuff. Will we be led to examine all this, to vote wisely in November's mid-term election? I doubt it. What we're apt to get is a rousing game of Trivial Pursuit. It's already underway. "Hot Button! Hot Button! Let's amend the constitution! Make new laws we desperately need to save America! No gay marriage! No flag burning! Anything that flames is a threat to the very survival of the American family!"

Well, honey, the world's on fire. And so is the financial security of most American families. Let's deal with the enormity of what's truly threatening us first. We can haggle over hot buttons and who's most morally pure after we put out the real fires that endanger us all.

I suspect no one on the Hill is listening. There's a litany of "The ends justify the means" coming from the White House. The old bait and switch game's in play. The shill games that divert attention; you watch the con man yank a gaudy bunch of paper flowers from his hat and miss the fact he's picked your pocket.

And here come the requisite cheerleaders, marching in lockstep toward the edge of the cliff, shouting: "Smear 'em on the

Left! Scare 'em on the Right! Who needs discourse? FIGHT, FIGHT, FIGHT!"

We deserve better. We'll get it only when we refuse to play the game.

Victory in Afghanistan:
The Dearth of a Nation

September 12, 2006

"As a result of the U.S. military, Taliban is no longer in existence and the people of Afghanistan are free." — *George W. Bush, September 2004*

Given the debacle in Iraq, given the Pentagon's own report stating the violent insurgency is growing there, given that the outlook for avoiding civil war is gloomier by the day, we have to look somewhere else to find something this administration has done right. It's not the economy or oil policy or the environment. It's not a president who's "a uniter, not a divider." It's not "restoring honor and dignity to the White House" or a scandal-free administration. It's certainly not the response to Katrina and the ravaged Gulf Coast. Nor is it accountability for their actions.

It's Afghanistan.

As Bush tells it "...the people of Afghanistan are building a modern and peaceful government." We sure won that one! Didn't manage to catch Osama — but we won the war, destroyed the Taliban and restored hope and sanity to a beleaguered nation.

Almost. It takes an economy to fuel a new government. Afghanistan is very busy making money these days. Last year they enjoyed a record yield of the crop they export for profit. Opium. 6,100 tons of it. Enough to make 610 tons of heroin. In 2005, 257,000 acres of farmland were devoted to the opium poppy crop. Today there are 407,700 acres producing opium. Their bumper crop is enough to drive down the price of heroin. A boon to drug dealers and addicts everywhere.

Much of the opium is being grown in the lawless Helmand province, a place wracked by a resurgence of Taliban-led militants. Their yield is up 162% and, according to a Western counter-narcotics agent, the Taliban is profiting from the trade. Drug traffickers are providing money and vehicles for terrorist attacks.

As conditions in Afghanistan deteriorate, President Hamid Karzai says the statistics on the resurgence of the drug trade are "...a disappointment. Our efforts to fight narcotics have proved inadequate."

Here's the new, improved Afghanistan: The "extinct" Taliban rises again. Violence, crime and terrorism are on the increase. A drug-based economy, with profits going to Islamic militants rather than to a "free and democratically elected government," flourishes. Osam Bin Laden roams free, planning the next strike against the U.S. and Britain.

No American doubted the legitimacy of taking action against Taliban-led Afghanistan after 9/11. That regime allowed al Qaeda terrorist camps to recruit and train extremists there. They sheltered Bin Laden, who openly admitted he and his thugs planned and executed the 9/11 attacks against this country. We invaded. So what went wrong?

The Bush/Cheney/Rumsfeld cabal pulled the bulk of troops out of Afghanistan before the job was done. After all, they had absolute, no-doubt-about-it, "slam-dunk" proof that Saddam had WMD, was in cahoots with al Qaeda planning 9/11 — and that a strike against the U.S. "in the shape of a mushroom cloud" was imminent.

We didn't build a peaceful, democratic nation in Afghanistan. We still aren't. Bush fiddles with the disaster in Iraq while Afghanistan burns.

One Fish, Two Fish ... Red Fish, Blue Fish

Oct 31, 2006

Dr. Seuss penned those words. His books were among my children's favorites. And mine. They were clever; they told us something about ourselves. Recently, we adults have been handed our own skewed version of Dr. Seuss's tale: Win State, Lose State ... Red State, Blue State.

We're no longer a multi-colored, multi-cultural map. We've become a politicized map of red or blue states. Seems there's no middle ground. We're labeled by color. Pre-sorted, tagged, set aside. We've allowed the Red State, Blue State mentality to define us. Red states are filled with people of faith; high-minded, morally superior, family-values folks who are right ... and Right. Blue states, sadly, are full of Godless left-wing liberals who are soft on crime, anti-family, unpatriotic Cut-and-Runners without courage or real values.

We like our labels. We like the certainty that we are who we are — and those of us in red states are surely a cut above those other folks. That certainty makes it much easier to vote. Go Red — Go Values.

All that glitters is not necessarily a string of priceless rubies.

Statistics from the Bureau of Justice, the National Center for Health Statistics, the Division of Vital Statistics, tell an interesting tale about Red State, Blue State.

● Of the ten states with the highest incarceration rates (2003), nine were red, one was blue. South Carolina ranked 6th.

● Of the ten states with the highest female incarceration rates (2003), all ten were red.

● Of the ten states with the highest execution rates (2004), all ten were red. South Carolina ranked 6th.

● Of the fifteen states with the highest rates of death by firearms (2003), all fifteen were red. South Carolina ranked 11th.

● Of the fifteen states with the highest suicide rates (2003), fourteen were red, one was blue.

● Of the eleven states with the highest-grossing gambling markets — excluding Native American gaming — (2005), eight were red, three were blue.

● Of the ten states with the highest divorce rates (2004), all ten were red.

● Of the ten states with the highest rates of illegitimate births (2003), nine were red, one was blue. South Carolina ranked 6th.

Well, now. There's a moral to every story. This one is clear: Contrary to conventional wisdom, red states have not cornered the market on moral rectitude or right-mindedness. Blue states have not been swallowed up by sin, vice and violence. The Keys to the Kingdom are not red; they're not stamped "Conservatives Only."

In his 2004 address to the Democratic National Convention Barack Obama said, "There is not a liberal America and a conservative America — there is the United States of America." It's time we remembered that. Neither red nor blue philosophy holds the sole solution to every problem, the single right answer for every wrong. Only a fool buys into the myth that one philosophy — one party — represents "values" and the other does not. It's cheap rhetoric. It's dishonest.

We've had enough of Red Fool, Blue Fool divisiveness. We're smarter than that now. Smart enough to think before we vote. Who's misled us? Who's accountable? More importantly, who's the boss?

We are. Dump the false, color-coded labels. Vote for positive change.

Malice in Wonderland: Fears, Smears and Leers

Nov. 7, 2006

Tick, tick, tick ...

A ticking bomb ... Bin Laden onscreen, threatening to kill us all ... a mushroom cloud ... the voice-over: "These are the stakes." The message? Vote Republican or get nuked. Bin Laden couldn't be happier. He's getting national airtime free of charge. Al Qaeda doesn't have to bother terrorizing America. In the run-up to the election, the GOP will do it for them.

A bare-shouldered white actress — hired to play the part — oozes lust from the screen. She met Tennessee candidate for senate Harold Ford Jr. at a Playboy party, she croons. "Call me, Harold," she purrs. The message? Harold Ford Jr.

happens to be black. You get the picture. One negative ad aimed at both racists and folks who hear "Playboy" and think "orgy." Did she meet or have a fling with the candidate? No. Did Harold Ford once attend a Playboy-sponsored Super Bowl Party? Yes. Ford says so himself. He went. He's single. He likes football. He likes girls. Dale Earnhardt Jr. drives a beer-sponsored race car. Does that mean he speeds and drives drunk? No.

A woman in silhouette performs an erotic dance. A voice-over warns us that Rep. Ron Kind (D-Wis) pays for sex ... The message? Ron Kind hires prostitutes. Does he? No. He opposed a move to stop funding for research on the subject at the NIH.

In New York, an ad accuses democratic candidate Michael Acuri of billing US taxpayers for phone sex. The truth? An aide, dialing a government office, got the wrong number. The phone numbers were identical but for a single digit. He hung up in seconds and dialed the correct number — it's all on the records. The cost of the misdial? $1.25.

Rush Limbaugh, his ignorance of the ailment as evident as his blustering right-wing bias, goes after Michael J. Fox for "going off his medication" so his Parkinson's tremors will worsen for TV ... or for faking it altogether. After all, Fox is an actor. The truth? Those terrible tremors are a side-effect of drug therapy for Parkinson's disease.

A study of TV ads in the top 101 markets, done by the non-partisan FactCheck.org at the Annenberg Public Policy Center, reports that both parties are guilty of negative ads. Democrats do it, too. But, the study says, the GOP stands out "for the sheer volume of the assaults on personal character ... while Democrats focus on policies of rivals or performance in office ... What stood out in the [GOP] ads was a pronounced tendency to be petty and personal and sometimes careless with the facts."

Rep. Tom Cole (R-Okla) says: "When people are looking at national issues that are not breaking our way, what you have to do is focus on your opponent. You've got to play the field's conditions. They demand very tough tactics."

Carl Forti, spokesman for the National Republican Congressional Committee, says: "You haven't seen the majority of the negative ads yet."

Iraq. The largest debt in US history. Tom DeLay. Duke Cunningham. Bob Ney. Jack Abramoff. Katrina. Domestic spying. Abu Ghraib. Gitmo. Halliburton. Discounting the relevance of the Geneva Conventions. Foley-gate. Lies. Cover-ups. Scandals. When you can't say something nice ...

There's a reason election day follows so closely on the heels of Halloween. Ghouls Just Wanna Have Fun.

Trick, trick, trick ...

Midterm 2006: Seein' Red and Singin' the Blues

Nov. 14, 2006

"Am I blue? Am I blue? Ain't these tears in these eyes tellin' you?"

If only Dubyah and his Good Ole Boys could sing like Billie Holiday ... nah. They hate blue. They don't even like purple. It's red or nothing.

Red alert: A victory for the Dems is a victory for the terrorists! Red alert: Do you want America to win the war in Iraq or not? Red alert: Those guys have no values! Do you want their "homosexual agenda" on Capitol Hill? Red alert: They want to tax you even after you're dead! Do you trust them with your money? Wait a minute — forget the money part. And forget the red part, too. The debt ... the deficit ... we're so far in the red we can't see our way out ...

What happened on November 7th? The American public saw red. Indignation about dishonesty, scandals and incompetence trumped fear.

In the final days, when it was clear voters were fed up with the mess in Iraq, Bush got testy. "What's YOUR plan?" he snapped at challengers to his failed war policy and his rubber-stamp-GOP hold on congress.

America answered: Might we remind you, Mr. Bush, that you are the one who rushed us into war without a plan in the first place? Too many of us believed you had one. Too many of us believed "Mission Accomplished!" in May 2003. Too many of us believed "The insurgency is in its last throes" in 2005. Too many of us believed "We've turned the corner in Iraq" too many times before we saw the light: If you "turn the corner" four times, Mr. President, you find yourself right back where you started. Too many of us believed "Stay the course" — whatever that was — sounded really nifty. Right up to the minute you changed the rhetoric, saying you never had been a "stay the course" kind of guy anyway.

By election week, we did not believe "... if you look at the general, overall situation, [Iraq] is doing remarkably well."

All the gerrymandering, all the smear campaigns, all the robo-calls and attempts at voter repression — all the Rovian terror-tactics — failed. We'd had enough of the old neo-con

Patriotism-'R-Us sham. Patriots do not necessarily march in lock-step to the same tune. Did we want the "homosexual agenda" you kept threatening loomed on the left? Given the Mark Foley scandal and cover-up, given the Ted Haggard fall from grace, it appeared we already had one in place. Was that closet-agenda of predator/hypocrite what we wanted? No. And you don't get to dictate the terms of morality anymore.

It was our turn. They were our votes. We used them to send a message: No more. No more one-party stranglehold on our government. We voted to repudiate the legal, ethical and moral wrongs this administration has done in our names. We voted for checks and balances again. For oversight. It's long overdue, Mr. Bush.

What happened? It's the accountability, stupid! The time has come. You can see red or sing the blues. You can go on being stubborn, deaf and blind or you can face the music — suck it up, admit you've been wrong and work with a bi-partisan congress for the common good. This time we're watching. And 2008 is not so far away.

Everything You Always Wanted to Know About Sects (But Were Afraid to Ask)

Dec. 26, 2006

There's a reason Baghdad is burning. Sects in the city. Sunnis and Shi'ites are killing each other just for being, well, Sunnis and Shi'ites.

If Dubya had been a student of history he'd have seen it coming. If he'd cared to learn a little about the people of Iraq before he invaded, maybe thousands of Iraqis and Americans could have been spared. And maybe our military wouldn't be caught in the middle of a civil — and religious — war today.

The Sunni and the Shia Muslims have been at each others' throats for nearly 1,400 years. No lie. It all started in 632 AD when the Prophet, Muhammad, died. They couldn't agree on a successor.

Shia Muslims believed that, since Muhammad was The Chosen of God, his bloodline was certainly holy. True divinity ran in the family. It's understandable. Christians embrace a similar credo. For centuries Europeans believed the same thing about their leaders. The Divine Right of Kings, they called it. Seems God was never too busy to pump up the red cell octane in the veins of royalty everywhere.

Shi'ites had double indemnity in their yen for succession-by-blood: Muhammad's daughter had married Muhammad's cousin, Ali. Together, they would produce an infallible line of Imams for Muslims. It was a done deal.

But Sunni Muslims had other ideas. They liked the notion of choosing a successor from among their most trusted religious leaders. No matter whose blood ran in his veins.

Where was the divinity in that? Some angry fundamentalist Shi'ite probably said something like "The only way to heaven is through the Son of the Prophet." Or the Daughter and Cousin, in this case. To which some equally strident Sunni replied, "Who died and left you the sole authority on who gets into heaven?" And the war was on. They've been at it for over a thousand years.

Clearly George W. Bush didn't know all this. If someone told him, he must have believed he could Shock and Awe 'em into getting along. We bombed and invaded. We meant well. After the fires went out, the bodies were buried and the rubble was swept into a tidy pile; after the Victory Parade where millions of happy Iraqis threw flowers at our feet, we'd give 'em democracy and convert 'em all to Christianity. Who wouldn't want to embrace the faith that brought Iraq all that peace, prosperity and freedom from Saddam?

Presto, change-o! Everyone would be friends, we'd have permanent military bases in the Middle East and control of Iraqi oil. Other countries in the region would be so impressed they'd fall in line like so many born-again dominoes. What could possibly go wrong?

Everything. We didn't learn a thing from Vietnam, where a total failure to grasp the complexities of the culture doomed us to lose the war. History repeats through ignorance. Ignorance breeds haste and hubris. Ignorance tainted U.S. foreign policy in Iraq from day one. And the 1,400 year long holy war between Sunnis and Shi'ites rages on, with our military stuck right in the middle of it.

Dubya was in an all-fired hurry to go to war. Couldn't wait a few months when former allies, Canada, France and Germany, asked him for a little time. Now he says he needs time to ponder "opinions and options" before deciding a "New Way Forward."

Too bad he wasn't inclined to such careful deliberation in 2003.

Mother's First Big Decision: The Name Game

Jan. 30, 2007

Anyone who thinks women have no real power needs a mental tune-up. Or a lube job. Or whatever it is you need when you're not running on all cylinders.

Someone once said, "The hand that rocks the cradle rules the world." There's no doubt about it. We women have it all over you men. We're the ones who teach our children what's right, what's wrong and where the soap goes when they sass us. Arguably, we have the power to shape the world by shaping our offspring. It's a mighty awesome responsibility and we begin worrying about it the minute a cheerful nurse hands us what we know to be the most beautiful baby ever born.

Too late. By then we've already been a little careless about what's really important for our baby's future. Mommy's first job is to name the child. Sometimes Daddy gets a vote but, more often than not, it's a woman's province.

I've had a problem with names for years. I don't think it's a great idea to name a baby girl after a mineral like, say, amber or crystal; or a jewelry store like Tiffany. Or a flower like daisy or rosie. Women have a hard enough time of it in the business world as it is. A CEO named Rosie Bush or Crystal Bowles or Amber Stuckey? Not a chance.

Last names are thrust upon us. We have to work with them as best we can. If your last name is High, you don't name your daughter Heidi or call your son Junior. And we should never name our sons after cities or states. Cheyenne Smith and Dakota Jones belong in the rodeo — not in the

White House.

Which brings me to Barack Obama. Or to his mother, who was certainly not scheming about his future in politics when she chose his name. She was from a small town in the midwest. Her husband — the father of her baby — was from a small town in Kenya. They met and fell in love while attending the University of Hawaii. She was white, raised a protestant. He was African, raised in the Muslim faith. They were a culturally blended couple; she named their son with his heritage in mind.

Barack is Swahili for "beloved." Hussein, the middle name, is a common choice in Muslim countries. Like John or Robert. Obama — well, it's his father's family name. A nice one, that's almost poetic when spoken. Barack Hussein Obama. A lovely, non-threatening name in the early '60s.

In today's political climate, however, it's a name that could qualify as a rhetorical WMD. Hussein. That could give you the heebie-jeebies. Saddam Hussein. Obama? What can I say? He's one letter away from getting stuck with Osama. It even rhymes, for Pete's sake!

So, until and unless the Right can find something bad to say about him, we're going to get a bellyful of the Name Game. Barack HUSSEIN Obama and "slips of the tongue" or the pen that give us Osama until we're scared out of our wits. We won't vote for a guy saddled with the names of our two worst enemies.

Life is hard enough. Mamas, don't let your babies grow up to be cowboys. Or proper-name-impaired.

A woman's place is in the House. And the Senate.

Feb. 6, 2007

Maybe it's time for a woman in the White House, too.

I like men just fine. My husband's a really nice guy. I've got a grown son and grandsons I adore. But male leadership seems to have gotten us in such trouble we might need a woman to straighten things out. There's plenty of conventional wisdom to support the gender change in Washington:

A woman brings experience to the table. We're experts in Health and Human Services, economics and diplomacy. Ask any woman with a family what she does. She keeps her house in order, sees to it meals provide essential nutrients, stretches every dollar, settles disputes and is the one responsuble for explaining why little Mikey can't whale the tar out of every kid he doesn't like, why little Sally can't spread nasty stories about kids on her "hit list," especially when they're not true.

A woman is less likely to send other women's children off to war. We're the ones who carried the kids — before and after birth. We're the ones who remember what our babies smelled like, how soft they were. And we're more apt to see that everyone on earth is some mother's child. Like our own.

Women would rather talk than fight. We believe in hashing everything out. Ask our husbands. Aggravating? Yes. Time consuming? Yes. Worth the effort to save the family? You bet.

A woman is unlikely to go too far down the wrong road. A bad neighborhood makes us nervous and, unlike most men we know, we don't mind admitting we're lost. We're quick to stop and ask for directions.

A woman in a lousy mood will cry, eat chocolate or go shopping. A man? He's more apt to holler and tear down the garage. Men like their Big Tools.

But a woman knows that words are often better tools than sledgehammers — and that, if the only tool you think you've got is a hammer, everything looks like a nail. Even someone else's children.

A Horse is a Horse — of course, of course

Feb. 20, 2007

Despite multiple surgeries and an extended stay in the spa-like U. of Pennsylvania animal hospital, thoroughbred Barbaro has died. A Kentucky Derby winner, a shoe-in to win the Preakness, he suffered three broken bones in his right hind leg. Most horses are put down when similarly lamed. Chances of survival are so slim it's kinder to put them out of their misery. But Barbaro was different. He was worth a fortune. Months of specialized treatment — and the staggering cost of such care — were deemed appropriate. Pound for pound, this was horseflesh worthy of extreme measures. Whatever the cost.

Meanwhile, back at the ranch, roughly 47 million Americans have no health insurance. Millions more are underinsured, unable to get — or afford — supplemental policies to offset the cost of catastrophic illness. Businesses are cutting benefits to protect profits while their upper management guys make record-high salaries. The average CEO of a Standard & Poor's 500 company made $13.5 million in 2005 while a minimum wage worker made $10,700. In the 1970s a CEO made 30 times the salary of an average worker. In Japan and Germany they still do. Here? A CEO makes 400 times what the rest of us do. "Average Joe" works a full year to earn what "Big Boss" makes in one day.

Our nation's largest employer offers health insurance benefits to fewer than 45% of their employees. 46% of the children of their 1.3 million employees are uninsured or on Medicaid. Their corporate profit for one year? Around $10.5 billion.

You can't blame big business types for wanting to make big bucks. You can't blame Barbaro's owners for trying to save their horse. His injury and his death were "Breaking News" stories on major outlets. America prayed for his recovery, grieved his passing. We're a nation of animal lovers.

But something's amiss in a country where the wealthy spend millions on healthcare for their animals while people — men, women and children — lose access to standard healthcare; where most of us are one major illness away from losing everything we own.

Sadly, none of us is apt to win the Kentucky Derby. Our illnesses and deaths are unlikely to make national news. Fair's fair, however, and it seems only fair that we have an equal shot here. Not to win the race, just to stay in it.

Black History Month ... and White Noise

Feb. 27, 2007

White noise: static; random noise; noise pollution.

February is Black History Month. Has a nice ring to it. Martin Luther King, Jr. was born on Jan. 15. Seems we missed the mark; maybe January would have been a better choice for celebrating the achievements of African Americans. Think of the symbolism: The birthday of Dr. King, the first month of every new year. But January has 31 days. A bit much. So we gave African Americans the shortest month of the year.

What are we getting, midway through February? News, news, news! An angst-driven (white) astronaut drives 900 miles in a (white) diaper to whack another (white) astronaut for dating her (white) fantasy lover. The death of a ditsy (white) blonde bombshell, famous for nothing but a burgeoning bosom, weight issues and a sad attempt to be an outrageous Marilyn Monroe clone. A faithless (white) San Francisco mayor admits publicly to diddling his best (white) friend's (white) wife. There's Britney, who went out to party hearty and left her (maybe white) underwear at home. And Paris (really white) Hilton, who was Britney's BFF for about 15 minutes. And Ted Haggard who, after three weeks of fundamentalist counseling, was cured completely of homosexuality; the dark stain of his sin bleached from his white soul in record time. Will Mary Cheney get her three weeks of righteous rehab, renounce her female partner, marry a good man and give that baby a daddy?

It's Black History Month. On Saturday, February 10th, a Black American, Barack Obama, announced his candidacy. He's in the race to win the Democratic nomination for president. Obama support groups sprang up like flowers after a warm, spring rain — nationwide. A serious, viable African American announces for president during Black History Month.

That's news. But we're getting little of it, sandwiched in between all the white noise in the mainstream media. And what we're getting is laced with "Is he black enough?" rhetoric. That's white noise of the worst kind.

Talking Trash: Ann Coulter Speaks at CPAC
March 13, 2007

The Conservative Political Action Conference held their annual meeting recently. A good thing. A chance for America to hear from conservative think-tanks, conservative candidates, conservative columnists/bloggers. Everyone's eyeing 2008. Everyone's got ideas about what's right — and Right — for a nation clearly at odds with current leadership in Washington. The time is ripe for elevated dialogue, for lofty ideas about the future course of the country. And everyone knows who claims both the moral high ground and divine sanction to lead us down the right path. We couldn't wait to be inspired.

What did we get? We got another toxic dose of Ann Coulter, right-wing writer/speaker who gave us such memorable lines as "Even Islamic terrorists don't hate America like liberals do," "Liberals can't just come out and say they want to take more of our money, kill babies, and discriminate on the basis of race" and, in referring to Oklahoma City bomber Timothy McVeigh: "My only regret with Timothy McVeigh is that he did not go to The New York Times building." Her elevated CPAC discourse this year included calling candidate John Edwards a "faggot." The audience laughed. Coulter tossed her blonde hair and preened.

Only after the fact, after media aired her invective and the public voiced outrage, did conservatives begin distancing themselves from such a slur.

Like they didn't know what kind of garbage comes out of Ann Coulter's mouth? At last year's annual CPAC bash Coulter referred to Arabs as "ragheads."

Good old Ann. She keeps spewing trash, some of it violent ("I think the government should be ... engaging in torture as a televised spectator sport, dropping daisy cutters wantonly throughout the Middle East and sending liberals to Guantanamo,") some of it ridiculous ("God gave us the earth. We have dominion over the plants, the animals, the trees. God said, 'Earth is yours. Take it. Rape it. It's yours.'"). None of it serves her party or the nation well. But they keep giving her a platform from which to spread her rubbish. Why?

Ann thinks she knows the reason. "I am emboldened by my looks," she says, "to say things Republican men wouldn't." She feels sexually sanctioned to spew. Heaven help us — maybe she's right.

Oedipus Wrecks: the Psychology
Behind the Yhrone

May 8, 2007

Psychoanalysts have had a Bush Analysis field day in recent years. They've made a cottage industry of long-distance exploration of George W.'s mind, trying to figure out why the president does the things he does. Some say it's a sort of Oedipal thing — a case of the son resenting Daddy. Competing with him, trying to prove he's a better king than Daddy was.

No one knows what drives this president to reject all opinions but his own, to summarily dismiss the ISG Report when his father's men comprised half of the group evaluating what went wrong in Iraq and how to correct it. But reject them he did, along with every suggestion made by long-time policy people in his own party.

He's like an overgrown kid playing follow-the-leader. He only allows his very best friends to play with him and he changes the rules of the game whenever he likes. It's his game, he's the "Commander Guy" and he'll only play with other kids who tell him he's always right. It makes for a very limited childhood and reinforces behaving badly. A "You can't tell me what to do — I'm the boss of you!" philosophy.

Dubyah won't listen to military brass who disagree with him — Eric Shinseki, Colin Powell. He jettisons them, installs others who'll keep their mouths shut and play.

But he's blindly loyal to playmates he likes best. No matter what they do. Rumsfeld was a disaster, even Republicans said so, but W. held on until he lost control of Congress in November and had no choice but to make a change. Wolfowitz, an archtect of the Iraq War who testified before Congress that Iraqi oil revenues would make war a cheap venture for the U.S., was shuffled by the prez to the World Bank. So the guy who was totally wrong about the finances, the cost of the war, was given a job managing money for the world's poorest people. Like they didn't have it tough enough already. Now Wolfie's in trouble for setting up his girlfriend in a cushy government job. Bush sees no fault in such abuse of influence. Wolfowitz should keep his job.

Alberto Gonzales corrupts the DOJ and lies to Congress about what he did, what he knew. He gets caught lying, swears he didn't lie — he only "misspoke." In his most recent testimony on Capitol Hill Gonzales said some variant of "I don't know" or "I don't remember" over 70 times. Conservative legislators were incensed over an Attorney General's best defense being "I don't know, I don't recall. But whatever it was I didn't know a thing about and whatever I forgot went on, even though I still don't know and can't remember — uh — I know that everything I don't know and can't remember was handled properly ..."

They call for his resignation. Bush's response? That Gonzales's testimony only strengthened his confidence in the Attorney General.

Oedipus Wrecks: One colossal adolescent blunder after another. Conservative or liberal, come 2008 we need a grownup in the Oval Office.

(Thank you, Jon Stewart, for the inspiration, the spot-on definition of the gist of Gonzales's spiel.)

America's Mayor:
"Rudy-Tootie, Fresh and Fruity"

May 29, 2007

There is no doubt that, on 9/11, while thousands were dead and dying, while smoke and ash, unimaginable debris, filled the air and streets of New York, only one duly elected leader was visible to a stunned and grieving nation. Our president, after being informed we were under attack, looked like nothing so much as a deer caught in headlights. His first responsibility as Commander-in-Chief was to finish reading My Pet Goat. Then he spent hours on Air Force One, flying from place to place. V.P. Cheney was hurried off to "an undisclosed location." We were left with Rudy Giuliani, ramrod straight, about the business of leadership. We all saw it firsthand: This mayor was in his city, right in the thick of it all. It was heroic. This was leadership. At its finest.

Except for one minor detail. There was a reason America's Mayor was seen wandering the streets of New York all day with a hankie over his nose. He wasn't intentionally visible to provide leadership to a nation badly in need of it. He wasn't leading a thing. Giuliani was in the streets because he had nowhere else to go.

After the first terrorist attack on the World Trade Center, on February 26, 1993, against the advice of his emergency preparedness experts, against the advice of public safety officials, Mayor Rudy Giuliani insisted the brand-spanking new, very expensive NYC Emergency Command and Control Center be placed inside one of the WTC Towers. Experts argued for a site in Brooklyn, a bunker distant from the WTC which had already been a terrorist target. America's Mayor chose to do otherwise — with catastrophic consequences.

FDNY, it appears, is no great fan of Giuliani's. Under Rudy's leadership, the city was lethally hindered in the immediate aftermath of the strike against the Towers by faulty communications equipment provided first responders by his administration; again, with tragic consequences.

Since leaving office, Giuliani has offered himself up as the "Terrorism Expert," founding his own consulting firm. Giuliani Partners sells expertise and solutions for a post-9/11 America. He's paid well to speak publicly, to share his success story in protecting New York. Sources say he's made $16 million in the last 16 months. A million dollars a month for expert advice, for the example of leadership in crisis.

Now he runs for president. As the expert in defending America against terrorism. He has the proven skills. The wisdom. He has the foresight.

Mayor Rudy Giuliani had the foresight to put the Command Center in the worst place at the worst possible time. He had the wisdom to ignore requests from public safety officials for new communications equipment that would work in time of crisis.

Like a tasty new offering at IHOP, he's garnished his image to a fare-thee-well. Rudy-Tootie, Fresh and Fruity. It's one dish I'm not buying.

Good Housekeeping: Adultery, Divorce and Politics

June 12, 2007

It's scary. That's the primary message — pardon the pun — during the Republican debates. Iraq, Iran and Muslims are scary. Raising taxes on the wealthy is scary. Any form of universal healthcare is scary. Arguing about corporate price-gouging and inflated CEO salaries is scary. A woman's reproductive rights are scary. Homosexuals are scary. Immigrants are scary. Foreign languages are scary. Evolution is scary. Liberals are both scary and scared. But worse, far worse, they say, is the fact that the American family is under attack.

Hillary Clinton's marriage is back in the news. Adultery and who's to blame and it's what liberal sinners do. It's practically genetic.

In his new book Tom DeLay has a thing or two to say about adultery. Bill Clinton's impeachment trial, he says, was one of his proudest moments. Except for the part about Newt Gingrich: "... I don't think that Newt could set a high moral standard ... during that moment." Why? Because Old Newt was in the middle of an affair with a 33 year old congressional aide at the time. And Newt's adultery, DeLay goes on, was worse than his own. While DeLay cheated on his wife, too, he didn't do it during the impeachment process. "There's a big difference," he says.

Marriage and family sanctity: The mantle of the right. It doesn't fit well.

McCain had an affair and divorced his first wife. Gingrich cheated and divorced, cheated again and divorced again. Giuliani divorced, remarried, cheated and divorced again. And Rudy's second wife learned he was leaving her when he announced it at a 2000 press conference. Nice going. During the divorce his wife said the new "other woman" was just the latest in a string of mistresses. He and his kids aren't on speaking terms.

Even much-touted Reagan heir-apparent Fred Thompson divorced his wife of 25 years in 1985. Reagan himself was divorced.

Marriage and family. They're at risk alright. They're under attack. But clearly the God-fearing Right has no legitimate claim to the family and marital moral high ground. When your best defense is "My adultery is better than your adultery" maybe you should stop posturing as the party of absolute family values, the standard bearers for old time religion.

Bill Clinton misled us about sex. A bad thing for families. George W. Bush misled us into war. A worse thing for families. Our children and grandchildren aren't apt to pay too high a price for all the marital mayhem among politicians. They will, however, suffer the consequences of a trillion dollar war, poverty, poor schools and a broken healthcare system. Let the pots stop calling the kettles black here and get busy cleaning up the mess in the Capitol Hill kitchen.

Deaf, Dumb and Blonde: TV, Ratings, and Bimbo Eruptions

July 10, 2007

MSNBC and CNN. Chris Matthews and Larry King, Ann Coulter and Paris Hilton. The vamping of hate-speak and the dumbing down of America. For ratings. For profit. And I watched. I should be ashamed.

Matthews hosted Arsenic-tongued Ann, who did her poisonous shtick in front of a live — and very young — audience. She went after John Edwards with a vengeance. Having already said "I'll just wish he'd been killed in a terrorist assassination plot," Coulter couldn't resist making reference to the Edwards' son, who was killed in an auto accident in the '90s. Edwards, she snarled, sports a bumper sticker on his car that reads "Ask me about my dead son."

Elizabeth Edwards, having heard quite enough, phoned in. She did Southern womanhood proud. "I ask her politely to stop the personal attacks," she said. "I'm the mother of that boy who died. These young people behind you, you're asking them to participate in a dialogue ... based on hatefulness and ugliness instead of the issues ... I don't think that's serving them or this country very well."

Coulter tried shouting over Mrs. Edwards while Matthews sputtered. We had one screamer, one stutterer and a single, Southern voice of reason.

Over at CNN, Larry King bumped an hour scheduled with Michael Moore, whose new documentary focuses on insurance company greed, the underinsured and a failed healthcare system. Why? Because Paris Hilton, sprung from jail, had something important to tell us. "I just want to let people know what I've been through," she simpered. Going to jail "... was the most terrifying day of my life." Truly, it was a nightmare for poor Paris. She did discover the Bible. She read it, she said, and used her jail time to "Figure out who I am." I waited for the revelation. Here's what I learned from the new, improved Paris:

Her DUI: She had only one drink. Honest. It was all unfair, really. People tell lies and the public doesn't really understand her. Jail was, like, traumatic. The cell was tiny (only about 8' x 12') and she suffers claustrophobia. She closed her eyes a lot, pretending to be somewhere nice. She'd like to "help" women in jail — but that statement was the extent of her plan. She's busy taping her TV show and will make two movies this summer. She's an Aquarius, and that makes her a "social" person.

Oh — and "I found out a lot about myself," she said humbly. So King asked her to name something she'd change about herself. Here it comes at last, I thought. Her born again wisdom. Paris took a deep breath. Whenever she's nervous or shy, she said, her voice gets all, like, high and squeaky. She'd like to change that.

Ann and Paris are two sides of the same American coin. The vicious and the vapid, famous for doing nothing of value. I watched. I listened. And I needed a shower.

Greek Prefixes, Smart Women and Obamaphobia

July 27, 2007

Clever, those ancient Greeks. They gave us art, literature, philosophy and the notion of a more perfect government. They gave us a language ripe for the picking. Greek prefixes, Greek root-words: "demos" (people), "kratos" (power). Democracy. Power to the people. What a word! What a concept! What's not to like?

They also gave us the hystera/hystero prefix — which means uterus. Hysterectomy. Problems with a pesky womb? If it offends you, cut it out. Not a bad thing. But there's also hysteria. You know, that hollering and screaming thing. Tantrums. Panic attacks. General emotional mayhem. And, for too many lo-o-o-ong centuries, the female's uterus was the definitive root of all disorganized behavior and thought. The womb made us a tad too flaky to be trusted to do more than have babies, cook and clean.

Hysteria has become an equal opportunity malady in modern times. These days men can be hysterical, too. Those Big Boys with all the power and guns can whip up a climate of hysteria any time they really need one. Dubya and his cronies have mastered the art. Saddam. WMD and the imminent threat of mushroom clouds poisoning every peace-loving American if we didn't invade ASAP, overthrow the madman with his finger on the nuke button and create a shiny new America-loving Iraq. Quick-like. They've kept us in line every step of the way by scaring us to death. Hysteria works.

The Clinton campaign seems to be sinking to hysteria mode lately. When Barack Obama said Bush's "zero-diplomacy unless I like you" policy is a poor approach, that he would be willing to begin talking to foreign heads of state — good guys or bad — within the first year of an Obama presidency, Clintonistas went ballistic. Suddenly the notion of diplomacy, of open negotiation, is akin to hopping into bed with a harlot after strangling your wife. Clearly Obama is too stupid to be president. Naïve. Irresponsible. Within days the "Obama will even talk to Holocaust deniers!" panic pill was dosed out like methadone at a drug rehab facility. It's hysterical.

I've always liked Hillary. She's smart, she's tough, she's

capable. But I'm mad at her for using the same old Bush-Rovian smear-and-fear tactics. She should be ashamed. She should be as sick as most women are of the hystera/hystero prefix and its use as a tool to deny us our rightful place in the world of "rational" men. This PMS-style over-reaction, the deliberate distortion of a rival candidate's intelligence and his intent, is nothing more than the same peddling of hysteria we've suffered for the last 6 1/2 years; it's Dubya's "We have to fight them over there so we won't have to fight them here!" nonsense in make-up and high heels.

It is unworthy of a candidate who says she represents change. It is especially unworthy of a smart woman who has had to weather the women's rights wars. The marketing of hysteria is beneath a strong candidate for the highest office in the land. It smacks of the same old dirty politics. Barack Obama has said — more than once — "We [Americans] are better than this." That sentiment should surely apply to Hillary, a powerful woman who is in a position to enhance the cause for women's capabilities trumping their wombs once and for all. The hysteria mode offends us. Cut it out.

Capitol Crimes and Misdemeanors: Honesty and Justice in Politics

Aug. 21, 2007

In a feisty discussion of politics last week a friend told me, "Face it. There ain't no justice and you all are partly to blame. Why don't you call a spade a spade, demand answers and rein them in? When will the media do more than serve as voyeurs or a steno pool for the power brokers in government?"

He may be right. This week the media gave us footage of the weepy farewell duo, Stinky and the Brain, and it was enough to reduce us all to tears. Dubya and Karl Rove, cutting the cord at last. There was the decided stench of dissembling in the air. Fleeing the scene of the crime(s), Rove mewled that old political saw, "It's time ... I just want to be with my family ..." Which begs the question: Which investigation, which subpoena, sir, is about to rise up and bite you on the keester? The CIA leak? Jack Abramoff? The Justice Department fiasco?

Maybe Rove only misspoke about his reason for leaving. He does that a lot. Often enough that he had to answer to the Libby grand jury over and again to "correct" his misstatements. Pols misspeak. They insist they're smart enough to lead the country but their memories fail them at critical moments and slips-of-the-tongue plague them both before taking office and after. Bush/Cheney et al misspoke about reasons for war, misspoke about the cost, the length, the hardship their war would entail. "Mission Accomplished" was a misstatement. So was "The insurgency is in its last throes." John McCain says he misspoke about his carefree (heavily armed) shopping spree in Baghdad awhile back. Giuliani admits he recently misspoke about all the long hours he spent — as long or longer than those laborers on site — sucking up the poisoned air at ground zero after 9/11. Mitt Romney, when asked why not one of his five strapping sons is in the military fighting the war he so ardently supports, claimed his sons' version of equally patriotic service to their country in wartime is helping him get elected. The lofty pursuit of a Romney presidency trumps bloody military service any day. "I misspoke," Romney said when the statement backfired.

To be fair, Democratic legislators who voted to authorize Dubya's Iraq War are queuing up in the "I misspoke" line rather than admit they were too cowardly to vote their common sense and conscience in the face of a "You're either with us or you're with the terrorists!" tack on the part of the White House. Can't get re-elected if you're an unpatriotic terrorist sympathizer, so go along.

Seems the powerful elite can slide by, doing or saying whatever they deem necessary to get or keep power, legal or not. Ethical or not. Unless it's about sex. And they never lie. They only "misspeak." Unless it's about sex; then a lie's a lie and somebody must be held accountable.

Ordinary folk can't get away with it. Lie little and your reputation is shot. Lie big — and you'll pay the price. We don't have the mass media serving as tail-wagging PR flunkies.

So we're supposed to believe a sudden yen for family time is Karl Rove's noble reason for getting out of Dodge? Right. I'll still respect you in the morning and the check's in the mail.

Born Again: The Faith-Based Initiative and Chinese Law

Aug. 28, 2007

Politix Lite. A little political humor is a good thing. Given the current state of affairs in this country, a sense of the ridiculous is even better. You have to go some distance to find a system as convoluted as ours has become. You know: "Federal debt is not really such a bad thing when Republicans do it. Sure — we're winning the war, the economy is (really!)

good and who needs health care? "

I found it.

In the PR war for the mantle of political idiocy, China has made a bold move. Even with another 17 months or so of Dubya's wit and wisdom ahead of us, we'll be hard-pressed to top this: According to the Chinese State Administration for Religious Affairs, a new law will go into effect come September. China has banned Buddhist monks in Tibet from reincarnating without government permission. The law, says a spokesperson for the government, strictly defines the procedures by which one is to reincarnate. It is "... an important move to institutionalize the management of reincarnation."

Well. That's a relief to every hard-working Chinese citizen. You can't have Buddhist monks reincarnating willy-nilly, whenever and wherever they take a notion to do it. Before you know it you'll have a bald, saffron-robed fellow meditating on every street corner, chanting some tuneless little ditty and expecting a free bowl of rice in the bargain. Not only that — if some thug goes after your wallet, beating you senseless in the process, the pacifist born-again monk won't lift a finger to help you. Karma and all. It wouldn't have happened if you hadn't done something creepy in a former life. You have it coming.

The point, actually, has nothing to do with protecting the citizens of China. It's about another kind of protection altogether. The Dalai Lama has been living in exile in India since 1959. Many of his flock — all those other monks — are living in Tibet. The Chinese government seems to feel that, if they succeed in barring these monks from reincarnating, there will be no new little Dalai Lama reborn to do all that praying and relief-of-the-suffering nonsense on Chinese soil. Once authorities have secured control of the reincarnation issue they can simply pick and choose the new Buddhist leaders. More mainstream, tasteful types, maybe, who dress better; who don't go around stirring up trouble about human rights, the poor, the sick and the hungry.

It may be that the Dalai Lama and the Chinese government strike a deal: Reincarnation at will as long as they keep it outside China and the Himalayan nation they seized over 50 years ago. How Buddhist monks will prove their adherence to the new law is yet to be determined.

One thing's certain. We'll never top this, despite our own current predilection with obsessing over who's-what-religion and why it matters. Whether it's ever a provable fact or not, the Chinese government wants reincarnation off the national agenda. Here it's mighty hard to get elected to public office unless you swear you're born-again. Whether you can prove it or not. Go figure.

The "Outsider": Role-Playing the Untainted Law and Order President
Sept. 11, 2007

It's official. He's in it to win it. A frustrated GOP offers up the Grand Ole Poseur: He's the new Ronald Reagan. Actor/lawyer/former Tennessee Senator Fred Dalton Thompson is off and running for the White House.

The collective conservative sigh of relief was powerful enough to alter the course of the jet stream; surely there's only fair weather and smooth sailing ahead. This guy has it all.

Experience on the Hill — just enough, not too much. Name recognition to die for, a face everyone knows and trusts. We've seen him in action. He's served us well as the serious, thoughtful District Attorney Arthur Branch on NBC's Law and Order. He dispensed legal pearls of wisdom every week for several years, never got flustered, seldom lost a case that really mattered. And every crisis was neatly resolved in under sixty minutes. You've got to believe in a guy who can do all that. Imagine what he could do in the Oval Office.

Not only has he got star quality, he's a bona fide regular guy. He wears blue jeans and tools around in a red pickup truck. He drove that old truck all over Tennessee in his '93 run for the Senate. Folks loved it. Most never knew the truck was pre-positioned a mile or two away from his stumping grounds. A luxury car or limo delivered candidate Thompson to the big red truck and he took it from there. The long-tall, plain-talkin' everyman arrived in red, white and blue average American style. It's all about image. You have to look the part.

He's an outsider, too. There's no "Washington Insider" tattooed on this old boy's forehead. Serving a term or two in the U.S. Senate does not make a man (or woman) one of those tainted insiders. That's a fact.

But there's more to the life and times of Fred Thompson than stints as a beloved TV DA or another Mr. Smith Goes to Washington-style pol. He's got a long history — 20 years or so — as a living, breathing lobbyist in D.C. One of his clients in 1982 was the Tennessee Savings and Loan League. On their behalf, Thompson lobbied for a bill to deregulate the S&L industry. The result? The final version of Thompson's pet bill is widely credited with laying the groundwork for the risky financial ventures, fraud and mismanagement that ended with the S&L collapse in the late '80s. U.S. taxpayers paid about $150 billion for the bail-out.

He lobbied for Equitas, a British reinsurance company handling billions of dollars of asbestos claims for Lloyd's of London. What profit-savvy insurer wants to face paying the claims of asbestos victims? Equitas paid Thompson $760,000 from 2004-2006 for his handiwork on their behalf.

A spokesman for Thompson said, "Many of the candidates from both parties have been lobbyists or have been lobbied ... in their careers. It is an honorable endeavor that goes back to the beginnings of this republic."

So, he's untainted. He's the new, improved outsider-insider. He's just like all of us. Except that the K Street gang — who've bought our government wholesale, kept the costs of gas and oil, health insurance and prescription drugs staggeringly high or wholly unaffordable for too many of us — can rightfully rejoice at a potential Thompson presidency. After all, he may say he's one of us, he may look like one of us, but he's one of them.

Poll Dancing: Questions, Answers And The Naked Truth

Sept. 13, 2007

Note: The questions I was asked in these polls do not deviate in the slightest from the truth. I have had to reconstruct them from memory, so the placement of "Press #1 or #2" may vary slightly from the actual poll; questions are paraphrased only to the degree that memory serves — so the words may not be in the exact order they were in originally, but I have not changed a meaningful word or the distinct flavor of the polling otherwise. Obviously, I have omitted the ordinary (and forgettable) questions. If it hadn't happened to me, I'd never have believed it. This is how it felt.

2008 looms large. Another national election, another chance to have our say, to opine from the voting booth. As soon as we know what we think. What we want. Who we want to give us what we want for four years. Some of us know exactly who we want. Many others, however, don't have a clue. It's all so confusing during primary season.

Thank God for polls. They're everywhere. They tell us who's in, who's out, and who's sinking faster than Dubya in a vat of truth serum. If polls tell us most people support, say, Giuliani over McCain or Clinton over Obama, we don't have to think hard. Or read much. Or learn a thing. No muscle tension headaches from all that exertion. "Most people" must be right. Only trouble is we don't know who those most people are or how they made their choices. None of us ever gets polled.

I live and work in South Carolina, a state as red as a ripe tomato. Nobody cares what we think. It's a given: We're a hardwired Republican bloc. The only polling experience we've ever had en masse was the 2000 George W. inspired pushpolling from some guy asking if "... you'd vote McCain if you knew the man was a liar and a cheat?" or "Would knowing John McCain fathered an illegitimate black child make you more likely or less likely to vote for him?" I can tell you, in all sincerity, I feel left out.

Or I did. Until a new, early primary date changed everything. Suddenly we're more important nationally than we've been since Cotton was King and we were first to secede from the Union.

My inbox becomes my gateway to the world of political polls. Folks want to know what I think, what my choices are apt to be. Heady stuff. I'm in the middle of a love/hate relationship with pollsters — and it's not entirely my fault. I'm polled online by PollingPoint. One of their polls gives me the opportunity to vote for every conceivable match-up: Clinton vs. Giuliani, Clinton vs. McCain, Romney, et al. Edwards is in there, too. It was great fun. Empowering and all. Except for one minor flaw. Barack Obama was not included. Odd, I thought, considering he's got the second spot, solidly ahead of Edwards. What did it mean? How did that compute in an accurate portrayal of the race to the primaries?

Zogby International offered me the chance to be a part of their Online Survey Panel. I jumped at it. I like Zogby. But even there problems arise. One of my online policy wonk pals lives in Chicago. She's a Zogby Panel member, too. We compare notes. On the same day that she was polled about politics and candidates I was polled about bottled water and tainted spinach. Look at my zip code, people. Does a rural Southerner drink Perrier? Dadgum! Some of us are glad to have a well and a clean bucket.

They did pose some near-political questions about China's propensity of late to poison us all with toothpaste and lead-laced toys. "Would you be willing to pay more for U.S. products you felt were safe?" I could answer "Yes," "No" or "Unsure." There was no "I'm not at all sure, given the regulation-free notion of good corporate policy these days, that a U.S. company wouldn't happily poison my family and me for profit" option provided. To their credit, they did ask this rural Southerner some agriculture-related questions. Maybe they were political. I might remember what they were if I were coversant in farm-speak. I'm not. We don't farm. I want issues of war, peace and diplomacy; healthcare, the environment, candidates who speak to me. I feel snubbed ...

Zogby's polled me a number of times since then. They've asked me how many five-star hotels I've frequented, which one most recently. None and none. They keep asking me, over and again, if my passport is valid. I keep saying "No" and they keep asking. Is this the MMPI of polls? Do they keep asking the same questions until they uncover some deep, fundamental truth? Am I anal retentive? Do I suffer a persecution complex?

Okay. Online polls aren't real anyway, I tell myself. The telephone poll is the standard, what matters most. I covet one, but none comes.

Until the second week in July. My phone rings and it is, at last, my turn. Mine. I'm polled by the kind folks at Rasmussen Reports. They've been tracking political races for over a decade. They are, they tell me, very accurate. I am, of course, thrilled. I like accuracy. And I get to be one of that esteemed "most people" crowd in the good old, red-white-and-blue traditional way. Chalk one up for a very smart, flaming liberal South Carolinian.

I take a deep breath, get my trigger finger poised to press #1 or #2 on my touch-tone. My nostrils flare like a racehorse. I'm hot to trot. First I have to answer all the usual stuff: My age, sex, party of preference, income. A warm-up. Then the fun begins ...

"Press #1 if you feel the country is on the right track. Press #2 if you feel we're off course." That one's easy. We're more than off course, honey. We're off the map. I press #2 and I feel good.

Now some of it gets a little complicated.

"Hillary Clinton chose to stay with her husband despite his infidelity. Does this make you more likely to vote for her (press #1) or less likely to vote for her (press #2)." I'm stuck. There's no "Press #3 if you don't give a rat's patootie what she decided to do about her marriage" option. I'd never choose not to vote for her over the infidelity factor. Ridiculous. But ... she's not my first choice for the Dem nod ... so I press #2, and I feel guilty about it.

Later, things get more bizarre.

"If Dick Cheney needed a kidney and asked for one of yours, would you say 'Yes' (press #1) or 'No' (press #2)?" There's no "If you're committed to using both of your kidneys for the foreseeable future but would humanely advise him to drink more water and offer to pray for him, press #3" option. I can't stand the guy. I might whack him one if I got the chance, but I wouldn't kill him. I'm a nice, church-going lady. I hesitate, but I press #2. At worst I'm passive/aggressive (ask Zogby). If he dies, he dies. There's always dialysis and he can afford it. He's got big Halliburton war-bucks and government health insurance that probably covers prescriptions for Viagra, acupuncture and hair replacement.

I'm beginning to have my doubts about this polling and accuracy business. I imagine hearing this next: "Would you rather shoot yourself in the head (press #1) or vote Republican in 2008 (press #2)?" Die or cry. What a choice.

Then this:

"Are you afraid of circus clowns? Press #1 for 'Yes', press #2 for 'No.'" What the — ?

What do circus clowns have to do with this? Is Bozo running? Have I missed something? I press #2. The best thing — at the circus — is a good clown. But I worry about it.

And it's over. The robo-voice thanks me and disconnects. I Google "psychology: fear of clowns" and the news is not good. There is a phobia. Seems the exaggerated-happy-face clown who beats up a smaller clown or kicks a dog scares some folks silly. You never know what evil lurks behind that big red smile.

The only memorable candidate Rasmussen mentioned was Hillary Clinton. The only issue, her marriage. The sole Republican featured was Dick Cheney — well, Cheney's kidney. And the clown? I'm still not sure about him. I think maybe he's that scary guy in the Oval Office now.

There's a lesson to be learned here. You can't entirely trust polls. One wrong answer in the Rasmussen Poll and I skewed the results. I should have pressed #1. I'm terrified of clowns.

The War and Mixed Messages: A Plan for All Seasons

Sept. 18, 2007

The Decider-in-Chief paid another stealth visit to Iraq the first weekend of September. Dressed all in Johnny Cash black Bush spent six hours there, surrounded by U.S. military, in the immediate neighborhood of a U.S. military base. He liked what he saw from that vantage point: Not a suicide bomber, IED, car bomb or insurgent sniper in sight. It was all good. He could assess the full range of progress on the ground from right there, long miles away from from the heat of battle, and cash in on a photo-op to boot. He left, one happy fella, on his way to the APEC summit in Australia.

Australian Deputy Prime Minister Mark Vaile met him as he arrived in Sydney, politely asking the POTUS how things were going in Iraq.

"We're kicking ass," the ever-eloquent Dubya quipped.

Another lofty pronouncement for posterity. We can add this one to the string of all-goes-well wisdoms we've been spoon fed since the early days of selling the war:

- Imminent threat!
- It won't take long and it won't cost much!
- Shock and awe will do it!
- They're gonna love us for this!
- Mission Accomplished!
- Well, looting and shooting in the streets just goes to show ya how messy freedom can be!
- What insurgency?
- Oh. That one. Well, it's in its last throes!
- A surge'll fix this — just wait until September!
- Well, I'm an October/November kind of guy.
- We need another six months — just wait until March 2008!

Been there, done that. In 1968 General William Westmoreland, tasked with re-marketing an unpopular, bloody quagmire in Vietnam, told us "We're seeing light at the end of the tunnel." Shortly after his pronouncement we got slammed with the infamous Tet Offensive and it was all downhill from there. It was a lousy case of the White House using military brass as a shield then — and nothing is different now.

General Petraeus, tasked with pulling an Iraq War rabbit out of his hat, gets stuck trying to stall for time before Congress. He's already told us there is no military solution; it's a diplomatic win or nothing and soldiers, no matter how brave, effective or patriotic, are not nation builders. Like many Americans and members of Congress, I felt sorry for an honorable man in an impossible situation.

Conventional wisdom: The new Bush strategy for Iraq? Kick this eroded can down the road, stay the course, play for time and run out the clock. Pass off this Iraq fiasco to the next president, let him (or her) deal with the inevitable "Damned if you do, damned if you don't" scenario.

Dubya's absolutely right. Somebody's ass is getting kicked here. At $2 billion a month, the economic ass-kicking is ours. Yours and mine. In the unthinkable ass-kicking of irreparable loss, it's our troops on the ground getting the proverbial boot; it's their blood being spilled for politics. There are more amputees coming home from this war than from any other since the Civil War.

They stand up, we stand down. That was the deal and we've been told for four years that we were almost there. To date, however, neither the Iraqi government nor their military can get on their feet. It may take years, they tell us now, before Iraq can defend or govern itself: "Insurgencies generally take nine or ten years to run their course." The Army says they cannot sustain this burden past March.

What's changing significantly and permanently on the ground in Iraq? Nothing but the body count.

Public Opinion Surveys and Pollcats: If It Stinks, it's Probably a Skunk

Sept. 19, 2007

"Bad wording is often the deliberate result of interested parties whose aim is to generate specific responses. One of the best tests of a poll is your reaction to it. Does it seem fair and unbiased? This 'smell test' is not foolproof, however. Seemingly innocent variations in phrasing such as 'aid to needy' vs. 'public welfare programs' can produce very different results." — Daniel Yankelovich, 2002 PBS interview with Bill Moyers

Face it. There are polls and there are polls. The notion of a perfect poll, one that accurately and fairly measures and reflects the opinions of "the majority of likely voters" everywhere, every time, is just that — a notion. And it's a dangerously far-fetched one. All polls are not created equal.

I recently had the chance to communicate with a real, live person who has a weighty opinion about what "some polls" are like. Rick Beaulé, a schoolteacher from Pennsylvania, worked his way through college. In 1992-93 he worked for Intersearch, a market research firm based out of Horsham, PA. The company was contracted to conduct surveys of various types — a quality control survey for Cigna Healthplan, a survey of TV coverage of the '92 Winter Olympics. Then there was the other one. It was political.

"It was the fall of '92, I believe, when a survey came in for a political race in the Philadelphia area," Mr. Beaulé wrote.

"At first the survey seemed as straightforward as the [others], asking for a general rating of each of the two candidates, but I soon began to notice differences.

"Among the most striking were long paragraphs ... that we were to read before asking a rating question. Often these paragraphs would contain words analogous to the following: 'If I were to inform you that Candidate X voted to raise taxes six times during his tenure in the legislature, how would that affect your [opinion] of the candidate? Positively, somewhat positively, not at all, somewhat negatively or very negatively?'

"Following that was another such question preceded by a paragraph detailing pay raises the candidate had supposedly voted for himself.

"(Then) was a long paragraph detailing something the other candidate had done that was positive, followed by a rating question about [him].

"Finally the survey asked the overall ratings of the two candidates again.

"It was plain to me that this survey was not intended to obtain opinions so much as to sway them. This seemed unethical to me. I went to my supervisor who sent me to the branch manager who stated that this was what we were hired to do and that the survey had been vetted by experts."

Mr. Beaulé requested — and was granted — permission to be removed from participating in that survey.

A female voter from the Midwest tells me she's been polled this primary season. Another telephone opinion poll. How did she feel about Hillary Clinton? Did she support HRC for the Democratic nomination? After responding that Clinton was not her first choice of candidates, as she remembers it, she was asked the following question: "Given that Senator Clinton supported allowing women who have just given birth to stay in the hospital for a minimum of 48 hours [after delivery], would you say your opinion of her is now much more favorable, more favorable, less favorable or much less favorable?"

Now, what sane woman in America would say her opinion was anything but "much more favorable" to a question like that? A childless, menopausal insurance company exec, maybe? Where's the positive percentage in such a weighted question? Whose "favorables" might rise accordingly?

"I felt that was kind of like asking if 'you still beat your wife,'" this voter went on. "I asked her [the pollster] questions about some of her questions but she didn't respond, which made me suspect the call was being monitored. She talked very fast, too."

A Virginia voter shares her experience: "I was polled during Democrat Tim Kaine's race for governor. I was asked a lot of questions about religion — like 'Would I be okay having a non-Christian governor?' Kaine is Catholic, which was apparently not Christian according to the crazy Southern Baptist zealots around here."

The Milwaukee Journal Sentinel Online reports that Oregon-based Moore Information called hundreds of Wisconsin voters about the '04 presidential race. Among the questions asked was this one: "Whose position do you think is closer to the truth — those 'veterans who served with John Kerry' and say that he does not deserve the medals that he received, or John Kerry, who disagrees with the veterans that he served with and who appear in the (swiftboaters) ad?"

This kind of push polling begs the questions: Who paid for this poll? Who stands to gain from this kind of "question"? Am I being manipulated?

Some polls are about as "fair and balanced" as Fox News, as "No Spin ..." as Bill O'Reilly. They're not about the business of asking what we think, they're engineered to tell us what to think. And there's money to be made for doing it. Maybe they think we're a few watermelons shy of a truckload. Well, we're smarter than they believe we are — and we've all got noses. If something doesn't smell right we know it. It's time to compare notes, ask questions and demand answers.

Scratch and sniff, America.

Palmetto Family Council's Stump and Straw Poll: Dancing in Dixie with the Devout

Sept. 26, 2007

Conventional wisdom, the polls and the SC press have been in agreement: Giuliani's in the lead. He's the man to beat. Tough enough. America's Mayor. When it comes to the threat of another terrorist attack, he's practically packing heat. Fear trumps family values any day of the week. Even on Sunday.

Not so fast. Maybe the South is looking for a new partner.

On September 20th, the Palmetto Family Council held their Stump and Straw Poll & Barbecue in Columbia. Nearly 600 conservatives attended the event, eager to share pork and politics with Republican candidates for the presidency. John

McCain, Fred Thompson and Ron Paul joined the crowd by telephone, speechifying for all they were worth. Romney sent his regrets via video; he was "busy raising money" for his campaign. Sam Brownback had to cancel; a vote and senate business kept him in D.C.

Only former Arkansas Governor Mike Huckabee and Rep. Duncan Hunter (R-Calif) came south to meet, greet and eat. Bluegrass music filled the air and sweet-tea (one word in the Deep South) flowed like — well, wine.

A grand time was had by all. Pols spoke to the issues of the war (for the most part, Hooray!), strong families (Yippee!), opposition to gay marriage (Hallelujah!), and ending abortion (Now you're talkin'!). No groundbreaking policy pronouncements were forthcoming. No matter. Like Dubya tells us, there's a lot to be said for consistency.

The Palmetto Family Council is a non-profit group formed in 1994 in association with James Dobson's Focus on the Family and the Family Research Council. Its mission is "... working through the centers of influence ... to present biblical principles ... committed to promoting those things that strengthen the family and decreasing those things that are destructive ..." They see the importance of victory in Iraq, frown on Hollywood, gay marriage and women-who-choose.

No less a Southern religious icon than Jerry Falwell suggested the ever popular social sins agenda might be side-stepped in 2008. What's more important than the family values dance card: adultery, sex, abortion, sex, gays, sex, the sanctity of marriage and stem cells? D-I-V-O-R-C-E? Nope. *National security*. We need a tough guy in the Oval Office. Someone who, no matter what his sins, will keep us safe. From al Qaeda. From Liberals.

Falwell gave the religious right tacit permission to hold their noses and change partners right in the middle of the old Texas Two-step. No more "It's all about moral character" song and dance. What would have driven them right around the family values-morality bend a few years ago is perfectly acceptable now. A candidate or two with fidelity problems and a fractured-family past? No problem. One who's happy to change his every position on sin and public policy to one-size-fits-all-believers faster than you can say "What exactly is a Mormon, anyway?" is just fine.

But the PFC is calling a new tune in South Carolina. Or a reprise of the old one — and it had a great hook and was easy to dance to, as the votes showed when they were finally tallied.

The three-hour event ended with the vote: Huckabee, 206; Paul, 179; Thompson, 43; Brownback, 29; Hunter, 25; Romney, 14; NC businessman Daniel Gilbert, 12; McCain, 10; Alabama physician Hugh Cort, 7; Giuliani, 5.

The only major candidate who chose not to participate at all was "I-don't-do-straw-polls" Rudy. When his absence by choice was announced, the crowd booed.

Seems the vote defied Jerry Falwell, conventional wisdom, polls and the press. Soft-spoken Baptist preacher Huckabee won the night. Anti-war Ron Paul finished a strong second. McCain was beaten by a businessman nobody ever heard of; Giuliani, the favorite, lost to both of them and to the Alabama doc. Last place.

Southerners can be stubborn. Ornery as hell. We may

come to the dance with one guy but if he steps on our toes, we'll darn sure leave with somebody else. At the end of the night we might just surprise everybody.

Jena 6: The Real Message and Why it Matters

Oct. 2, 2007

This is the New South and we're proud of it. We've come a long way since racial intimidation and violence made headlines.

The Civil Rights Movement, as much as the white South resisted it, changed us for the better.

We were dragged, some of us kicking and screaming, into an era of tolerance and racial harmony. We're color blind and the days of lynching uppity black folks in trees is far behind us. That's what we tell ourselves. But if you scratch the civilized, enlightened surface something ugly is still there.

The Jena 6 case ripped off the scab. It all began with a single tree in a Louisiana schoolyard. White high school students congregated there. Everything was fine until a black student asked — and was granted — the permission of school administrators to sit there, too. A few black students wanted to share the shade.

The next day three white boys hung nooses from the tree. They were not expelled for committing a threatening racist act, for conspiracy to incite a racial incident. They got in-school suspension. It was "only a prank."

The day after that, several of the high school's black football stars organized a peaceful, silent protest under the tree.

The school panicked and called the police. Reed Walters, the local district attorney, came to address the student body. According to news reports, Walters is said to have looked at the black kids in the audience, waved his pen in the air and said, "With a single stroke of this pen, I can make your life disappear."

NPR reported that, the next night, 16-year old Robert Bailey and a few black friends went to a party attended mostly by whites. Bailey was attacked and beaten. Tensions escalated.

There was another racial scuffle outside a convenience store in which a white student pulled a shotgun from his truck.

Bailey and his friends got the gun, took it to Bailey's home. Bailey was charged with second-degree robbery and disturbing the peace.

The white boy who pulled the weapon was not charged with a thing. Neither were the white kids who beat Bailey the night before. But six outraged black students were arrested and charged with aggravated assault against a white boy.

They did the crime —no doubt about it. Thankfully, their victim was not seriously hurt.

He was checked over at the hospital and released, went out with friends the same night. D.A. Walters increased the charges against the Jena 6 to attempted second-degree murder.

Violence — no matter the perpetrator — is no answer to any problem. Aggression is intolerable. If you commit a crime, you should answer for it. But there's something terribly wrong with a justice system so clearly weighted against people of color.

A black kid is beaten and nothing happens. A white kid

gets it and somebody's crying "Murder!" before you can say "Is this lop-sided justice fair?" or "Does the punishment fit the crime?"

And it all started with the powerful and disgusting implied threat of extreme racial violence: Nooses hanging from a tree. The real message? "No niggers allowed. Or else."

Where's the tolerant I'm-no-racist white outrage in Jena? Where is the New South? We should be speaking out, demanding equal justice.

And we should be ashamed if we're silent.

Barack Obama Rallies Rock Hill, South Carolina

Oct. 7, 2007

I don't want to do this. I've been dreading the trip all week.

Saturday, October 6th. A hastily rescheduled stump speech in upper South Carolina — the do-over for the one Senator Obama canceled on September 20th so he could stay in Washington, vote again for futile legislation to end the war. I was disappointed then. I was eager for that rally; this guy had been pushing all my buttons for months. I wanted to be there, see it up close, feel it, write about it: "The Visionary Speaks!"

But I don't want to go now. Polls and pundits tell me this is a campaign — and a candidate — circling the drain. He might be a great guy, he might be an intellectual with soul, he might draw huge crowds, he might have garnered nearly a hundred thousand new donors in the third quarter and collected enough cash to raise the Titanic but it's a done deal. Prevailing wisdom says HRC's nomination is inevitable.

He's speaking in a very small southern city. In a high school gymnasium. And I'll have to tell the truth: A small, passive crowd, a tired speech. A tired candidate on his way out.

I travel the hour-long trip with a group of women. They are Obama activists. They are all African Americans, mine is the only white face in this small crowd. "It's frustrating," one of them laments. "I keep calling and folks are still saying 'I don't know yet ...'" Much of the ride is silent. My stomach sinks.

We arrive at Northwestern High School, a large, multi-building campus. The first sign that there's life left in the Obama movement is the parking lot. Too many cars, too little space. It looks like Super Walmart on Christmas Eve. Folks are parking across the street. I almost smile. Almost.

We walk some distance. There are Obama volunteers everywhere. I wonder if there are more of them than there are of us. We open the door to the gym and I relax. There is a thrumming, a pulse of sound and energy, a large gymnasium filled with people. We have arrived fairly early and already the seats are full, the floor a mass of humanity. It's a racially diverse crowd; black, white, Hispanic, Asian. There are young and old, the well-dressed and the rural poor in clean but worn clothing. There are small children riding the shoulders of their dads.

My friends go off to find seats, if they can. I pull out my steno pad and begin working the crowd. I meet Democrats,

Independents and a surprising number of Republicans. About half of the twenty or so attendees I speak to are committed to Barack Obama. Many are "leaning his way." They cite his stance on the war, healthcare and education as primary reasons. I hear "charisma," "judgment," "speaks to diversity," "the need to heal." I hear, more than I expect to hear it, deep concern about the way the rest of the world sees this country after six years of George W. Bush. Republicans tell me they like Obama. "There's something about this guy ..." they say. They can be swayed. The sole concern for any of them is one word: Experience.

I meet a twenty-four year old fellow who smiles and tells me he is most definitely Republican. He's a Huckabee supporter, he says, for one reason: "I'm pro-life — and it means the world to me." On every other issue, he goes on, he's solidly with Barack Obama, especially in the areas of foreign policy and the war. "What if Huckabee fails to win the nod?" I ask him. He smiles again. "Then I'll vote Obama."

The music ramps up, Sam & Dave singing "Hold On, I'm Coming." The crowd noise swells with it. Congressman John Spratt appears on the stage, an enormous American flag on the wall behind him. He looks almost boyish, his cheeks flushed as he begins introducing the Senator from Illinois. It's hard to hear him over the crowd. There are, he tells us, over 2,000 people here. I learn later that event organizers had to turn people away. We are an overflow crowd.

Barack Obama springs onto the stage and the roar is deafening. I'm a veteran of NASCAR crowds; I've sat on the second row at Darlington Motor Speedway when the green flag dropped and 43 muscle-cars sped by at 165 mph. I know noise. 2,000+ Obama supporters and others give any race I've ever attended serious competition in the clamor department. A hush falls. Obama scans the room, grins at us. A lone voice hollers "How ya doin', Senator?" Barack laughs and waves. "I'm doin' good!" he hollers back and the tone is set.

This is no stump speech, no passive crowd of listeners. This is a 45 minute interactive revival meeting. We are in the "big tent" — that all-inclusive space where the spirit takes flight and everyone goes with it. There is no podium in sight. There are no notes. Barack Obama, mic in hand, is a man in motion. He walks the walk while he talks the talk, gestures with his free hand for emphasis. Choruses of "Amen!" and "Yeah!" and "You're the man!" punctuate his oratory. He hears the crowd and they know it. I'm on the gym floor with the standing throng; I watch them react. They move to the cadence of Obama's words, rising from flat-footed stance to tip-toes, arms in the air swaying or clapping. The Republicans I've spoken to are equally taken with the mood. Enthusiasm like this is contagious.

He's had a little spat with Hillary Clinton, Obama tells us. It's about his willingness to meet with all world leaders, even the bad guys. It's about EXPERIENCE. "Naïve Obama!" he declares, "Naïve Obama will lose a propaganda war! Well, I'm not worried about a propaganda battle with some petty tyrant! Strong countries and their presidents talk to their adversaries! ... We're not afraid of any other country ... Experience does not equal judgment! Age does not equal character! [I should] wait longer? Why? To be more like the folks in Washington?" The crowd goes wild.

The Senator from Illinois speaks to the issues of equal justice, war and diplomacy, healthcare and education, poverty, the environment and our dependency on fossil fuels, oil money for terrorists. He speaks to the need for parents to step up to the plate and be responsible for their children. The crowd grows louder, more enthusiastic with each challenge for change. Obama slows the pace. "It won't be easy," he warns us. "I'm asking you to make the sacrifice ... 'cause none of it will come cheap ... I'm asking you to make the hard choice ... to be responsible ... to hold your president and your government accountable ..."

The roar of approval, sacrifice or no, is ear-splitting.

"We can change the world!" Obama cries out. The masses respond in kind. The litany begins. "FIRED UP! READY TO GO!!"

I back out of the gym while Barack and the crowd chant the campaign mantra. I want to watch the exodus, measure the impact of nearly an hour of the Message of Hope. Folks come out dancing, still chanting. There are hugs and high-fives. "You hear that?" one man shouts. "He's takin' it to her about experience!" "Amen to that!" someone answers. I assume they are talking about Hillary.

It's over. We're leaving. Music pounds from the speakers again; Jackie Wilson this time. "(Your Love Keeps Lifting Me) Higher and Higher." I'm exhausted. My feet are swollen from two hours of walking and standing. But I'm singing along with Jackie: "Now once I was downhearted ..." and I'm dancing my way two blocks to the car.

Michael Medved:
'Six Inconvenient Truths about Slavery'

Oct. 9, 2007

He's at it again. No kidding. Self-styled right-wing moralist and movie critic Michael Medved holds forth on the issue of slavery in America, and it's a non-issue. According to him, hey — that shameful era in our history wasn't all that bad. Really. He may well prove that the more the white man changes, the more he remains the same. Medved offers up his "Six Inconvenient Truths" and one wonders if he's into revisionist, white-makes-right history or racism revisited:

● Slavery was an ancient and universal institution, not a distinctively American innovation.

Well, goody for us! Everybody else was doing it, we didn't invent it, so get out of here with all that guilt and shame business.

● Slavery existed only briefly, and in limited locales, in the history of the republic — involving only a tiny percentage of the ancestors of today's Americans.

Yeah, Mikey! Slavery only lasted from 1670-1865. What's 195 years, give or take? And the tiny percentage of slave ancestors? If you count white folks in the overall tally, you're on the money. Besides, who doesn't remember those great explosions of African immigrants who crossed the Atlantic in steerage to grab their fair share of the American Dream?

● Though brutal, slavery wasn't genocide: live slaves were valuable but dead captives brought no profit.

Good point. All we did was kidnap a few Africans, fracture established family units in Africa and then go on to break their patriarchal family model by refusing our slaves the right to marry and splitting up slave families by selling off the parents or the kids whenever the notion struck us. After all, they were worth some serious money! Could have been worse. We could have murdered all of them rather than only the uppity ones.

● It's not true that the U.S. became a wealthy nation through the abuse of slave labor: the most prosperous states in the country were those that first freed their slaves.

Well ... actually the slave-owning Southern colonies were more prosperous than the Northern ones during most of our pre-revolutionary history and that wealth was largely due to slave labor. Cotton, tobacco, rice, indigo and all. Prosperous after the slaves we freed? We didn't go bust down here until after we lost the Civil War — and slavery along with it.

● While America deserves no unique blame for the existence of slavery, the U.S. merits special credit for its rapid abolition.

Repeat: 195 years of slavery. "Rapid abolition" took what? Five or six generations followed by years of one of the bloodiest wars in history and half a million Civil War dead? A quick fix. Painless, too. No blame here — and kudos for conscience!

● There is no reason to believe that today's African Americans would be better off if their ancestors had remained behind in Africa.

Dang straight! The destruction of black dignity, the black psyche, the black family unit, rape, lynchings, denial of human rights and education, a hundred years of Jim Crow?

They should be grateful we brought them here. Definitely. And no one can prove otherwise.

Michael Medved. The Great Right Apologist for White America. When is a crime not really a crime, a sin not really a sin? When Medved says so. You go, boy!

Burying Jim Crow: A New Democratic South

Oct. 11, 2007

Will the climate ever be right for a Democratic resurgence in the South? Fair weather or not, an early primary translates to the power of the South Carolina vote to play The Decider in a critical election. Or the spoiler.

The two top Democrats are a woman and an African American. We may tolerate a Clinton candidacy — but how will this southern state respond to the notion of a black president? Jim Crow may have been blown away by the liberal highs in 1965, but that racist storm front spawned a bunch of little bastard squalls all over the Deep South before he breathed his last.

We don't much like change down here. We liked the climate just the way it was before The War of Northern Aggression ended badly and Yankee emancipation was crammed down our throats. We were punished with Reconstruction. It was a long, bitter cold snap, but we rose again with Jim Crow to keep us warm. We were Jim Crow Democrats for nearly a hundred years, until Yankee Liberals co-opted our Democratic States' Rights Party, turning Jim Crow on his head. Strom joined the new Conservative GOP and so did we.

Recently I was privileged to interview two retired Southern journalists about the Old South and the New. Both were editors of small newspapers during the Civil Rights Era. Both are veterans of decades in the newspaper business: Ed as reporter, editor, owner/publisher and past president of the South Carolina Press Association; as reporter, the first woman in the state to edit a newspaper and past vice-president of the SCPA.

Ed: "... the Democratic Party here [once] encompassed both 'Democrats' and 'Republicans' ... both were known as Democrats. The few registered Republicans sometimes 'picked' a candidate at a small social gathering. [But] in election news coverage back then ... to win the Democratic nomination was the same as being elected.

"No doubt it was race issues that caused the 'right turn' and as civil rights moved forward the Democratic Party in South Carolina moved steadily backward."

Both Ed and Betty made the hard choice: They would cover civil rights, particularly the integration of South Carolina schools, fairly. In doing so, both editors embraced the "liberal" view that the real story was a human rights issue.

Betty: "Republicans were the anti-integration party. In my column I tried to get my licks in on why [integration] was necessary — just driving by those poor 'colored' schools should have been reason enough — and I stressed the fact that everybody bleeds the same color ... I covered NAACP meetings and reported the facts: No violence there; their young people were told to always be respectful ...

"Threats were made against me for those editorials, so arrangements were made with the county sheriff for someone to keep an eye on me as I did the daily traveling my job required. It was unnerving and I admit I did worry about my family.

"... there were family issues, too. My husband's two older brothers had a talk with him, telling him he should 'make her quit writing all those awful things' ... he refused."

Ed: "There were Ku Klux Klan rallies and the more acceptable 'Freedom of Choicers' [rallies], some led by politicians ... [that] made a lot of noise without violence erupting.

"I was sitting in front of hundreds of screaming rednecks at a Klan rally ... the Grand Kludd (or whatever he was called) passed around a copy of my newspaper in which I wrote an editorial advising people to stay away from the event. That editorial was noted in his speech ... When it was over I didn't waste time getting to my car and ... out of the field while the cross was burning."

Both editors suffered the consequences of standing firm for what they believed to be morally right, from threats to the loss of advertising revenues when merchants were angered by their pro-civil rights reporting. Both agree the solid Right bloc still holds today. Neither sees a dramatic shift coming in 2008. Lynchings, burning crosses, poll taxes, literacy tests and segregation, the old Jim Crow Laws, all are a thing of the past. But the Jim Crow squalls: felony disenfranchisement, which denies the right to vote to offenders in a justice system heavily weighted against African Americans, impacts the southern vote; intimidation tactics, like those used in Florida in 2000, frighten minority voters away from the polling place; poverty, unemployment and fewer opportunities for advancement leave a substantial segment of the population feeling hopeless. Little has changed for them. They've come to believe elections don't matter; promises of "better weather" have been made and broken too often. They stay home on election day. Jim Crow lives on.

Ed and Betty did offer different responses to my final question. "Is the South ready to vote for a woman or for an African American for president?"

Ed: "No and no. I live in a [coastal] area that is mostly Republican and getting more so every year. The change here [now] is not racially motivated, it is the Northern retirees moving to the beach. They strengthen the Republican Party two or three to one over the Democrats. Property values and fixed income concerns [top] the list these days.

"I ... would have no qualms about voting for Hillary or any other Democratic nominee. If ever there was a time to be a 'yellow dog Democrat' it is now. In the primary I intend to vote for the candidate with the best chance of whipping the Republican nominee."

Betty: "I live in an enclave of Bob Jones Republicans, but I have hope. So I'll say 'yes' to both questions. I hope that either Hillary or Obama wins the primary."

The GOP has, for now, a steely grip on the South. How does the wind blow in South Carolina? From the Right. But a finger in the wind tells us there's a change coming. Against all odds, Barack Obama has a strong, well organized campaign on the ground here. A new front may be coming along to clear out the last of the Jim Crow lows. Lightning has yet to strike, but there's ozone in the air and a definite rumbling in the distance. It sounds like hope.

W.'s War, Dithering Democrats and Fractured Family Values

Oct. 18, 2007

Campaign 2008: It's the War, Stupid!

At $2 billion or so a week, follow the money. The cost of the unending debacle in Iraq is hitting us all. Right where it hurts. Health care crisis? Education? Social Security/Medicare? The environment? Crumbling infrastructure? No money, no money, no money.

But some folks are paying a higher price than others. While 99% of America fights the "Patriots' Lapel Pin Battle" and Shops for Freedom, the other 1% — our military and their families — pay the price no one wants to talk about. It's time we did.

M is a military mom, S is her only son. S has served five tours in Iraq and awaits orders for his sixth deployment. He has spent the bulk of his late twenties and early thirties at war. She has spent the time living in fear.

M: "S was a punctual, neat orderly kid, methodical and logical in his thinking. He was smart, made good grades. He wanted a career in the military right out of high school in 1993. I was proud of him. I encouraged it. He's very brave, patriotic, loyal and an excellent soldier who has served fourteen years and plans another six years at least.

"His feelings about the military have not changed. He loves it. [But] his feelings about the war upset me. He says we are not helping but hindering the situation there by our presence. I asked him if the 'mission' was what he initially thought it was when he returned from his fifth deployment in late June;

I asked 'What is the soldiers' inside consensus about the war?' S is torn between his loyalty to the military and their 'mission' ... he says they all feel they are not accomplishing anything there ... morale is low, deployments are too frequent. They've missed half of their lives for the last five years ... the cost has been high: deaths, injuries, divorces, fatherless/motherless babies, brokenhearted parents ... who sent their kids to serve without a clue they would be called upon to die so that corporations can gain wealth.

"S has been stressed beyond all reason. One of the ... atrocities of this war is the constant fear of being deployed over and over when you are trying to make a life for yourself, to have some family time before everyone is dead. The knowledge that he will be sent back weighs heavily on his mind. He lost his wife because the [mulitple] deployments were too much for her. He's in a serious relationship now and is constantly afraid he will lose his new family ... family life is lived at a fast pace, cramming as much time together as you can while he's home. It certainly isn't 'normal.'

"He's more impulsive in his spending [now], buying whatever he wants, living hard. He was never this impulsive before. It worries me ... it is as if his attitude is 'I'm going to do what I want because I may not be here next year.' S has changed ... drinking more in recent years. His girlfriend worries, too. She says he is drinking more hard stuff. I can't say [the drinking] is all because of this war, but the constant threat sure doesn't help. We all try to self-medicate with something.

"How many times will S and his comrades be sent back there and how many times can he be sent before the odds catch him? He doesn't deserve this, nor do his troops and their families. I favor reinstatement of the draft ... to spread the responsibility, the sacrifice and the pain around equally. We should have done it years ago when we saw we were being spread so thin and that this war won't be 'won.' [The draft] will make people resist war. The only way [they] really pay attention is if it involves [their] son, daughter or family member.

"I felt, when the Democrats took the House and Senate, that something was finally going to be done. I was very disappointed when Congress 'rolled over' after the election, didn't take a tougher stance. I think they are too cowardly to fight back. I don't believe in withholding things from the troops, but we must stop funding this war. Short of cutting funds, nothing is going to stop it. S and I have lost almost all faith in our government. The soldiers' lives have been pawned enough for politics and corporate gain. It's sickening.

"It will be up to the next poor president to end this thing. There was never an exit plan. S believes that Barack Obama comes closest to offering sane policy for ending the war and even then, Obama says, it would take a year to bring the troops home. S believes there will always be troops there to protect the companies involved in construction and oil production ... Halliburton, Halliburton ...

"I won't vote for Hillary Clinton. Hillary isn't Bill Clinton. He's a non-threatening conversationalist. She is a threatening conversationalist. She does remind me of Bush when she sets her jaw and says things like 'Fighting the war in Iraq is fighting terrorism.' That scares me. [Doesn't she] know yet that the terrorists who attacked us weren't part of Saddam Hussein's Iraq? What is wrong with these people?

"I think Obama, who was against this war in the first place, has the right idea. Get out of Iraq. He wants to shake up Washington and that could be a very good thing. I just wish we knew his plan ... his execution of his plan. This is what I hate about primaries and elections ... they tell us whatever we want to hear, then they seldom come through with any of it. But, of all the Democratic candidates, [Obama] is my favorite so far.

"S gave me 'that look' when he told me [about another deployment], where his face gets very sober, his lips pout out a tiny little bit, only the little bit a mom would notice ... I will always see my little boy in his face, no matter how many lines sprout from his eyes and forehead or how gray his hair is getting ... He is expecting orders for Iraq soon. He just came home in June, but he'll go back because he remains loyal to his country. He will do what is asked of him.

"Please, somebody, please — this war has to stop! His sixth tour! Please pray it isn't so. I can't do it again yet. I know he can't either."

This is an American family. A proud military family. Good people who have believed in their government, who have chosen to serve their country. In the lofty "Family Values" atmosphere, touted so often and with such ownership and vigor by the GOP, these families were the first to offer themselves in time of war. The price they pay, in blood, in pain and loss, is far too great when they are the minority, when the war drags on and on with no one else stepping up to shoulder any share of the burden.

Multiple deployments and the fracturing of military families is not "supporting our troops." Far from it. This is the flagrant abuse of a courageous, loyal military and the families who are left behind.

The Patriots' Lapel Pin Battle: Fighting the Good Fight

Oct. 23, 2007

Only in 21st century America, land of the soft, spoiled armchair warrior ...

We've been bogged down in a war with and occupation of Iraq for nearly five years now but, unlike, say, WW II, this nation is not fully engaged. Far from it. We sacrifice nothing. No rationing of sugar or gasoline, no maps on our walls with pins marking the front, no families gathering around the radio every evening for war news.

While 1 percent of the population — the military and their families — bear the entire bloody burden of the real war, the other 99 percent of us are busy Shopping for Freedom. And we've had our own tidy little battle making headlines lately: Partisans declaring war on Barack Obama for failing to sport the tiny American flag pin that is surely the measure of both patriotism and fitness for office. No red, white and blue lapel pin, no support for our troops. To his credit, Mike Huckabee says it's a non-issue. He doesn't fly the flag on his suit all the time either. His patriotism, however, is unchallenged.

As the Lapel Pin War raged in the media and good Americans fired off rounds of deadly condemnation, a military family in the Midwest spent every ounce of energy they had cramming in as much happy time as possible while their loved one, a veteran of fourteen years in the military, was home from his fifth tour in Iraq. He expects orders for his sixth deployment very soon. He's spent the bulk of his late twenties and early thirties at war. His family has spent those same years living in fear.

This proud military family will not be voting Republican in 2008. They like Barack Obama. Unless something changes between now and primary day, they say they'll vote for him. The political banner on their wall might read: "It's the War, Stupid!" Obama's judgment in 2002, when he spoke out against the pending invasion of Iraq as rushing into a "dumb, rash war," one that would leave our troops stuck in a bloody quagmire with no way out, with inconceivable consequences and at unimaginable cost, has proved prescient. They like his plan for phased redeployment. They don't care what trinket adorns his suit coat. Symbolism is a cheap commodity when bullets, RPGs and IEDs are real threats to real soldiers — and one of them is your son, your daughter, your husband, wife, father, mother.

This military family, like too many others, has sacrificed enough. This military mom says, "How many times will [my son] and his comrades be sent back there and how many times can he be sent before the odds catch him? He doesn't deserve this, nor do his troops and their families. I favor reinstatement of the draft ... to spread the responsibility, the sacrifice and pain, around equally. We should have done it years ago when we saw we were being spread so thin and that this war won't be 'won.'"

Our troops don't have the luxury of time to fret about who's wearing a lapel pin and who's not. That's not their war. Tragically, there's a time when too many of them wear the American flag, big and bold, for everyone to see. It's draped on the coffins of those who, after one too many deployments, find their luck has run out. They get to come home then. To stay.

'Truthiness' Candidate Colbert Surges in Political Poll

Oct. 30, 2007

According to a Rasmussen Reports poll conducted between October 19-21, South Carolina comic Stephen Colbert has found his political base. There's grassroots support for the Comedy Central satirist who announced on Jon Stewart's Daily Show that he was "considering whether or not to consider running for president in 2008." He needed to think about it, he said, in a typical "tease" a la contemporary GOP and Democratic pols who like to play with the public a bit before making the big announcement. They want us to convince them they ought to run. Pretty please?

If he did decide to enter the race, he told Stewart, he would run in South Carolina only — in both Republican and Democratic primaries. That way, he went on, he could "lose twice," and that takes serious political chutzpah.

On his own show, The Colbert Report (which immediately follows the Daily Show), Stephen announced his candidacy that very night. After fifteen minutes of deep thought, he said, he was ready to declare for president. The studio audience cheered, music blared and red, white and blue balloons fell like rain from political heaven.

Pollster Scott Rasmussen wasted no time putting his automated finger on the pulse of America. In a survey of 1,200 likely voters offered the chance to "vote": in a Clinton vs. Giuliani vs. Colbert race, Hillary got 45 percent of the vote, Rudy 33 percent and Colbert 13 percent; in a Clinton vs. Thompson vs. Colbert match-up, Hillary got 46 percent, Fred 34 percent and Colbert 12 percent.

Colbert's base is the younger voter. In the 18-29 year old demographic, Colbert got 28 percent of the vote in a race with Clinton and Giuliani, 31 percent in a race with Clinton and Thompson. Rasmussen Reports states that "Colbert, running as an independent, attracts more voters under 30 than the GOP candidate." Young voters are sold on him — against all Republican comers.

Respondents to Rasmussen's poll believe Democrats can be trusted more than Republicans on the key issues of Election 2008 with the sole exception of national security, where the GOP has gained a slight advantage.

Colbert, who is pulling double-digits in the poll among all age groups and enjoys the lead among younger voters, has only to energize his base and stake his claim on an issue to sway older voters. Since he's stronger against the GOP field, I'd suggest that he dump the Dems and run as a Republican in the S.C primary. He can certainly separate himself from the field and it may be that national security is his issue du jour. If he lays a more daring plan on the political table for Keeping America Safe, say, bombing the entire Middle East into the Stone Age, permanently occupying the region and renaming the whole of it Exxon-Mobile America or the Halliburton States of America, he might just win this thing. A campaign slogan like "The New Manifest Destiny — And Free Gas for Everybody!" ought to do the trick. He'd find himself in the Oval Office come January 2009 with a mandate like no president has ever had to play with ...

And Scott Rasmussen could take the job as the Colbert

administration's Pollster-in-Chief. It was Rasmussen, after all, who saw the trend emerging in the summer of 2007 when he polled likely voters and asked the key question: "Are you afraid of ... clowns?"

Apparently we're not.

Reactions To The MSNBC Debate in Rural SC
Oct. 31, 2007

Richardson tanked, Edwards spanked and Hillary was out-flanked.

Bill Richardson lost any notion of support with his "Holier Than Thou" speech to others onstage about their piling on Hillary Clinton. After a minute or so of sermonizing, he was debate-watchers' toast. The consensus? "She says she's a big girl. She can take it. What's he running for, anyway? Veep in the new Clinton administration?"

So say a group of rural South Carolina women who watched — and rated — the performances of the candidates at the October 30th Democratic debate. There were seven of us; four African Americans, three Caucasians. We're longtime friends, all of us political activists. We range in age from 54 to 89. We're the women who volunteer, who phone-bank and get out the vote for every election. And we don't always agree on every issue, or on a candidate.

I have to be honest (that rule really does apply at Huffington Post) and tell you this is an Obama crowd. Four of the seven of us support his candidacy. The other three are undecided. Two of them have been leaning toward Hillary since late spring; the woman thing, the experience factor.

But Barack Obama did not win the night and Hillary Clinton was anything but "inevitable." In the post-debate straw poll among those of us who felt strongly enough about performances to vote, John Edwards was the clear winner with four first place and one second place votes. Obama took one first and two second place votes. Hillary's best showing was a single third place — Joe Biden finished ahead of her. Edwards' tougher tone won the hearts of Southern ladies who are ready, as one of them put it, "... to stop all this monkeying around and tell it like it is!" Edwards got cheers three times, for three powerful statements, all of them directed at Hillary. In response to HRC's vote in favor of Kyl-Lieberman, Edwards turned his well-coifed head in Hillary's direction and said "... if Bush invades Iran six months from now ... are we going to hear 'If only I knew then what I know now'?" Every woman in the room was on her feet then, steno pads waving like flags, feet stamping and hollering. No one, it seems, is happy with that second concession to the Dubya Doctrine.

The women were moved when Edwards, on the subject of Iraq, said "If you want combat troops over the long term and no timetable for withdrawal, then Hillary Clinton is your candidate" and again when he spoke of passing on all our problems to our children and grandchildren rather than dealing with the hard realities ourselves. We're all mothers, most of us have grandchildren. We worry about the world we're leaving them.

Electability is a concern among this group of women. We're tired of losing. Chris Dodd got points for laying on the table the "unfair Clinton baggage" the HRC campaign brings with it. It's a real problem, that visceral hatred, and we have to face it. Re-energizing the far-Right is a Halloween ghoul of the worst sort here in the South. "The best we can hope for," one of the women watchers lamented, "is that those folks keep fighting amongst themselves over Rudy and Romney and stay home on election day." As much as some of us like Hillary, we worry that her nomination will incite the Right and cost us the White House. "We just cannot afford to lose," another of the women interjected.

Obama, the group said after the debate, got off to a slow start but did well overall. What he didn't do was hit the high notes that Edwards did. They responded well to Obama when he spoke to the issues of honesty and transparency in government, taking Hillary to task over lobbyists, about not facilitating the National Archives' speedy release of Clinton White House documents so the public can see evidence of her eight years' experience in impacting public policy. They cheered when he, unlike HRC, said he would lift the salary caps impairing Social Security solvency. "I'd be happy to contribute more if I made that kind of money," one said. "We need to start taking care of one another."

These women are torn about Obama's going on the offensive. It makes for schizophrenic support. They want him to hit back. No. No, they don't. He's better than that ... but maybe he really should ... or not. They were happy Edwards did it for them.

It's worth mentioning that Joe Biden made everybody's top three. He was forceful, they pointed out, and showed the wisdom of longtime public service in a positive way

Dennis Kucinich did amazingly well with the group. They loved his single-payer, not-for-profit healthcare plan — a fascinating development, since two of them are in the business of health and life insurance. We all loved Kucinich's repeatedly bringing up impeachment. Dubya is not popular here. None of us liked the tenor of Brian Williams' "Will you pledge ..." question about Iran and nuclear capability. It sounded aggressive. When Kucinich scolded Williams and the MSM for their culpability in "ratcheting up the rhetoric for war" by framing questions in such volatile terms, he got applause. Pencils flew over paper as he spoke, checkmarks prominent next to his name. I thought he'd finish in the top three right up to the moment he said he'd seen a UFO. There was a collective groan. "No one's gonna take that man seriously now," someone muttered.

At the end of the night the only candidate to drop out of the top tier was Hillary. Edwards, whether or not he won their votes, had a few new fans. The Obama bunch said they'd still vote for him, but would like to see an Obama/Edwards ticket. Biden won both attention and respect. Dodd got a big nod for having the courage to tell us the 800 pound gorilla in the room is more than a specter of Halloween and that we'd darn sure better acknowledge it. Richardson became the non-candidate who panders for position with the frontrunner. Speaking of frontrunners, one of our group made two points: "It's sad," she said, "that more people probably watched the "Dancing with the Stars" results show than the ... debate, but there might be a lesson [there]. The early frontrunner, the one almost everyone assumed would be in the finale, was booted from the show ... who knows?"

And then there was Dennis Kucinich, who can win our hearts with lofty ideals only to shoot himself in the foot before our heads are ever engaged. It's important to note, however, that he is clearly the happiest candidate on any stage. We watched him and his gorgeous young wife in a lip-lock after the debate. It was worthy of any lusty Harlequin Romance book cover. If only Al and Tipper had looked so steamed-up in 2000.

Hillary Clinton:
That Ain't No Way to treat a Lady

Nov. 6, 2007

The pre-Halloween Democratic debate proved to be the first really interesting evening since the (endless) debates began. On either side. The code of conduct on the Left has been "make nice." They've been so slavishly polite to each other that a debate between Democrats comes off as a love-fest. I keep waiting for a chorus of "Kum By Yah" before the thing's over. On the GOP side we have a battle over which of them is the most conservative ("I am!" ... "No you're not — I am!"), who is more like Reagan, which is quicker on the draw. Mitt Romney joined the NRA in 2006 to ensure his inclusion in the "tough guy club."

On Oct. 30 the Democratic gloves came off. And the target of the man-handling was, for the most part, Hillary Clinton. She's staked out her claim as the most hawkish of liberal candidates on Iraq, Iran and the "War on Terror." She is tough. Tough enough, she tells us, to handle the job. But the buzz in the media and the online political community after the debate has been a different story. "MSNBC set her up and all those men were piling on the only woman ..." The Clinton campaign tsk-tsked over Edwards and Obama daring to stoop to confrontation. They're supposed to be the nice guys. Obama pledged a kinder, gentler campaign and broke that promise ...

I watched the debate with a group of women, all of us politically engaged. There were six of us in my den, another hooked up to us by computer. Four were African American, three Caucasian. While one commented that Tim Russert might have been biased against Hillary, we all agreed it was about time clear distinctions were made between candidates.

In reference to Hillary's vote in favor of Kyl-Lieberman — labeling the Iranian Republican Guard a "terrorist group" and cracking the door for another Iraq — John Edwards turned to her and said, "You cannot give this president an inch ... if Bush invades Iran six months from now ... are we going to hear 'If I'd only known then what I know now'?" The women in my watchers group cheered. We do not want to hear those words spoken about another disastrous invasion. None of us were happy with a second concession to the Dubya Doctrine on Hillary's part and no one saw Edwards' question as a personal attack.

There was enthusiasm for Obama's argument for honesty and transparency in government, taking Clinton to task for cash from lobbyists and failing to facilitate the National Archives' release of Clinton White House documents so the public can see evidence of her "eight years' experience" in impacting public policy. Clinton clearly waffled in her response, first blaming the National Archives for being bureaucratic, then backing off when Russert reminded her it was Bill Clinton who asked the Archives to hold all documents until 2012.

Chris Dodd got a collective nod for laying on the table the

"unfair Clinton baggage" the HRC campaign brings with it. That visceral hatred, fair or not, is a real problem and we have to face it. Dodd had the guts to tell us the 800 pound gorilla in the room is more than a specter of Halloween and we'd better darn sure acknowledge it. His pointed disagreement with Hillary about her apparent support of issuing drivers' licenses to illegal immigrants in NY got the women's attention, too. Not because they all agreed with him, but because, again, when confronted Hillary moderated her position. Both Edwards and Obama called her on it.

No candidate called her any names, no one attacked her personally. She lost points among the women's group because, as one put it, "She habitually refuses to answer some questions and tonight she kept trying to shift her position."

We like Hillary. All of us. She lost ground with some of us, but it was nothing personal. And neither was there an unfair attack during the debate. We worry about her electability and her performance did nothing to alleviate that concern.

As to the Bad Boys "piling on" — if the Clinton campaign can't handle a tougher Democratic debate without crying "That ain't no way to treat a lady!," how will they ever deal with the down-and-dirty GOP frontal attack that's sure to come if she wins the nod?

Any Little (South Carolina) Boy
Can be President? Not a Chance.

Nov. 13, 2007

Native son Steven Colbert is a gone goslin'. South Carolina Dems couldn't get his name off the primary ballot fast enough. In a 13-3 vote, the Democratic Executive Council rejected a Colbert candidacy. The repercussions — for the South Carolina Democratic Party in general and the Obama campaign in particular — are right tawdry.

Online howling commenced with a bang bigger that the first shot fired in the Civil War which, for those of you who don't know your history, was fired by South Carolinians. Political bloggers and commenters alike are on us like white on rice. Clearly, South Carolina Democrats are not really, well, democratic. Obama supporters are at fault, the power behind the Democratic/democratic lapse. It's tacky bidness down here in Dixie.

Inez Tenenbaum, former superintendent of education and a member of the Obama camp, lobbied to get Colbert's name off the ballot. She said she could not imagine Iowa or New Hampshire "letting a comedian on the ballot." And we sure do want to be like those folks. Don Fowler, longtime S.C. pol and former chairman of the DNC, maintains that, while there was some concern among Obama supporters about losses in the young voter demographic, it was not the reason he opposed a Colbert candidacy. He compared Colbert to Nader in 2000; a bit of a stretch, if you ask me.

Here's the truth as we Palmetto State liberals see it: Barack Obama had nothing to do with this. Fowler hit the Confederate nail on the head when he said "[South Carolina] would be the laughingstock of America." Council member Lumus Byrd, who voted in favor of Colbert, said we would be exposed to ridicule. All the things we don't like aired in public — the wrong flag flying in all the wrong places, lousy schools, our dicey racial history — would be fodder for Comedy Central and the nation. For a South Carolinian with identity issues (and we sure, Lord, have 'em), a Colbert candidacy is anything but Comic Relief. We've got problems enough down here. Politics is only funny after prime time. Late at night. On cable. We Southern liberals dose up on Jon Stewart, Steven Colbert and Bill Maher like public policy Prozac. They keep us from imploding.

It's not fair to blast S.C. Democrats for political hanky-panky. What we're guilty of is piss-poor political management. In this state, Republicans are much better at the machinations of slate-building. They have a built-in filter for ensuring their candidates are worthy: It costs $25,000 to get your name on their primary ballot in the first quarter. By the time Colbert threw his clown hat in the ring the Repub filing fee was a cool $35,000. It takes some serious bucks to run as a right-winger. Democrats, in true egalitarian fashion, charge about $2,500. Colbert refused to pony up the GOP's asking price. Too much to pay for a satiric candidacy. He's a comic — not a total fool.

That left the Left as the sole loser in the event of a Colbert Comeuppance; in a close primary race, a few thousand votes impacts the outcome. Not fair. We're sick of losing. It makes us right cranky.

Let's face facts; even if the Right didn't charge out the wazoo, those guys don't have the sense of humor God gave a huntin' dawg. Colbert would be unlikely to cost them any "real" votes. When they vote funny it's because they're laughing ... all the way to the Corporate America Military-Industrial Complex National Bank. And that's the truth(iness).

The Religious Right: Looking for Mr. Goodbar

Nov. 20, 2007

In 1975, Judith Rossner's novel, Looking for Mr. Goodbar, was a shocking read. The protagonist, a meek schoolteacher, cruised bars late at night when insomnia and need propelled her into a desperate search for something to ease her pain. "Mr. Goodbar" was her code name for the perfect man; the answer, she believed, to all her problems.

But she looked in all the wrong places, picked up candidates for her salvation high on booze and lust, took them home with her if they looked sort of right, sounded sort of right. She hopped into bed with one after another but, after copulation — and inevitable disillusionment — she ordered them out of her house. This sad chick had problems taking the time necessary to meet the right guy in the right place or getting more than sound-bite familiarity with him before taking him home to her bed. When she finally met the man who wouldn't agree to leave, the book reached its grisly, unavoidable end: He killed her.

Campaign 2008 seems to have pitched a number of evangelical leaders into a Mr. Goodbar identity crisis. There are online "Evangelicals for ..." sites for a host of GOP candidates. Evangelicals for Mitt Romney declare "[He] is the best candidate ... He's not a flip-flopper on abortion — he's a convert ... He shares our values and he's fought for those values in hostile territory — the Liberal state of Massachusetts." Translation: He was for abortion before he was against it and an entire northeastern state is nothing less than an American Baghdad. The guy deserves a Congressional Medal of Honor for risking life and limb on the battlefield. As to the issue of his Mormon faith, they say: "Let's leave the absurd religious litmus test to the Democrats." Implication? Anyone who raises questions about Mormonism is a left-winger. Now that's a new twist. The right has been accusing the left of having no religious litmus test at all for forty years. Liberals are notorious for overlooking a candidate's religious preferences altogether.

Utah-based evangelical pastor Jason Epps says Mitt is, indeed, a flip-flopper. Further, Dr. Epps writes, "... his Mormonism makes me extremely nervous. I would never vote for a person who actively supports the [LDS] teaching of a doctrine that Jesus Christ is Satan's brother ..." Dr. Epps is an active supporter of Mike Huckabee.

Focus on the Family's James Dobson says he could never support Giuliani, McCain or Fred Thompson because of their personal and/or political lapses. He threatens to support a third party candidate if Rudy gets the GOP nod.

No mention of endorsing Huckabee, who's the candidate most likely to faithfully represent the evangelical conservative point of view. He's strongly pro-life, pro-family, a Baptist minister. He even worries about poor people. But prevailing wisdom dictates he is a man who cannot win this thing. Endorsing a sure loser takes, well, faith.

And there's CBN's Pat Robertson, who has very publicly

endorsed "fidelity- and marriage-impaired, mob-connected, pro-choice, pro-civil unions for gays" Rudy Giuliani. One might suspect Robertson was holding his nose when he made that choice. Or that he's one evangelical leader who's in this race for the power – not the glory.

The evangelical vote is no longer in lock-step monolith mode. Some of them, in their imperfect wisdom, are cruising for the "perfect man," and that includes trading off deeply held religious convictions for the slick, sound-bite pick-up line of national security. It means electability. The biggest gun looks fine in a dark, smoky room. Times are tough for Republicans. They want a sure winner to take home.

So did Theresa Dunn, that schoolteacher Judith Rossner wrote about 30-odd years ago. Theresa learned her lesson the hard way: The perfect man may be the best looking guy at the bar, his come-on may be smooth enough to give you goosebumps. But once you let him in, Mr. Goodbar is apt to leave you mighty cold.

The Half-truth, the Untruth and Consequences

Nov. 27, 2007

"I would never vote for Barack Obama. Never. He's a Muslim!"

He won't put his hand over his heart for the National Anthem. He won't wear a flag pin, either.

Yeah ... and according to another deliberate smear campaign, one waged by the Bush camp in 2000, John McCain had "fathered an illegitimate black child ..." Who'd vote for a guy with the morals of an alley cat?

The "whisper campaign," the rumor mill, cranking out lies or distortions based on "partial truth" sure gets the job done. After beating Dubya soundly in the 2000 New Hampshire primary, John McCain lost, big time, in South Carolina when the Bush campaign turned dirty and deceptive. John and Cindy McCain had adopted a little girl from Bangladesh. She was black. Since she was orphaned, she might have been illegitimate. So, if your aim was to ruin the guy, you could twist the truth, say he'd fathered an illegitimate black child and tell yourself it really wasn't exactly a lie. It's politics, after all. The public, while swearing we're sick of dirty campaign tactics, swallows the filth and forgets who shovelled it.

The 2008 version of the "black bastard" story is "Obama the terrorist." He must be one. His name is strange, he's not white, he went to elementary school in Indonesia for a few years. And his daddy was Muslim. Really.

The truth, for what it's worth (and that's not much during campaign season) is this: Senator Obama's father was born and raised in Kenya — where most everyone is Muslim. Sort of like most everyone here is Baptist. He was not a faithful, practicing Muslim, nor was he a significant figure in Obama's life. Like too many red, white and blue American dads, he walked out on his wife and child.

Barack Obama is an active, practicing Christian. He's been a member of Trinity United Church of Christ in Chicago for about 20 years.

Does he wear a flag pin? No. He stopped wearing one when it became clear that Cheney, Rumsfeld, et al, took great care to sport their patriotism in miniature while lying to the public about the war in Iraq, refusing to pursue a new course to end the war while more and more American troops were maimed and killed. Obama made a statement: Lapel pins are a poor measure of either love of country or support for our troops.

Yeah, there's a photo of Senator Obama, standing erect for the anthem, with his hands at his side. There are dozens of others in which his right hand is placed squarely over his heart. I've seen one of George W. Bush with his right hand on his belly during the anthem. Disrespect? Indigestion? Lousy aim? Does it matter?

One last thing. About John McCain, who suffered a devastating smear campaign right here in South Carolina: Dubya, Rove and Reed fingered the wrong perp for fathering an illegitimate black child. It wasn't McCain. It was Strom Thurmond, who fathered a child with his family's black maid in 1925. Given the oppression of African Americans back then, I doubt she had much choice in the matter. Thurmond never acknowledged Essie Mae Washington-Williams, although he did secretly contribute to her support while she was growing up — that would have been about the time he was running for president. As a segregationist.

A Good Race for the GOP Finish Line? It's Debatable.

Dec. 4, 2007

Wednesday, Nov. 28. Another GOP debate. I watched. Can't help myself. It's rather like going to Darlington or Charlotte for a NASCAR event. I settle in my seat, a drink handy, and wait for the green flag to drop.

What's so addictive about these debates? Why the NAS-CAR comparison? It's the certainty that some super-drivers are going to bump-draft the others, some are going to spin, some are going to blow an engine, some are going to wreck — and maybe take out a few others before they hit the wall.

This race was more remarkable for car trouble than for the big pile-up coming out of the fourth turn on the last lap. Romney, Giuliani and Thompson, running a little loose, got dinged. Paul, Tancredo and Hunter never quite got up to speed — not enough down-force. McCain only qualified as a past champion. Mike Huckabee skillfully avoided contact; no small feat when you consider he drove with one hand while waving happily to fans with the other; he's mastered the outside groove.

There was a lot of spinning, some of it dangerous. Like when a young Muslim woman from Huntsville, Alabama asked the candidates what they would do to repair our image in the Arab world since the invasion and occupation of Iraq. A caution flag was in order. But Rudy put the pedal to the metal, invoked 9/11 and vowed to continue fighting the war on terror. He isn't worried about what Islamic terrorists think (and apparently, they are the Arab world.) Those are the folks, he says, "we want to offend." McCain, who loves a fight to the finish, pledged to continue the surge because it's working, we're winning, and the troops love it. Duncan Hunter spun the full length of the track: Not only will he fight on, but those folks had better remember how we Americans tend to the world's needs during disaster and never fail to defend the underdog. Dadgum. We're darn near perfect and we don't apologize. To anyone.

Engines sputtered like someone had laced the hi-test octane with water. Rudy sputtered over charges of financial han-ky-panky when, as America's Mayor, he charged New York for trips he made to the Hamptons while cheating on wife #2 with wife #3.

Mitt Romney, however, won the Goody's Headache Award for poor engine performance.

On whether or not he believes the Bible, verbatim, is the literal word of God: "Absolutely ... .uh, er — yeah. Um — um — I maybe interpret it differently — um ..." On torture: He refused to answer the question, "Is waterboarding torture?" He sputtered, spitting out the "no candidate should tell" national security spiel. McCain bumped him from the rear; it's a yes or no question, a defining position and military experts in interrogation say it's torture. Period.

On the issue of gays and lesbians serving in the military: In '94, it seems Romney said he looked forward to the day they could serve with honor and dignity. Now he's against it. When moderator Anderson Cooper reminded him of his prior position, Mitt's engine misfired so badly his car flip-flopped down the back straightaway.

It wasn't much of a race. Most of the cars are back in the shop getting realigned, getting engines rebuilt, their carburetors cleaned out. The winner? Mike Huckabee. For surviving without incident.

Dear Hillary, What are you thinking?

Dec. 11, 2007

How desperate can a few sagging poll numbers make a presidential candidate who tells us she's not only the toughest, most experienced Democrat in the race, but the smartest?

Apparently desperate enough to drill past the scurrilous innuendo and mine for the rock-bottom ridiculous allegation. If you can't unearth a 24 carat scandal in Senator Obama's past, invent one. He "seems to have character issues" you tell us, because his health care plan doesn't satisfy you. If it's not your plan, then he must be hiding something really nasty. Oooooh! A character flaw! That's bad enough strategy, Hillary, but your Kindergate ploy is the mother-lode. Can't find gold? Try a little brass.

Accusing Obama of harboring some nefarious ambition to take the White House because he wrote an essay in kindergarten? Are you serious? You're suspicious because a five year old African American child dared pen "I Want to be President When I Grow Up?" That's a reason for voters to worry about Barack Obama's character? His moral authenticity? Are all of us vulnerable to attack because of things we said — or wrote — in kindergarten?

When I was that age I told everyone who'd stop long enough to listen that I knew exactly what I wanted to be when I grew up. I wanted to be a ballerina. And a nun. Both. At the same time. What does that say about my character? That slyly pursuing both careers simultaneously would ensure success when dancing became a habit? Have I lost all credibility as a writer, a mother of three, a protestant? What am I hiding?

Am I a liar or a flip-flopper?

Aw, Hill, this kind of campaigning doesn't look good. If a few polls rattle you this badly, impair your judgment to this degree, what can we expect from you as president? And you tell us there's more of this attack mode coming? "Now the fun begins," you say. Will the real Hillary Clinton please stand up?

There was a time you spoke with outrage about a "vast right-wing conspiracy" and "the politics of personal destruction." You were morally offended by the tactics; you were above all that. Until now. Until the going gets a little tougher than you expected it might be. Extremely unattractive posturing, honey.

A little friendly advice seems to be in order: If you're really the smart, policy-savvy, experienced, ready-to-hit-the-ground-running-as-first-woman-president you say you are, stick to issues of public policy. For Lord's sake don't go bringing the "who's got the better character" hoo-hah into the mix here. It'll backfire on you. The questionable morality dilemma is not Barack Obama's. I know it's mighty irritating when this uppity young fella's popular vision for change in governance punches a few holes in your mantle of inevitability, but you'll never win by playing dirty. Especially if you look ridiculous. And with all that experience of yours, you know a smart politician doesn't expose her own weakness. It's not fair, but the prevailing wisdom is those troublesome character issues are your problem, not his. Best to keep that baggage in the closet — where the weight of it doesn't land in your lap.

The Obama/Oprah Effect?
A Record-Breaking Crowd Gathers in SC

Dec. 18, 2007

The skies over Williams-Brice Stadium are a clear Carolina blue, the temperature a balmy 70 degrees, and more than 29,000 Southerners have come together to hear Michelle Obama, Oprah Winfrey and presidential hopeful Barack Obama speak to the need for a climate of change to spread from the White House to a nation desperate for a new beginning. It is the largest crowd ever assembled for any presidential candidate, we are told. Here. In South Carolina. There is a sense of history in the making and the crowd loves it.

But South Carolina isn't done yet in the "record breaking" department. Before the event begins in earnest, thousands of attendees pull out their cell phones and call thousands more undecided South Carolina voters whose names and numbers were provided them by Obama volunteers as they entered the stadium. The result? Another record broken by South Carolinians, who set a new one for the Guinness Book of World Records: The largest phone bank. Ever.

The tone is set for the rally. It is a day of unabashed optimism, of confidence in both the candidate and the outcome of the January 26th S.C. primary.

Michelle Obama comes onto the stage beaming, waving both hands overhead. "Hello, South Carolina! Man! What are you all doing here?" Her greeting is met with a rousing chant: "Obama! Obama! Obama!" She speaks briefly about her husband as a leader who "gets it" about the poor; a leader who can touch the soul of the nation and unite us for the common

Photo by Martha Hamilton

Someone asked me when it was I first believed (that this man could win not only the nomination but the White House.) My answer? That day — Dec. 9, 2007, at Williams-Brice Stadium in Columbia. That multi-cultural crowd, that overwhelming response to a candidate. It was "... the hour I first believed ..."

good. "It is not the time to be afraid," she says. We've had enough of the politics of division and fear. She introduces Oprah Winfrey, "A woman you know you can trust."

Ms. Winfrey, in a bright yellow jacket, has the crowd on their feet, their response to her thundering applause and cheers. "It is amazing grace that brought me here today," Oprah declares. "Amazing grace. I've never done this before. I've been disappointed in politicians; I've had some apathy going on ... but apathy is the attitude that disappointment is normal."

It is time, she tells the crowd, to step out of the box. She believes in Barack Obama, she says, because she knows him well. "There is no veil of political rhetoric about him," she says. "He has an ear for eloquence and a tongue dipped in the unvarnished truth."

Oprah tells the hushed thousands in the stadium to "see right through people who try to tell us experience in Washington is more important than good judgment." Or good character. Or having a conscience — "Barack Obama actually has one."

The Carolina crowd loves this woman whose roots are in the South, like their own; whose path was not an easy one, like their own. They trust her judgment, and it shows in their response to her as she speaks.

"It's Obama time!" Ms. Winfrey exclaims. "It's Obama time!"

Barack Obama appears onstage and 29,000+ Southerners rise to greet him. The sound of their voices as they call out his name can be summed up in three words: A sonic boom.

And Obama is Obama. "Look at this crowd!" he declares. "Look at this crowd! It is unbelievable ... I am grateful for this day — all praise to God — look at the day the Lord has made!"

Obama's speech is everything we've come to expect from him. He is impassioned; he speaks to issue after issue with both "Yes! We can!" and the caveat that it will take effort and determination from all of us. The fact that 47 million Americans have no health insurance enrages him. There are too many families, he tells us, losing everything they own because of health care crises. We can't afford college for our children. We can't save money. We can't retire with dignity. No Child Left Behind is a failure when funding for it is also left behind. The "haves" are well-served by government while the "have-nots" are ignored and an ill-considered, futile war without end is costing us over $10 billion a month that could be better spent right here. Minimum wage, he insists, must be raised to keep pace with inflation. "If you're working — and working hard — you should not be poor in America!" he tells us. The Carolina crowd is on it's feet. They're "Fired Up! Ready to Go!"

The event is an inspiring one. In the flesh, Barack Obama leaves no doubt he means exactly what he says, that he is exactly what we see: A young man who loves his God, his family and his country. On Sunday, December 9, 2007, more than 29,000 South Carolinians and other Southerners feel they have been witness to history.

They made history. They leave celebrating a candidate they believe in — and that, many of them are saying as they exit Williams-Brice Stadium, is reason enough for hope.

Happy 'Holidays' from Bill O'Reilly?

Dec. 25, 2007

Bright lights, parades, Santa, creches with sweet little baby Jesus smiling up at his adoring mother. Giggling children, wild with anticipation. It's that wonderful time of the year — or it ought to be.

For some of us the dreaded War on Christmas goes on. It's getting to be sort of like the other one — the Iraq quagmire we love to hate — we just can't seem to find a way out of it. Faux News' Bill O'Reilly is ready, once again, to make use of his second amendment rights, armed and dangerous and firing away at the Happy Holidays crowd. If you won't holler "Merry Christmas!" exclusively, you're the enemy. If you shop the store with a Happy Holidays banner on display, you're a secular collaborator. Christmas is Christmas, it's for proper Christians only and you'd better watch what you say about it. The O'Reilly Parsing Posse is on the prowl. Holiday is a no-no. And this is war.

In Australia it appears that a jolly old Santa who can't control his jolly old laughter and cuts loose with "Ho-ho-ho!" has stepped over the line. In major fashion. He's offensive to women everywhere with his "Ho" reference. Which three hos is he talking about, anyway? Is he pimping the holiday? Who knew? The jolly old elf is prostituting Christmas. And he's been getting away with it for years.

Is nothing sacred anymore?

Not much. Seems we're a world of "Christians" so taken with buying up the shiny stuff — and with declaring war on one another — that we've forgotten what the gift of the season really is. It's non-denominational. It's the season of love. And maybe the best gifts we ever get aren't the biggest, shiniest boxes under the tree.

I wrote about a military family last spring, one whose young son was in Iraq on his fifth deployment. He finally came home in July and he is awaiting orders soon for his sixth tour. But his family has had him safe at home for five months now and he will be spending Christmas with them for the first time since the invasion of Iraq. This military family doesn't care if it's Merry Christmas or Happy Holidays. They're apt to holler whichever phrase pops into their heads these days. They don't worry whether or not, to some folks, Santa's shout-out sounds like "Get Your Jollies With One of These Babes Right

Here!" either.

They'll attend Christmas Eve services, exchange gifts, laugh, love, hug and eat too much. For this military mom the real war, at least for awhile, is on hold. Her Christmas miracle is celebrating with her son; she's been praying, since 2003, for a season of peace.

This family's gift is one my family has been privileged to enjoy with them. I want to share it with all of you. Let's get all the war and politics out of the way for a few days — both the real, deadly ones and the ridiculous battles over semantics. Let's let it be what it is, the season of love and of peace.

Happy Holidays, ya'll. And "Ho-ho-ho!"

Bugged by a Ron Paul supporter

Jan. 1, 2008

An average day in my home office begins with a flood of messages. Sixty or more of them, all politics. My inbox is rarely empty and most of the incoming messages demand attention I'm not willing to give them. Folks want me to know who they're supporting for president in '08, who they love, who they loathe. And why. And why don't I write something nice about their guy, anyway? The delete key is my favorite computer option.

Recently, one message really got me. It's been bugging me ever since. A young Ron Paul enthusiast sent me The Modern Day Ant and Grasshopper. You know, that old fable about the industrious ant who works all summer long (no vacation for him!) getting his house ready, stocking it with food for a long, hard winter. The grasshopper, who thinks the ant is a fool, spends his summer drinking and dancing. Winter comes. The ant is warm and cozy and well-fed. The shiftless grasshopper, without food or shelter, dies in the cold. Moral of the story? "Be responsible for yourself!"

The modern day version begins the same way. A hard-working ant with foresight and ambition; a lazy, selfish grass-hopper who fritters his time away. But this new fable takes a turn. Come winter, the grasshopper calls a press conference to complain that he's suffering extreme poverty while the ant has plenty — and a BMW. Major news outlets get involved, exposing the plight of poor grasshoppers in America. The public is deeply disturbed when Oprah and Kermit the Frog discuss grasshopper poverty. Every liberal and minority activist in government gets involved, persecuting the ant. He never paid his fair share of taxes, they say. He didn't hire an equal number of minority green bugs either. He's fined for that and, because he hasn't enough money to pay his retroactive tax hike, the government seizes his house.

Naturally, in this fable, the case of the ant and the grasshopper goes before a panel of liberal federal judges appointed by Bill Clinton from a list of single-parent welfare recipients. The ant loses the case and disappears into the snow where, it appears, he dies. Clearly he's punished for doing all the right things. The grasshopper gets the ant's house and all his food. Of course the lazy grasshopper abuses the property; the house falls apart and the grasshopper (we all know what they're like) is killed in a drug-related incident. His abandoned house is taken over by a gang of spiders and there goes the neighborhood.

It's a simplistic little tale and the moral is clear: Poor folks are poor because they're all lazy substance abusers. All of them. No exceptions. They get exactly what they deserve and the rest of us owe them nothing. The American Way, according to Ron Paul and his admirers, is endangered by taxes and social programs for the underprivileged. Give a grasshopper an inch and he'll take your house and all your food, leaving you to starve in the snow. It's the Darwinian principle at work; the survival of the fittest — and the richest — is the new American Dream.

How sad. How frightening that decent people fall for a brutal, shallow coda and see, in an inane, prejudicial rewrite of an old fable, a new perfected truth. The have-nots are simply bad bugs. Good bugs, like you and I, aren't responsible for the least of these bugs. Step over 'em. Step on 'em. They've got it coming.

How Do You Lose Inevitability? It Takes a Pillage

Jan. 8, 2008

For an experienced politician who crowed "I'm the only candidate ready to hit the ground running from day one!" Hillary Rodham Clinton was clearly not ready for Iowa. Barring a miracle, Barack Obama's insistence on taking the high road, his message of hope and the promise of real change will win the day in Clinton's "firewall" New Hampshire as well.

The Obama Effect is proving to be more a movement than a campaign. And it's moved Hillary to both emotional outbursts and attack mode, some of it wrapped in the same speechifying. If Bill Clinton "felt our pain," Hillary is asking us to feel hers — while the claws come out.

What happened?

The pillaging of Clinton invincibility was the result of no insurgency, no frontal attack by a more powerful enemy, no sly rebel sniper lying in wait to take her out. The Clinton wounds are self-inflicted: A tin ear for what the public might really want in new leadership. Macho-posturing to prove she has bigger b- , no, let's be civil and call it more "testicular fortitude" than any man on the campaign trail. She wanted to prove she can roll right over the big boys. She's hard. She's tough. She can fight this war with the best of 'em. She can beat 'em. Anywhere. Any time.

She invoked the bloodied ghosts of Partisan Wars Past. She's survived those attacks; she knows how to give as good as she gets. She can draw blood and that makes her the only real winner among Democratic hopefuls. They lack her experience. They're all pretty words and no action. Change? Not as important as Experience in D.C. Hope? Get real. This is war, you silly idealists, and the battle-hardened veteran is the only logical choice.

America heard you, Hillary. And it seems what America heard was more of the same old angry gridlock waiting to happen. Battle lines are drawn. The enemy is identified. We elect the gal who's kept her hands fisted, jabbing, jabbing, looking for the glass jaw, going hard for the knock-out punch.

It's not over yet. Democratic insiders, the power brokers, have been solidly tied to the Clinton War Camp. The dogs of the War Room, Bill and Carville, will have their day. The machine may emerge intact and muscle you farther down Primary Road. But the people, Hillary, are telling you something.

We don't like the tactics and we don't like the message.

We're war-weary. We're sick of Iraq and we're just as sick of the Capitol Hill/Oval Office warfare that's been raging since the '90s. We don't want that old baggage back in the White House. We really do want change we can believe in. We really do believe we are better than this; that we can still set aside our partisan differences, stop the smears and the name-calling and invest our energy in the common good of a decent nation. We want idealism again — we're worth it. We want hope and we want a president who knows what's worth fighting for and what isn't. We want communication and progress, not a bloodsport.

America heard you. Do you hear us?

South Carolina and the Audacity of Hope?

Jan. 15, 2008

"... I'll tell you who I'm voting for. I'm voting for Hillary Clinton. We need to get Bill Clinton back in the White House. Barack Obama's a fine young man but he [has] no business running for president ... No way is any black man getting elected president in the United States of America — not in my lifetime and not in yours! If he gets elected there'll be rioting in the streets the likes of which [you've] never seen. And they'll kill him. They'll kill him."

— October, 2007, a 67 year old Pageland African American voter

The Obama campaign has been nothing if not a phenomenal movement. I've been following Barack since he declared for president in February 2007, covering events, interviewing voters. The bulk of Obama's support, early on, was very white and very liberal; idealists who were against the war in

Iraq, worried about health care, education, poverty and a toxic political climate where Republicans hated Democrats, Democrats hated Republicans. The senator from Illinois had a record of bridging the great divide and getting things done during his tenure as a Democrat in the Illinois legislature. Conservatives liked him. Independents liked him. His message of open communication, of both sides listening to each other and working together for the common good resonated with folks who wanted peace — in D.C. as well as in the Middle East.

He was the long-shot of all time. Broad support in the African American community was hard to come by; they feared for his safety, the Clinton mystique was strong and there was little faith in the electability of Barack Obama. White America could not be trusted to back a black candidate for president. But the Obama movement took hold. Massive volunteer support nationwide grew in size and in commitment. "Impossible" became "Maybe" as crowds at Obama events numbered in the enthusiastic thousands again and again.

Then came the Iowa caucuses and a predominantly white state said Yes to the Audacity of Hope. The notion that "White folks won't vote for and African American" was blown away. Even here, in South Carolina, where the Clinton candidacy was seen as an impassable juggernaut, the momentum shifted.

In a WCSC (CBS, Charleston)/Survey USA poll of 3,000 likely voters statewide on the eve of the New Hampshire primary, Barack Obama won 50% of the vote to Hillary Clinton's 30%. A twenty point spread. Edwards trailed with 16%.

South Carolina, home of the Dixiecrats and Jim Crow, re-

garded as a racist haven by much of the nation, was poised
to make history. New Hampshire, where Obama was behind
Clinton in double digits only a few weeks ago, was suddenly
in play. Media hyped a major upset: Obama by a wide enough
margin to cripple the Clinton campaign. The mainstream media set the stage and prevailing wisdom was that, if Barack
didn't beat Clinton by at least ten points, well ... maybe she was
inevitable after all. He lost, in what was very nearly a statistical
tie, by 2.6 percent. He did tie HRC in winning NH delegates.
He won nine, she won nine. He is, as the campaigns move on
to Nevada and South Carolina, ahead of Hillary Clinton by
one delegate. On Jan. 26 it's our turn. Does a very slim majority of New Hampshire voters dictate the outcome here? Does
support wane because another largely "white" state wasn't a
clear, commanding win for the African American candidate?
Does race matter more than intelligence and humane governance? Does gender matter in "toughness"? Do we want a
whole new approach in Washington or do we want to reprise
the Clinton administration?

Joe Biden predicted that the next Democratic nominee for
president would be determined in South Carolina. It seems
we matter now, and that's uncharted territory for us. It's pretty
potent, folks. Who are we South Carolina Democrats anyway?
What do we believe in? How courageous are we willing to be
on Jan. 26, 2008?

South Carolina in Black and White

Jan. 19, 2008

At the end of the day Campaign 2008 in South Carolina is about the "politics of personal destruction" — and of fear — after all. Lessons learned from the Lee Atwater School of Scorched Earth Political Warfare still frame the debate and the tactics here.

Years after the Willie Horton ads and the George W.-inspired "John McCain fathered an illegitimate black child ..." push-polling mortally wounded the presidential aspirations of Michael Dukakis and Senator McCain, we are suffering Lee Atwater redux. South Carolina's claim to political fame seems to be a remarkably high tolerance for the fear-and-smear campaign. We red, white and blue Southern Christians do love our occasional wallow in the pig sty.

We're at it again. John McCain is no war hero; he's a coward who sold out to his North Vietnamese captors to save his own skin. Huckabee pardoned more Willie Hortons than Dukakis ever dreamed about turning loose on an unsuspecting public. Mitt's a bona fide member of a religious cult. Democrats? They're all tax and spend baby-killers who'll surrender to al Qaeda and pitch us into the fiery pit of socialized medicine — which we all know is communist hell.

It's right ugly down here.

And the ugliest tactical assault by far, the most damaging, is about race. The targeting of Barack Obama is breathtaking in its depth and breadth, playing to deeply held fears and bigotry.

Those of us covering the campaigns know that South Carolina's African American voters did not rally en masse to hop aboard the O Train. In the early days of the Democratic race for the nomination, black support for Hillary Clinton was rock-solid. Southern African Americans love the Clintons, who have been consistently sensitive to issues of racial parity. She would win their vote. We writers, who spent time listening to African Americans in their barber and beauty shops, in their churches, heard the same argument time and again. A sixty-seven year old gentleman, waiting his turn in the barber's chair, told me "I'll tell you who I'm voting for. I'm voting for Hillary Clinton. We need to get Bill Clinton back in the White House ... Barack Obama's smart and he's a fine young man, but he's got no business running for president ... No way is any black man getting elected president of the United States of America — not in my lifetime and not in yours!"

South Carolina blacks were slow to believe Barack Obama could win.

Until December and the Obama/Oprah Event, when 30,000 South Carolinians, black and white, rallied for the senator from Illinois. Until Iowa, when a very white state said "Yes" to an African American candidacy. The notion that "White folks won't vote for a black man" was blown out of the water. The momentum shifted. Pro-Obama meetings doubled and tripled in size. On the eve of the New Hampshire primary a WCSC (CBS, Charleston)/Survey USA poll of 3000 likely voters statewide underscored the strength of the Obama surge: Barack Obama had the support of 50% of the respondents to Hillary Clinton's 30%. John Edwards trailed with 16%. A staggering 20 point spread for Obama. If you could trust a poll. If that lead held ... South Carolina, home of the Klan, Dixiecrats and Jim Crow, was poised to make history.

Doubt was defeated and fear kicked in. The specter of assassination has haunted the Obama campaign here all along. America has not been kind to her visionaries, especially those of color, and success has bred violence. An electable Barack Obama may be an endangered Barack Obama. For journalists on the ground with the campaign, the question most often asked by the South Carolina African American voter was no longer "Can he win?" but "Can he survive a win?"

That concern is well-founded. The politics of racist fear and loathing has surfaced in South Carolina since the New Hampshire primary. A viral campaign is in effect here; a massive e-mail assault, "Who Is Barack Obama?" is underway. Thousands of South Carolinians are getting the message: Barack HUSSEIN Obama is a Muslim. All Muslims are terrorists. So he's the Manchurian Candidate who will hand us over to radical Islam and destroy America from within. Everyone is talking about it.

A sixty year old white liberal woman who has not voted Republican since 1968 told me "I voted for Bill Clinton two times ... I don't like Hillary. I don't like her one bit. But I got an e-mail about Barack Obama — he's a Muslim ... he won't wear the American flag pin and he won't put his hand over his heart for the Pledge of Allegiance. I just can't vote for a Muslim no matter what he says or how good he sounds ... Barack Hussein Obama scares me."

A thirty-something white voter, who has no internet access, also quoted the viral smear, chapter and verse, as her reason for being adamantly anti-Obama. When asked where she got her information she said, "Why, we got copies from members of our church!"

And that's where we are: South Carolina blacks are afraid of an assassin's bullet and, as one put it, "... the death of our leader and the death of all our dreams, all over again. We just can't take it. Not again." South Carolina whites say they're afraid of a Muslim in the White House.

White Democrats here have been skittish about Obama. The mantras of "Inexperience" and "He can't possibly win" and the "Muslim/radical madrassa myth," for too many of us, may be little more than the thin veneer of the New South — the one concealing a splintery racism with a mellow sheen of respectability. We're not racists. We're not bigots. Not anymore. We'll vote for a qualified black man, honest we will. But we won't vote for an anti-American, unpatriotic closet Muslim. No way in hell.

The 527, the PAC or the candidate who stooped to conquer, who gave us the Big Terrorist-in-Waiting Lie as cover so we can vote, guilt-free, against an African American, may just win the day here on January 26th. Unless there are enough black South Carolinians who refuse to abandon their principles or their candidate to fear; unless there are enough white South Carolinians who are willing to abandon the politics of character assassination and racism. We stand to learn a great deal about our courage, about the content of our character. Maybe we've outgrown the destructive stereotypes. But it's a mighty tall order, rising above long held fears and bridging the great divide of South Carolina in black and white.

The House that John Built

Jan. 22, 2008

What person, with a heart and a Bible, doesn't love the story of John Edwards' rise from a dirt poor South Carolina mill worker's kid to a brilliant career as a lawyer who battled big business and the health care/insurance industry on behalf of ordinary Americans like you and me? Who wouldn't celebrate the success, socially, financially and politically, of such a Southerner; one who fought his way out of poverty? One who became a U.S. senator and a candidate for president?

And who among us (the big heart and Bible folks) is too hard, too selfish, to resist Edwards' populist message? His passion for the poor, for the powerless? His whole life's work, he tells us, is — and always has been — a fight for America's poor. This battle, he says, is personal. He will raise up, from the depths, this nation's needy like the wreckage of the Titanic. It's a Herculean task he embraces because the poor are always with him. They are always foremost in his heart, in his mind.

You've got to love that message. For the unabashed bleeding heart liberal like me, his words resonate like a rare symphony. He can move me to tears.

But there's something wrong with this melody. There's a flat note running through the music. Something's off.

It wasn't the four hundred dollar haircut. That was easy enough to dismiss as a non-issue. If he wants to pay that kind of money to be well-coiffed, it's his business. In this world you gotta look the part.

But John Edwards' new home in North Carolina is another story. This populist with a heart of gold and a passion for poor folks built himself a 21,000 square foot mansion. Twenty one thousand square feet for two adults with two children still living at home. How much room do four people need to roam around in? How much does it cost to heat and air condition that thing? How much energy does it waste? When is so much personal wealth squandered for luxury morally offensive? How many Habitat houses could have been built with the excess cash if, say, the Edwards' had opted for 5,000 square feet of opulence and invested the rest of that money in the battle for decent low income housing? How many bright poor kids could have been educated, lifted out of poverty permanently, with that kind of cash?

And that takes us back to the haircut, which becomes a bit of an issue after all. If Edwards needs his style maintained every two weeks at that price, he spends $800 a month on his hair. $9,600 a year for trims and blow-dries.

There is a dissonance here; a disconnect between the populist melody and the reality of the composer's lifestyle. If the poor are always with him, if his avowed mission in life is the plight of those powerless, disenfranchised, needy folks ... how does he justify personal priorities which allow for selfish, excessive, conspicuous consumption in the face of such need? What's the real message in such a life? What he says or what he does?

Voters need to give serious thought to the issue of a man's personal priorities before going to the polls. This is the house that John built. Come primary day, I reckon he ought to have to live with it.

S.C.'s 'Shame On You Award' Goes to Hillary Clinton

Jan. 27, 3008

South Carolina stunned everyone on Saturday night. Pundits will be parsing the exit polls, the numbers and an unexpected Clinton rout for a month of Sundays. Those of us who live here, who work here and have been on the ground with the grassroots campaigns, have our own take on the two-to-one margin in favor of Senator Barack Obama, on the significant surge of support among white liberals.

No one expected white South Carolina Democrats to exceed 10-13% of the Obama vote, but they doubled expectations and they did it in the privacy of the voting booth — when no one was watching. An argument can be made here for folks having voted principle over prejudice, for having made a stand for a better brand of politics. One thing is sure: South Carolina Democrats are saying they rejected the Clinton tag-team match. We like our mud-wrestling confined to sleazy night spots and late night cable. It's entertainment. We don't want it in our political discourse. Not anymore. That's big news.

But there's another story in South Carolina. At the end of the day, it may speak louder and define the character of a candidate in starker terms than any stump speech or pundit's perspective. It's a human story about what happened here on primary day — and what happened in Columbia after the polls closed.

When exit polls indicated an uncomfortable, even embarrassing, margin of victory for Barack Obama, Elvis left the building.

Hillary Rodham Clinton left for Tennessee faster than a jackrabbit when the hounds are loose. It was not the wisest decision she could have made.

Clinton staffers and supporters rallied in Columbia Saturday night. It's what you do. Even when it's hard. Even when you know the win has slipped through your fingers. You rally for your candidate. You cheer her on; you keep the faith. And your candidate is with you. She gives as good as she gets in optimism, in rousing support. She reminds you it's not over, that she's with you and will soldier on. And she thanks you — up close and personal — for all the hours, the hard work, the commitment, the emotional and financial investment you've made on her behalf.

The Clinton folks did their part and they deserved better than they got. They worked every bit as hard as Obama and Edwards staff and volunteers; they cared every bit as much. They didn't slink away to lick their wounds when the vote didn't go their way. They came together in the face of a loss that hurt and they did it for their candidate.

Hillary Clinton did not join them. She wasn't there to console them or encourage them. She wasn't there to thank them, either.

Somebody wins the Shame On You Award in every election. The South Carolina Democratic Primary trophy of shame goes to HRC, hands down. She wanted to win big here. She did. And it's a shame.

I Am Woman ... Misogyny, Ambivalence and the Clinton Campaign

Feb. 1, 2008

"How do we beat the bitch?"

That's the inflammatory question a Republican asked John McCain at a televised November campaign meeting in South Carolina. Lousy language. Bad form. Worse, the questioner was a woman who looked like your next-door neighbor. The one who gets her hair done every week and never misses a Sunday morning at church. Video of the historic/hysteric moment was posted on Youtube; the thing was viewed nearly a million times.

Candidate Clinton is the woman everyone loves to hate. Hillary-for-President? They're fightin' words.

Internet social networking sites are especially fertile ground for misogynist seeding; anti-Hillary groups spring up like ragweed in pollen season and, before you can get your hankie out, everybody's sneezing. Facebook is the home of groups like "Hillary Clinton: Stop Running for President and Make Me a Sandwich" and "Life's a Bitch, Why Vote for One? Anti-Hillary '08." Myspace hosts "Citizens United Not Timid" — catch the acronym. It's enough to make you sick. It's largely male rage, both inexplicable and vicious.

Off-line, more than a few Southern gentlemen have told me "I'm sorry. I simply will not vote for a woman for president of the United States." They can't say why. When challenged, they revert to "There's just something about [Hillary Clinton] I don't like. (Read: 'If there's anything I can't abide, it's a woman with PMS and a smart mouth')."

Pollsters and media talking heads have slavishly postulated the odds of a woman winning the White House (Are We Ready?) and the percentages have been all over the map. On a good day, somewhere around 60-67% of Americans, give or take, claim they'd have no problem voting for a woman. Easy enough to say, of course, and P.C. But a finger to the touch screen, in the privacy of the voting booth, may tell another story altogether.

What about the other 33-40%? The ones who won't say they'll vote for a woman? Does that mean any woman — or just the one who's running now? Sociologist C.J. Pascoe, researcher with the Digital Youth Project at Berkley's Institute for the Study of Social Change, has said, "This would not be happening if it were Elizabeth Dole [running for president]." Can we take that to mean a conservative woman seeking the highest office in the land might not provoke the rabid misogynist reaction Hillary Clinton does? Why is that?

How has the Clinton campaign responded to Feminazi Fever? What positive steps have been taken to ameliorate a bad situation? To describe the campaign — and the candidate — as ambivalent is an understatement. There have been missteps along the primary path that nearly put their campaign cart in the ditch.

Hillary tells us, in no uncertain terms, she's smart enough and tough enough to serve as our first female president. From Day One. And she's absolutely right. Nobody knows the issues any better and nobody seeking the nomination, on either side, is quicker with a sharp comeback or an equally sharp elbow to the ribs. Like the low blow or not, "This is politics, not bean bag ..." as the HRC team likes to say.

Point taken. But she can't have it both ways and here's where Clinton campaign ambivalence kicks in. The gender game is in play, and HRC won't pick a side.

First it was a debate last fall. John Edwards challenged her, on her record and on her rhetoric, fair and square. She bristled, and by the next morning Clinton surrogates were crying foul, accusing the "bad boys" of ganging up on the lone woman.

A third place finish in Iowa added impetus to the gender game. By the time Hillary got to New Hampshire and South Carolina, hubby Bill was in full armor, astride his white charger and going after his distressed damsel's enemy with a lance as big as an intercontinental ballistic missile. Sir William would eviscerate all comers, and he wouldn't necessarily play by the rules of chivalrous behavior, either. Hillary's response when it backfired? "He did it because he loves me." A fluttering, feminine Hallmark moment for the masses.

The NY State Chapter of NOW sprang to Hillary's defense, too. When Senator Edward Kennedy, a longtime proponent of women's causes, endorsed Barack Obama, they attacked. Ted Kennedy was a traitor, a betrayer of all women, they cried. Whatever candidate he (and niece Caroline Kennedy Schlossberg) believed was best for the country, he should have supported the woman, because she's a woman.

We have loathsome, mindless misogyny on one side of the bell curve and gender ambivalence on the far side. We have woman-bashing "Get thee to the kitchen, wench!" on the one hand and "I'm as tough as you are, buster, get out of my way!" coupled with "I'm vulerable, too — and that ain't no way to treat a lady!" on the other. Both are destructive and dishonest. Both are bad for the process and bad for the country. Intellect, strength, character and capability know no gender. There's no logical or practical reason a woman can't run this nation as well as any man. Better than most.

That said, a strong, smart woman who's well-qualified to serve as president doesn't need to play the game on both sides of Gender Street. If she does, she gets the disrespect she's got coming, adds momentum to the misogynist movement. The Clinton campaign cannot control the knuckle-dragging misogynist. What they can control is an unfortunate pattern of ambivalent behavior that feeds the beast — and take their campaign setbacks on the chin, like the other guy has always had to do.

In the Promised Land of enlightenment and gender parity, what's good for the goose is, after all, good for the gander.

God is Good: The Quiet Christian (R)evolution

Feb. 6, 2008

The Super Tuesday Southern Surge for Mike Huckabee may have surprised media talking heads, but it came as no great shock to those of us who live in the South. Old Time Religion resonates down here and a candidate who says he wants to amend the Constitution to ensure that hallowed document is more Southern Baptist Bible-friendly doesn't scare most of us one little bit. He's apt to hear a rousing "Hallelujah Chorus" come primary day.

Many super-conservative Southerners want their government to Get Right With God (that'll solve everything) and there's only one way to do it. They're not alone. Evangelicals and religious fundamentalists nationwide have been wooed and

won by the far right. Conventional wisdom? They're all alike.
They're a voting bloc as solid as the Berlin Wall. Or they were.
Outside the Deep South the Ultra-conservative Christian Wall
is being dismantled in much the same way as the communist
one was — brick by brick. And not by some external, atheist
liberal insurgency, but by committed believers who see a broader, more tolerant, more inclusive vision of the Christian ethic.

There is a quiet Christian revolution underway. It's not
some brand-spanking new pop-culture fad. The movement is
decades old, a force of faith arguing for reason, for peace, for
commitment to addressing the needs of "The least of these
..." both here and abroad. These evangelicals do not want an
American Theocracy. They are not interested in power politics
or photo-ops in the Oval Office. These evangelicals see war,
genocide, poverty, disease, illiteracy, intolerance and greed as
the primary evils loose in a suffering world. Led by progressive
Christians like Jim Wallis and Tony Campolo, this burgeoning faith-based group has kinder, gentler priorities. They work
in concert with like-minded people of all faiths, Christian and
non-Christian, for social justice. They're a growing movement
and they've got momentum.

What they haven't got is the kind of rapt attention the MSM
has given the rabid religious right. Why? They're boring. Their
leadership is not given to outrageous pronouncements like
"We ought to take out Chavez and Ariel Sharon had it coming"
Pat Robertson or "You can blame homosexuals, feminists and
abortionists for 9/11" Jerry Falwell. When Tony Campolo said
"Mixing religion and politics is like putting together ice cream
and horse manure. It doesn't hurt the horse manure, but it ru-
ins the ice cream," the media yawned. There's no percentage
in covering the rational, reasonable Christian when the other

guy is hollering hellfire, brimstone, divine retribution and the occasional political assassination.

The old school ultra-conservative evangelicals/fundamentalists successfully narrowed the entire moral universe to a single, hot-button battleground where the enemies were gays, lesbians, desperate women and the families of those stricken by catastrophic illness with no hope of ever recovering. Pro-family meant only one kind of family — their own. Pro-life did not extend to protesting the commission of an immoral war for oil in which hundreds of thousands die, are maimed, are orphaned, are displaced. Too many of them innocent babies and small children. These Iraqi little ones are, according to a fifty-something year old South Carolina dyed-in-the-wool pro-lifer, "Collateral damage. Too bad." War is hell. But if it's ours, it must be righteous.

Slowly, surely, there's a moral climate change coming. The new evangelical is rising. There's evidence of it even in the resistant South. The fact that warrior John McCain defeated Southern Baptist Mike Huckabee in both the South Carolina and Florida Republican primaries lends credence to a shift in priorities.

There's more:

She's 37, a wife and mother of three small children. She's a Phi Beta Kappa with a demanding career in academia. She's also a South Carolina born and bred devout evangelical Christian who gets tears in her eyes when she speaks of the love of God and what that love means in her life. She is opposed to abortion as a casual means of birth control, but she's pro-choice. She is not a member of either party; she's not a single-issue voter. She makes her choice of candidate only after careful study of both issues and potential nominees, bases her decision on what she believes is best for her family and her country. She did not choose Mike Huckabee. She supports Barack Obama.

She's a forty-something African American professional who voted for George W. Bush twice. "Because he was a praying man, a born-again Christian who said he was for family values. It was a mistake. Just because they say they're believers doesn't mean they're gonna do the right thing. This war — this war — they won't fool me again." She'll vote for a Democrat in 2008, she says. Either one who gets the nomination.

He's sixty-two. He's a white, conservative Southerner, a pastor who believes the Bible is the absolute, inviolable word of God. He's a religious fundamentalist who is passionately pro-life. After considering war, poverty, the plight of America's working poor and a world in need of uplifting leadership from the United States, he passed on the South Carolina Republican primary. "I voted on the 26th," he says, blushing. "I voted for Senator Obama."

Given the Huckabee Southern Surge on Super Tuesday, when the inevitable Christian (R)evolution is flourishing, the South is apt to be the last bastion of the narrow, unyielding brand of Old Time Religion. This is where the dwindling population of religious dinosaurs will breathe their last. Their time come and gone.

Amen to that.

The Boomer Girl First Wave:
The Fractious Feminine Mystique

Feb. 11, 2008

The women's vote in Maine, media wise ones told us, would likely be enough to tilt the caucuses in Hillary's favor. Didn't happen. Some of those reliable women voters had other ideas. We're left to figure out what went wrong — at least with a portion of them.

It's a dangerous game, trying to pigeonhole the psyches (or the votes) of first generation baby boomer girls. Like Hillary, we're sixty-ish. Like Hillary, our life experience has made us occasional Masters of the Mixed Message. To understand where we are, you have to understand where we've been:

Our mothers deferred to our fathers, wore housedresses and were attached to the kitchen by an invisible umblilicus. Mother knew a thing or two, but Father Knew Best.

We played house, secretary and school teacher. We played with our blonde Barbies well into pre-pubescence. We didn't menstruate; we had "The Curse." We didn't talk sex; we talked "The Black Act" or "The Dirty Deed." By definition, sex was only full-fledged, unadulterated intercourse. We could do anything — and everything — else except the conventional act itself and say, in all honesty, we never had sex. We could be good and bad simultaneously.

We grew up wanting to be good girl/bad girl. What began with Barbie ended with Sandra Dee/Marilyn Monroe. And it was true: Blondes had more fun.

We were in our mid-teens in 1963, when Gloria Steinem shimmied herself into a bunny suit, worked a stint at a New

York Playboy Club and wrote about the objectification of women. She was a leggy, frosted blonde who lived the high life in New York City and looked entirely too good toting a tray of cocktails. Some of us, awkward, thick-ankled and smelling of Clearasil, missed her message. Not because her point of view wasn't relevant and feminist, but because our Barbie/Sandra/Marilyn complex got in the way. We didn't trust a woman who looked that good in a bunny suit telling us we needed a man like a fish needed a bicycle. Easy for her to say — she could ride any bike she liked.

Lots of us married young. We were smart, but college was the place too many of us were sent to find a Mr. Right who'd be a really good provider. When we opted for yards and yards of white tulle rather than a little old piece of sheepskin, Mother and Father didn't mind a bit. Especially if Mr. Right was in pre-law or pre-med. We were good girls.

We missed Betty Friedan's The Feminine Mystique in 1963. We were too young for the first edition. So we had no idea "... the full time homemaker role is stifling ..." or that we'd been trapped in the Netherworld of Domesticity with festering penis envy and without realizing we had "brains as well as breasts." By the time we got that message the deed was done — and re-examining our choices was too risky. We tried not to think about it.

Then Germaine Greer told us we had no idea how much men hated us or how well we'd been taught to hate ourselves. She said a Women's Revolution was in order and scared us half to death. We were unarmed. And we were getting depressed. Maybe Steinem, Friedan and Greer were bad girls.

We looked to other role models who made us feel better.

YES, WE DID

Phyllis Schlafly, who was almost as blonde and hyper-coiffed as Barbie, told us what to do in perilous times. Feminism was bad for us. The ERA? Forget it. It was practically communist. We saw good old Phyllis on daytime TV while we folded laundry, baked bread and nursed our babies. We might be exhausted, we might be bored; we might be a little blue because, unlike the Sandra Dee-Bobby Darin movie marriage we'd grown up on, ours had no romantic soundtrack. But we were saving the American Family single-handedly. Our husbands, our children and posterity would be forever grateful to us. Phyllis told us so. We failed to notice that she was too busy flying all over the place, getting rich preaching the Happy Homemaker Doctrine, to tend to her own family 24/7.

And we had another blonde helper. Marabel (The Total Woman) Morgan had the answer to the Who-Am-I?-Bored-Housewife-Blues. We had only to put on a happy face, understand our men, forgive them their trespasses and all would be well. We wanted more? Easy. All we had to do was get buck nekkid, wrap ourselves in Saran, slap a big red bow on our heads and meet hubby at the door at 6:00, ready to stop, drop and roll. Forgive, forget and say Yes!

Coming of age in an era of such radical feminine duality was enough to drive us over the edge.

By the time we got serious-blonde-with-a-sensible-headband Hillary in the '90s, we were screwed up in more ways than one. Even those of us who'd foregone the early marriage, finished grad school and done great things, were screwed. We felt guilty if we'd done the domestic thing. We felt guilty if we hadn't. But ... Hillary Rodham Clinton had done it all. She was a smart professional woman who was raising a really nifty kid. We loved that. She'd married a Mr. Right who'd made the Big Time and called her an equal partner. We loved that. Then came trouble and Hillary's caustic "stay home and bake cookies" line and "I'm no Tammy Wynette standin' by my man ..." We turned off faster than a far-right Republican at a pro-choice rally.

Truth is, we first wave boomer girls have a love/hate relationship with Hillary Clinton. She didn't fall far into the good girl/bad girl trap, but she's neck-deep in the SOFT GIRL/HARD WOMAN one and the mixed message doesn't set well. She epitomizes the yin and yang of our perpetual struggle to come to grips with our place in the world and, because she swings both ways, we can't be expected to stay the course with her just because she's a woman. This woman seems to be as confused as we are. Maybe she's too much like us: Conflicted enough to keep dog-eared copies of both The Total Woman and The Feminine Mystique on her mental bookshelf. So maybe some of our sisters in Maine reverted to form and stayed home.

Mormons and Muslims and Things That Go Bump on the Right

Feb. 12, 2008

The Super Tuesday Southern Surge for Mike Huckabee effectively killed Mitt Romney's candidacy. Pundits can talk Mitt's flip-flopping on the issues to pander to the GOP base (which he certainly did) until the cows come home, but the bottom line is this: In poll after poll fully 39 percent of conservative Christian evangelicals say they won't vote for a Mormon for president. Even if hell freezes over.

And it's a tough winter for the GOP, with an unpopular president, an unpopular war and the economy circling the drain. They need all the votes they can muster come November. Romney's religious persuasion, no matter what he said, was troubling to a significant bloc of conservative voters. Odd, too, when you consider that Mitt's father, George Romney, was a bona fide Republican governor of Michigan for eight years. 30-year veteran Sen. Orrin Hatch (R-Utah) is Mormon as well — and as far as I can tell, neither of them brainwashed their constituents or strong-armed them to leap into an off-brand Christianity. Or a cult, as some hysterics have called it. Donnie and Marie are Mormons, too. Everybody likes them.

Republicans are left with John McCain, who doesn't suit the hard line conservative base, either. Folks attending the Conservative Political Action Conference, when Mitt bid the Campaign Trail a fond adieu, wept. The same crowd booed Senator McCain. They like Romney's church better than they do McCain's politics.

They're left with Arkansas governor and Southern Baptist minister Mike Huckabee, too. He's a really friendly type, like George W. was. Frankly, I like the guy. He's funny. He knows how to deliver a punchline. He knows how to play bass guitar. But last fall, when the NIE (National Intelligence Estimate) was made public and we all learned that Iran had suspended its nuclear weapons program in 2003, Governor Huckabee didn't know what in tarnation everybody was talking about. He was the only candidate, of either party, who "didn't get it." Sort of like Dubya in 2000. A nice guy who means well and attends the right church doesn't always perform too well in the Oval Office.

Maybe Mitt, flip-flopper or not, had a better grasp of public policy. But the "Mormonism is a cult" myth cut deep at a time the GOP can't afford to lose another chunk of voters. We're not well-served when a candidate is cut off at the knees because some unsavory folks distort the facts — and the significance — of his religious faith. We're not well-served when equally unsavory folks do worse and lie about a Christian candidate, labeling him a Muslim (and a threat to democracy) because a father he never knew and a stepfather who didn't raise him were of Muslim heritage. That's scare tactics. Dirty, bump-and-run politics.

Solutions Not Speeches? I've Got a Secret

Feb. 16, 2008

The Clinton campaign is still trying to find its voice. We've been through Experience is Everything, Tough Enough and Ready to Lead on Day One. We've had a few bars of You Want My Human Side? Here's Your Humanity! thrown in for good measure. But none of them seems to have worked well enough to silence the soaring rhetoric of Change We Can Believe In.

So the Clinton camp has minted a shiny new mantra: Solutions Not Speeches. Barack Obama may have good ideas, his words may inspire you from Milwaukee to Dallas to Columbus to Philly and back, but Hillary Rodham Clinton is the one who has the solutions. It's what she does. That particular recipe for success is hers alone and she wants to be held accountable.

Let's have at it.

The Solutions mantra begs the question, "Huh?" We're hard-pressed to find an example of a major positive solution to a critically problematic issue here. We do remember the early '90s, when Hillary took on the wholly admirable task of finding a solution to the impending health care crisis. She headed the President's Task Force on National Health Reform. Many of us were thrilled. We'd voted Clinton, we'd gotten two wonks for the price of one, and we could see the handwriting on the wall if something wasn't done to rein in big pharma, greedy purveyors of insurance-for-corporate-profit-only and health care consortia who were (happily) in bed with the aforementioned.

She failed. There was no solution in sight. There were, admittedly, powerful forces at work against health care reform. But a significant part of the problem with the Clinton-led task force was this: The tenor of Hillary's process got plenty of attention — and much of it was not so good. There was an air of secrecy, of policy-making behind closed doors; there was an information blackout which fueled a right-wing argument that a secret cabal of policy wonks was about the business of plunging us headlong into creepy socialized medicine and depriving us of both quality care and our physician of choice.

Does that approach to solution seeking sound familiar?

Fast forward to 2001, to Dick Cheney's National Energy Policy Development Group. Like Clinton's task force, Cheney's was secretive, met behind closed doors and withheld information from the public.

His motives were certainly not the loftier ones of Ms. Clinton, but they shared a similar philosophy about the solutions game; a patronizing, paranoid exercise in furtive, convoluted power-play politics. It was politics as usual, characterized by a total failure to inspire public trust, to build consensus, to effect any positive change at all.

Had Hillary adopted the "Hope, Change and Transparency" Obama approach (not everyone outside your circle of wagons is your mortal enemy), maybe there wouldn't be 47 million Americans without health insurance today. Maybe Senator Obama has a point worth noting when he says "... all of us have proposed plenty of solutions in this race ... The problem ... is not a lack of good ideas. It's that Washington today is the place where good ideas go to die. They're the victim of petty partisan politics, point-scoring, and special interest influence that's out of control ... the real question ... is who can change that ... and actually get something done?"

A nifty new campaign slogan changes nothing. A fruitcake is a fruitcake. Nobody really likes 'em, but hey, it's Christmas and it's what you do. Years ago Johnny Carson, joking about how hard, dry and inedible fruitcakes are, suggested there's only one of them in the entire world, no one wants it, so the same damn cake keeps getting passed around, year after year, until some fool will eat it.

Seems the Clinton campaign is this year's fruitcake. They keep re-packaging the thing as if putting a shiny new bow on top will make the cake easier to swallow.

America's response, with notable momentum behind it, is that we want something different. We don't want a "new voice" ad campaign and we won't be satisfied with changing the wrap and ribbon on the same old cake. We want a better recipe for finding solutions. One that works. We want a president who knows we need to change not only what's being done in Washington, we need to change the gnarled, negative, counterproductive way it's being done.

And that's no secret.

Politicians, Pundits and Silly Season

Feb. 19, 2008

Nobody got it right about Campaign 2008. Mainstream media conventional wisdom pointed to the inevitability of a Giuliani-Clinton match-up in November. On the Right ... if Law & Order Ersatz Reagan Fred Thompson didn't jump in quick, who could best America's mayor? On the Left, well, Edwards might have been an eloquent voice for the poor, Obama might have injected a dose of civility-with-the-Right and Hope into the dialogue, but who'd ever overcome the powerful Clinton machine when Bill and Hill called in their chits? They were flush with cash and organized on the ground. From day one.

Dadgum if the American voter didn't upset the apple cart. Once the caucuses and primaries began all media bets were off. Voters eliminated everyone but John McCain and Mike Huckabee on one side, Hillary Clinton and Barack Obama on the other. Hillary went bust and Obama is suddenly the one with the cash, the grass roots movement and the momentum.

Now practically everybody's in a lousy mood. It's no fun being wrong. Tongues are wagging before brains are engaged.

We expect that from candidates, who get tired and cranky on the bumpy campaign trail. Especially this one, which seems to have gone on forever; a full year already of stumping, stomping and endlessly debating-for-TV has inspired some fabulously silly rhetoric:

John McCain, when asked if he supported Dubya's vision of keeping U.S. troops in Iraq for another 50 years, said "Make it a hundred. That would be fine with me." (War without end, amen, amen.)

McCain, again, on change and hope for a better future: "... The promise of a better future is not always clear." (If he can't see it clearly, where is he leading us?)

Joe Biden, for no apparent reason: "You cannot go to a 7-11 or a Dunkin' Donuts unless you have a slight Indian accent ... I'm not joking."

Hillary Clinton, when asked what qualified her to deal with leaders in Iran and North Korea: "... we face a lot of evil men. And what, in my background, equips me to deal with evil and bad men?" (The crowd — and the candidate — yowled at the clumsy reminder of scandals past.)

Hillary, following multiple Obama wins, says caucus states don't really count (too many volunteer activists), small states don't count like big ones. South Carolina and Louisiana? While she respects African Americans, we are, after all, densely populated with them. (All votes are not equal.)

And there's the media, with MSNBC leading the pack. David Shuster says the Clinton campaign somehow "pimped" daughter Chelsea into pressuring super delegates to support her mama. Chris Matthews, who often prattles faster than he thinks, said this about Barack Obama's ability to inspire and energize large crowds: "[We understand] the feeling most people get when they hear [his] speech. My, I felt this thrill go up my leg! I don't have that too often." (Don't know exactly what he meant to say — and I don't really want to.)

There are primary miles to go before we sleep. No rest for the weary. And it begs the question: How much more inane can it get?

America — Love It or Shove it

Feb. 21, 2008

Oh, the shame of it. The ungrateful, unpatriotic, uncouth comment that shocked the sensibilities of real Americans everywhere: Michelle Obama, speaking in Milwaukee, says "Let me tell you, for the first time in my adult life, I am really proud of my country. Not just because Barack is doing well, but I think people are ready for change ..."

Partisan pundits and bobble-head political spouses are quick to blanch and gasp, "Why, I'm always proud of my country!" They mean that thing, too. There hasn't been a moment — not a single one — that they haven't been 100% proud of America. America, right or wrong. The disinformation campaign that launched a disastrous, deadly war for corporate gain in Iraq? Guantanamo? Abu Ghraib? Black sites? Illegal spying on U.S. citizens and the outing of a CIA operative? Where's the shame in that? None of it matters. A real American is an unfailingly proud American.

Clearly, Ms. Obama has a problem. Or somebody's going to make her one.

No matter that what she's proud of is a dynamic this nation has not seen in decades: Citizens, by the millions, are shrugging off the cloak of apathy, getting energized, engaging in the political process, registering to vote. Caucusing for change. Voting for better government.

But she said those words ... heavy, hot-button words which, out of context and leached of intent, can mean whatever partisan politicos want them to mean. So they matter. And, for those who've been carping about "only words" and "empty words" and "words without work," the about-face is stunning, indeed.

Words have always mattered. The mighty pen and the sword thing, you know? Michelle Obama's words inadvertantly touched a raw American nerve and everything old is new again.

"Adult life," for those of her generation, came to full flower in the mid-eighties. The nation had suffered through the long, bloody quagmire that was Vietnam, an ill-advised war begun without understanding the culture of the country or the enemy we faced. The United States was bitterly divided for years — the dirty, anti-war, sex-and-drug-crazed, protesting hippies squared off against the mainstream, morally superior, my-country-right-or-wrong establishment. The words du jour? Bumper stickers everywhere, shouting "America — Love It or Leave It!" The first Golden Era of "Either you're with us or you're with the enemy" politics was upon us and there was precious little middle ground.

The combination of an endless bad war, bad leadership and bad public policy was lethal to optimism and activism. Politics turned deadly dishonest. Watergate exploded, the Nixon administration imploded and the American public lost faith in good government, turned off and dropped out.

The aftermath of war and Watergate set the stage for the self-absorbed "Me Generation" seventies and the callous

"Greed is good — poor folks wouldn't be poor folks if they were willing to work hard like I do" eighties. The nineties brought the man from Hope. A new, more idealisitc generation took the reins of power only to falter. All that promise wasted through vicious partisan politics and self-inflicted scandals.

Apathy, anger and disillusionment have characterized much of the last half-century, peaking under the Bush II administration. We're back to the bad war, bad leadership, bad public policy quagmire, laced with arrogance, scandal and criminal behavior on the part of leaders who promised us the restoration of honor and dignity and a "faith-based" renaissance of relief for America's poor.

Now is no time for a new "America — Love It or Shove It!" mentality to take root again. Ms. Obama spoke to her pride in the American peoples' willingness to re-engage, to rise above fear, prejudice, disillusionment and apathy. She referred to her pride in their willingness to rise to the challenge for fundamental positive change in governance, and rightfully so. It's been a long time coming. The American voter is finally about the business of overturning the tyranny of ideas which effectively censored critical thinking, muzzled the voices of those who would say "Whoa! I love my country, but this is wrong ..."

She's not alone in feeling proud of — and a little awed by — this groundswell of public political re-engagement. Who knew we still had it in us? We're surprising ourselves.

The Wages of War? No Sweat

Feb. 26, 2008

Houston, we have a problem.

And Dubya has finally owned up to it. The economy is not so good, folks. We're making less money, paying more for everything from soup to gas, Wall Street has the flu and folks all over the country are losing their homes.

In an interview with NBC, George W. denied there is any connection between the Iraq War and the faltering economy. Zero. Zip. Nada. We can afford our little war — shoot! — it's only costing us somewhere between $2-3 billion a week. That's not so bad, is it? At that rate we're only paying $432 million a day. $18 million an hour. For a country as rich as we are, that's practically pocket change.

When confronted with the cost of the war, Dubya grins that sweet, wacky grin of his, cocks his knotty little head and says, "I think actually the spending in the war might help with jobs ... because we're buying equipment ... and people are working ..." Which begs the question: "Huh?" Anyone you know made any war equipment lately? Opened a war equipment shop on Main Street? Own a piece of Halliburton?

No matter. Dubya has it all figured out. "I think the economy is down," he says, "because we built too many houses ..." The failing economy, he goes on, is only "adjusting" to all those houses we built. Silly us. This from the president who said "Thanks to our policies, home ownership in America is at an all time high." (September, 2004) and "We're creating ... an ownership society in this country, where more Americans than ever will be able to open their door where they live and say 'Welcome to my house, welcome to my piece of property.'" (October, 2004) It's enough to make you misty-eyed, ain't it?

A Bush spokesman said that long after folks (like us) forget all about Baghdad and Abu Ghraib, this president's legacy will be the Great Ownership Society. George W. is, after all, the architect of the Home Buying Surge in America. He does enjoy a good surge. How did he do it? Well, one way was to push the "easy home ownership" doctrine. Bush urged the private sector to "unlock millions of dollars" for the purchase of homes. He wanted poor folks to have homes, too. And that's a grand idea. Let's go after 'em. But his "easy" way was the free market, who-needs-regulations-when-there's-quick-money-to-be-made method, and predatory lenders of all stripes came out of the woodwork, advertised to a fare-thee-well, and lured folks with little money to buy bigger and better houses than they'd ever dreamed possible — because the easy money's right here for ya! These scam artists fast-talked right past the poor folks' subprime pitfall featuring mortgage payments that could double or triple over time. So folks who could just barely afford the payments on the houses they bought found themselves stuck with payments they couldn't possibly afford later on. Imagine buying in at, say, $800 a month. Say you keep the same job (remember, wages aren't going up by much) and, two years later, your payment is $1,600. Three years later? $2,400. You're in foreclosure before you can say "Honey, find me the phone number of that fella we borrowed from — "

If you do try to find that fella, well, it won't help, because your home loan has been sold and resold to so many mortgage companies you can't find it to save your life. Or your house. And it's your fault the economy is going belly-up.

Ask Dubya. The $18 million an hour occupation of Iraq has nothing to do with it.

The McDevil Made Me Do It:
Drive-thru Fast Food Religio-political Fare

Feb. 28, 2008

We have been to the mountaintop and we have seen the other side ... It's not the fertile green valley we were promised; there are no clear pools or shady glades. There's no abundance of sweet fruit. It's smoke and ash and charred earth. It's a dark road lit by garish neon: "Today's Specials: Godless Heathen Scandal Sandwich! Delusion Dogs! Your choice of Muslim or Messiah Milkshake! Quick Serve! Cheap!" Nothing of nutritional value is served there. The Holy War of American politics is toxic to living things.

There have long been Mormons and Muslims and Things That Go Bump on the Right. Scary politics. The fear doctrine has worked so well they've refined it. In recent years their new, improved American ideal is a construct, a narrow doctrine of patriotic righteousness. It's not enough to love your country and your God. The uber-candidate (the only one who can keep us safe) must love a nation he/she sees as already perfected (America need not change, thank you very much, she's perfect just the way she is) and a singular God (don't give me your take on religion — there's only one way to heaven and it's mine). Civil discourse, rational parsing of differences on the issues, public policy, vision for humane governance, are no longer necessary. Or even desirable. It's all about perception. Fast food perception and mass marketing. Wrap that sandwich, slap a label on it and shove it through the drive-thru window. Plenty of folks'll eat anything if you sell it right. It's all in the advertising. Consumable politics has been reduced to "evil food" and "good food." The public has only to grab the good sandwich and wolf it down on the way to the mall.

Mitt Romney couldn't sell his Family Values Fried Apple Pies no matter how hard he tried. And they were fine looking pies, too. Critics can talk Mitt's flip-flopping on issues to pander to the GOP base (which he certainly did) until the cows come home, but the bottom line is this: Nearly 40% of uber-conservative Righteous Patriots say they won't vote for a Mormon for president. Even if hell freezes over. They know a Cult Burger when they see it and that's one sandwich they're not buying. Keep repeating (evil) Cult Burger long enough and Mitt's off the menu.

These Righteous Patriots don't like Barack HUSSEIN OSA-MA either. They've been shrieking "Boo! Muslim Sleeper Cell Sandwich — Salmonella!!" for nearly a year now. But folks are still ordering up a double-decker of Hope and Change, all the way, with a side order of Inspiration. They say it's tasty — and they feel better after every meal. They feel so much better, in fact, that they've rediscovered a bloom of good civic health and boundless energy to work for change they'd lost after a years on a starvation diet. They're coming back for more and bringing friends with them.

The Righteous Patriot's having none of it. Something's got to be done about this guy before the entire country is addicted to health food.

If the Muslim packaging won't stop him, maybe the Devil will. Righteous groups are circulating nutritional warnings: The

End Time is near and the Anti-Christ is coming. "I feel in my soul that [Barack Obama] is the Anti-Christ," one Internet Believer wrote. "He's too good to believe in ..."

On another right-wing site there's "Something supernatural about Obama?" and "The Mystery of the Obama Cult." These Righteous Patriots aren't entirely sure the Democratic front runner is actually the Satan Sandwich, but "... what is happening ... is starting to scare even those liberal reporters at CNN! They are referring to him as a 'Messiah-like figure' and talking in terms of 'the Second Coming!' ... Maybe he is the Anti-Christ!" What a marketing ploy! Who wants to buy a "Beelzebub Burger and Hotter'n Hell Fries? Like an infamous Russian Marxist once said, "Keep repeating a lie often enough and it becomes the truth." It's the Golden Rule of good advertising.

The Muslim/terrorist and Anti-Christ scare campaigns are singularly egregious fabrications, but the Smite Makes Right doctrine is nothing new. What is new is the foray into a similar brand of scurrilous false advertising on the part of those who share the liberal vision for better government. When a Democratic candidate and her surrogates employ terms like "deluded" followers and "cult-like rallies" and "screaming and fainting" to marginalize the (obviously air-headed) supporters of a rival candidate, maybe we've gone a bit too far down the dark road. When one liberal candidate mocks another by comparing him to an ersatz Messiah calling his flock to go up in rapture when "... the sky will open, light will come down, celestial choirs will be singing ..." — well, what can be said in defense of cooking up the progressive version of the Crappy Meal?

The McDevil made me do it?

New York, New York: McCain and the Liberal Media

March 4, 2008

It was dumb. The New York Times ran a titillating front page story sniffing around the fringes of Senator John McCain's candidacy. In 2000, the NYT reported, McCain had a bona fide lobbyist on the bus. Vicki Iseman, blonde, bubbly and thirty years younger than candidate McCain, was along for the Straight Talk Express ride. She was so cozy with the guy-who-spurned-all-lobbyists that anonymous sources inside the campaign told the Times they had to intervene—to block her access and to "protect the candidate from himself." The inference was positively scandalous. It appeared that Senator McCain was in bed with a lobbyist—in more ways than one.

Trouble is, the story pretty much stopped at inference. It looked bad, but "Where's the beef?" was a fair question. Don't run the story if you can't back it up with something a little more substantial than "anonymous sources" who are easily labeled "disgruntled former staff trying to get even."

The New York Times did for John McCain what the candidate could not do for himself. The GOP base and right-wing radio jocks were not willing to back his bid for the White House. Some threatened to bolt—or sit out the election—if McCain won the Republican nomination. He isn't conservative enough. They don't trust him. They don't like him. Enter the NYT, hinting at scandal, and the Right rallied behind their red-headed stepson, reunited like a squabbling family after crisis intervention counseling. They loathe the liberal media more than they do the family member they can't tolerate. And the Times, they'll tell you, is the worst of the elitist, left-wing newspapers.

We may never know if the New York Times might have found a crack in McCain's wall of "impervious-to-lobbyist-influence" credibility. He had his hand in the cookie jar until the Keating Five scandal threatened his career. He reformed after that. He'll swear to it.

And the Times may have gotten it all wrong. They've been wrong before, in a big way. They printed every pro-Bush, pro-Iraq invasion story Judith Miller penned for them in the run-up to the war. The truth, that Miller was nothing more than a stenographer copying Cheney/Libby propaganda word for word and reporting disinformation as fact, was a long time coming. Too late we learned she was a shill for an administration determined to go to war. Too late we learned the liberal New York Times had adopted a right-wing war posture which made invading Iraq palatable to innumerable readers who might not have trusted George W. Bush but did trust the Times to dig deep and get the story right. They didn't. They got it wrong and we're still paying the price.

Poor reporting, poor editing.

Whether or not the McCain/Iseman story had legs is irrelevant. Solid editorial judgment is neither liberal nor conservative. Such judgment would have meant a solid story. Or no story at all.

The Vast Right-Wing Conspiracy Strikes Again...

March 11, 2008

...No kidding. Clinton campaign aides have resurrected Whitewater/Lewinski-gate special prosecutor Ken Starr. He's come back—and he's Barack Obama.

That's what they're saying. Barack Obama is the new Ken Starr. In light of the Clinton campaign's "Let's throw everything at him but the kitchen sink and see if anything sticks" attacks in the final few desperate days before the March 4th primaries, the Obama camp says it's going to get tough and fight back. The Democratic front runner dared challenge Hillary to release the Clinton's tax returns and the political horse puckey has hit the fan. We're back to the '90s and The Vast Right-Wing Conspiracy.

Obama made his own income tax information public shortly after he entered the race for the Democratic nomination. He didn't have to do it—and most candidates don't until after they've won their party's nomination. But the Senator from Illinois has a bee in his bonnet about transparency and accountability in government. He's sponsored two bills, SB453 and SB2030, in an attempt to change deceptive practices in federal elections and requiring pols to report bundled contributions by lobbyists and non-lobbyists alike. In releasing his own financial data, Senator Obama underscored his argument that the murky status quo in Washington must be challenged. And changed.

Bill and Hillary have been dragging their feet about releasing their tax returns. At first Hillary said she'd do it the old fashioned way—after she wins the Democratic nod. When pressure mounted for earlier disclosure, especially after she lent her own campaign $5 million in January, she said she "didn't have time" to do it. She's too busy. When the Obama campaign asks the same question other Democrats are asking, The Clinton camp shrieks "Ken Starr!" Which makes the rest of us, I reckon, the vast right-wing conspiracy.

This hyperbolic over-reaction to a simple request as "proof of another conspiracy to persecute the Clintons" is peculiar, indeed. Eight years ago, when Hillary Clinton was running for the U.S. Senate in New York, she made quite a fuss about her opponent, Republican Rick Lazio. Seems he was way too slow in releasing his tax returns and that was mighty suspicious. One of her staffers went so far as to dress as Uncle Sam and disrupt a Lazio event. You just can't trust a guy who won't come clean about his taxes.

No matter. It's politics and politics is war. All's fair.

Desperate times call for desperate measures and, in the run-up to March 4th, Clinton had lost eleven states. She had to win in Ohio and Texas or the war was over. She had to take down that uppity speechifier real quick-like. And she did. She did just what her campaign threatened to do—threw everything at him. Including the kitchen sink. Whoa, Nellie! When the entire contents of the kitchen are flying, who has time to call foul when the meat cleaver slices and dices whole chunks of truth along with the intended victim?

You have to do what you have to do. You can glue the broken things back together later.

But what do you do when the good Senator Obama you trust, the one who refuses to dive into the politics-as-usual gutter, opts to draw the line? What if he really fights back? He could. There's plenty of nasty stuff in the Clinton closet; there's a bogeyman or two hiding under the Clinton Campaign bed. Hillary's eight invaluable years of experience fighting the good fight in the Clinton White House? Fair questions might be these: "What lofty battle was it you spent most of those years fighting and what did you win?" Fair answers might be: "The Great Whitewater/Lewinski Scandal Wars. I fought for personal and political survival. I won the battle, but the country lost the larger war."

And who will be to blame then, Ms. Clinton, for picking on you? Who will be responsible for dirty politics, for bringing up all the old Clinton scandals and reminding the public that, just maybe, we don't really want to go back there?

A fair answer might be: You're responsible. The Obama campaign has studiously avoided the seamy side of the Clinton legacy. You're the one who brought it all up again—when you labeled your opponent "Ken Starr."

"And to the republic, for which it stands, one nation, oh-my-God! ..."

March 16. 2008

The Founding Fathers must have been prescient. They tried to warn us, with their separation of church and state proviso, that dangerous times lay ahead. And a rabidly nationalistic religious zealot with a yen for political power and glory would have been their worst nightmare. I doubt any of them ever envisioned the advent of multiple religious zealots vying for the top spiritual spot, but here we are.

There's a game of Religious Fundamentalist Tag afoot on the political playground. Whoever whacks you on the head hardest and hollers "God'll getcha!" loudest gets sole ownership of the truth and wins the game. If you protest the rules of play you're not Born Again, you don't have a personal relationship with your Savior and you're out. You're listening to Satan, you're a lascivious liberal and you hate our troops.

Praise the Lord and pass the rhetorical ammunition! The hateful, outlandish verbiage has been flying like bullets outside the Green Zone ever since. Jerry Falwell declared that feminists, abortionists, gays, lesbians and the ACLU were partly to blame for the 9/11 tragedy — the Good Lord don't love ugly and America had it coming for bad behavior. Pat Robertson said "I totally concur." Right wing heavenly hyperbole has since promoted everything from homophobia to censorship to political assassination. We've gotten used to it.

But it's hate-speak. Divisive, dangerous, enemy-baiting, intolerant hate-speak. It's nuts, so are those who traffic in it, and they're not about to give up the limelight.

Uber-moralist Pat Robertson very publicly embraced philandering candidate Rudy Giuliani. The Odd Couple appeared together for the formal blessing and Rudy was tickled pink. There was little reference made to wholesale hypocrisy (the Lord can't abide a hypocrite,) the media had nothing much to say and no one owed anyone an apology.

John McCain has his own religious nuts in tow. San Antonio's John Hagee, whose aggressive, militaristic pro-Israel-at-any-cost philosophy extends to expanded hostilities in the Middle East which include war with Iran, has hopped aboard the Straight Talk Express. While the fundamentalist view is that all those Israeli Jews we should fight and die for are go-ing straight to hell anyway — because they're Jewish — Ha-gee needs Israel to be Israel. He can't get to heaven without that real estate in the right hands. Besides, Islamic heathens are satanic and he hates 'em. He doesn't like Catholics much, either. They're a "false cult system," therefore all Catholics must willingly embrace the "great whore." Can those liturgy-crazed Episcopalians and Lutherans be far behind?

Ohio's Rod Parsley has joined Team McCain, too. Candi-date McCain says Parsley is "a spiritual guide." Who doesn't need a little spiritual guidance now and again? But this reli-gious nut says "... our country cannot truly fulfill its divine purpose until we understand our historical conflict with Islam ..." He maintains that we were founded, as a sovereign na-tion, "in part, with the intention of seeing this false religion destroyed ..." And if that's not reason enough to duke it out to the death ASAP, Christopher Columbus wants us to do it. "It was to defeat Islam," Parsley says, "among other dreams, that Christopher Columbus sailed to the New World in 1492."

While a few eyebrows have been raised at the endorse-ments of Hagee and Parsley, there's been no public outcry. The MSM and good Americans everywhere seem to accept Senator McCain's word when he says he hates their sins, but he loves these sinners. He needs those votes and he gets a pass.

But when Barack Obama's pastor, the Rev. Jeremiah Wright, dares speak ill of the United States all holy hell breaks loose. There's something sinister going on in this man's church. When he rails against the white power elite (and most of them are white) — those corporate multi-millionaires and billionaires who get richer by the day on the backs of the working poor and the mortally wounded middle class — this African American preacher is a diabolical threat to God and country. When, in outrage based on a long, ugly national history of racism and classism, he cries from the pulpit "... God Bless America? ... God damn America!" there is no exception to be made for righteous anger. There is no understanding that his anger is deeply rooted in his personal experience, growing up Black in perilous times for minorities. None. If he were a loyal, God-fearing American he would never imagine that the last thoughts of the Black American lynched in the Deep South might be "God damn America!" Nor would Black Americans beaten, hosed, attacked by police dogs for doing nothing more than peacefully marching for equality, think such a thing. Nor would the staggering percentage of young Black Americans rotting in prison because they have no resources to buy better justice.

Certainly, the Clinton campaign tells us, they have done nothing to provoke either African American anger or a raw reminder of the racial divide. You know they wouldn't do that. Not intentionally. Intentional or not, by the time Geraldine Ferraro got through speaking her piece, targeted white America got the hot-button message: Barack Obama is the unqualified Affirmative Action Negro trying to take the job away from the Highly Qualified White Candidate.

The Rev. Wright reacts hotly to these perceived racial slurs; he seems to have a history of occasional raging rhetoric from the pulpit. He's hardly the sole religious leader who's ever taken the hellfire and brimstone path on Sunday morning.

There's nothing in Senator Obama's past, in his voting record or his writing or his rhetoric, to indicate that he shares Jeremiah Wright's rage against the system. He has, in fact, made it clear he renounces this volatile part of his pastor's message. The way Obama has chosen to live his life would indicate he's telling the truth. Many of us, if we're honest, renounce at least some of what our own pastors preach at us. I'm neither evangelical nor fundamentalist; I'm a mainstream protestant. Contrary to form, my pastor believes all abortion is a mortal sin, a crime. He believes stem cell research is an abomination and that Terri Schiavo was murdered. We disagree, totally, vocally and openly, about these issues. But I can still love this man because the core of his ministry and his hands-on pastoral energy are spent addressing the issues of poverty and homelessness both here and abroad. I do not leave my church family when the broader message is one in which I believe.

So maybe Senator Obama deserves the same consideration. Maybe he deserves the same political tolerance given Senator McCain.

And maybe we need to consider which message from the pulpit is truly the more dangerous, sinister one. Pastor Wright's anger about social justice in America? Some of his words are ill-chosen. Some of them are hurtful, even hateful. But he's no Robertson, Hagee or Parsley. He's not using the church or the name of God to incite bloodlust for wholesale war against other nations, other faiths. He's not preaching Islamic genocide. He's not peddling the Apocalypse so he can rise up to heaven, buck-nekkid, in a Rapture of his own design and on his own timetable. The far-right religious nuts need Armageddon sooner rather than later. They're tired of waiting for God to get the job done.

There's clearly sound reasoning behind the separation of church and state. The Founding Fathers were smarter then than some of us are now. Or maybe they had an epiphany on the Road to Democracy and saw what was coming.

The Man Act, the Mann Act and Moral Wrecktitude

March 18, 2008

I don't want to dwell on the seamy particulars of N.Y. Governor Eliot Spitzer's fall from grace. Suffice it to say he had a nasty habit of frequenting high class hookers and, in the pursuit of his extracurricular fun and games, this Harvard Law grad violated the Mann Act when he transported at least one young woman across state lines for the purpose of—well, you know. With his educational background and a career built on prosecuting the bad guys and bad gals (prostitution rings,) it's useless to argue the point that maybe Spitzer didn't know he broke the law. So I won't. Clearly, he thought he was above the law.

I won't judge him either, except to say that I wouldn't mind whacking him upside the head with a skillet full of hot lard. For hypocrisy.

For what he's done to his wife and kids. I still harbor the same yen to clobber Bill Clinton.

So, this is not about Spitzer's Folly. There's a larger issue. It's about perception. Perception is not about fact, it's about the appearance of fact. It's about how things look, entirely true or not. Here's the popular public perception that worries liberals like me:

Why is it that so many Democrats can't seem to keep their pants zipped for God, country and party? They may be in the (idealistic) right about war, sane gun control policy, poverty, fair taxation and accessible health care, but any willing woman with a little cleavage and legs that go all the way up is reason enough to derail an entire career.

Why is it that so many Republicans seem to have Super-Glued their flies shut (with the possible exception of young male pages on the Hill or airport restrooms)? They can't resist the lure of a good war. They indulge in the Reverse Robin Hood urge to steal from the poor (and the middle class) and give to the filthy rich. They might avoid military service, drive under the influence and lie about going to war and staying there, but sex? Naw. That would be a sin.

On the Right, illicit sex has become the ultimate obscenity. On the Left, it's illicit violence.

Why is it that so many Democrats are perfectly satisfied with a little female dominance while their Republican counterparts lust after world dominance? It must be a guy thing. And it begs the question: Which phallic symbol is more lethal to the American psyche—the unruly male member or the big, badly used bullet?

Some days all we can say is this: A pox on both your houses.

It's 3 a.m. — You Want this Guy Answering the Phone?

March 25, 2008

If there's anything we can count on, presidential hopeful John McCain tells us, it's his vast experience in Washington. He knows his stuff. Well, most of it. By his own admission, he doesn't know much about the economy—but he's the foreign policy expert in this man's race. He knows who the enemy is and he knows how to win a war. Even if it takes a hundred years. Wanna be safe, America? He's our best bet.

While the Democrats are still slugging it out for the nomination, Sen. McCain is off to the Middle East. Being presidential. Looking every inch the commander in chief.

Except for his little blunder in Jordan. Speaking about the Iraq war to members of the press in Amman, candidate McCain, dour and deadly serious, said Iranian operatives are "…taking al Qaeda into Iran, training them and sending them back." He was certain of it. Dead certain. When pressed by media to elaborate, McCain said "It's common knowledge and has been reported in the media that al Qaeda is going back into Iran and receiving training and are coming back into Iraq from Iran, that's well known…"

Sen. Joe Leiberman, who was standing just behind McCain and fidgeting, stepped forward and whispered into the Republican nominee's ear. He was looking dour and deadly serious, too. He talked, McCain listened. Then the would-be 44th President of the United States of America, the would-be Commander in Chief of the United States Armed Forces, red-faced and uncomfortable, said, "I'm sorry. The Iranians are training extremists. Not al Qaeda."

Oops. Okay. So he made a mistake. So he only thought it was common knowledge that Iran has been busy training al Qaeda. He only thought he read it in the paper or heard Wolf Blitzer say it. No harm done. Anyone can get a little confused about which enemy is getting what training in what country.

But John McCain is not just anyone. He wants to be president. He says he's the most qualified candidate in the race. And that means we have the right to expect that he has his facts straight—especially in matters of life and death, of war and peace in the Middle East. We can't afford another mistake.

If he wins in November, we need some assurance that we're safe. When that infamous White House crisis-is-brewing phone rings at three a.m., waking President McCain and demanding a dead certain response, I sure hope Joe Leiberman is lying in bed right next to him. Otherwise, I won't sleep a wink.

Faith and Politics? Be Not Afraid ...

March 26, 2008

It's the Social Justice Gospel.

It's not black or white. It's not exclusively Southern Baptist or Pentecostal or Presbyterian or Catholic or Jewish or Muslim — it's all of us. Sometimes it might be angry, but it's not hate-mongering. It's not war-mongering. It's not rabid nationalism masquerading as "patriotism" or raging intolerance masquerading as "religion." It's not the evils of abortion-abortion-abortion or gays-gays-gays. It's not hellfire and damnation. It's not anti-any-faith-but-my-own-brand-of-Christianity dogma.

On Wednesday, March 19, I was fortunate enough to go to The Carter Center in Atlanta to hear a compelling argument for a citizen-driven movement for change in America. Progressive evangelical leader Jim Wallis spoke to the need for a revival of faith in a nation whose government is broken; whose moral and ethical compass is spinning, leaving us lost, isolated from one another and from the truth. And before all you ardent secularists and faith-is-the-big-myth folks start hollering "Oh, no you don't! I'm not buying your religious hocus-pocus!" let me share a few quotes from Jim Wallis' message:

"Religion has no monopoly on morality ... for the last twenty-five years this country has been afflicted by the Religious Right ... God is not American — or Republican ... the idea of the common good also has secular roots ... a whole new denomination has emerged — the 'spiritual but not religious' ..." Wallis, who, like Barack Obama, was against invading Iraq from day one, maintains that we must leave behind the "exclusive use of war to fight evil."

Great moral shifts in this country have often begun in and been fueled by our communities of faith. Broad social movements arise to change bad public policy: Reforming child labor law, the abolition of slavery, civil rights, voting rights, ending war. Fiery rhetoric from both the pulpit and the secular public square moves us to demand change for the common good. And when we act together, when we believe the larger truth of our humanity is more important than our individual differences, when speak as one voice, we expose social injustice. We effect positive change.

It's never easy. Sweeping change calls for self-examination. The truth is too often ugly and those who hold up the mirror, demanding that we look at ourselves, are seldom well-loved for having done it. We are fond of cosmetics; pretty, shiny things that mask our flaws. We want to be free to love ourselves, to believe in only the best of what we've done, of who we are. An honest look, in bright light, in the American mirror tells us this:

YES, WE DID

We breached the borders of the New World uninvited. We refused to assimilate or learn the language. There was land and wealth to be had and we wanted it all. This was our Manifest Destiny. So we took what we wanted, shoving Native Americans out of the way — and none too gently. We began with thievery and ended with genocide. When we wanted cheap labor, we participated in the kidnapping and enslavement of free citizens of Africa. We believed "... all men are created equal ... ," but slavery, child labor and denying women the vote were acceptable in our new democracy. We brutalized people of color. We stripped Japanese Americans of everything they owned and condemned them to the American equivalent of concentration camps during WWII. We have an ugly history of participating in the overthrow of duly elected leaders of other sovereign nations when it served our national interest; often, that "interest" was greed-driven. We wanted their natural resources and we wanted them cheap. We've propped up murderous tyrants when it suited our purposes. We have used lofty terms like patriotism, liberation and democratization to justify our actions.

We have been, and we remain, an imperfect nation. The inner struggle to do the right thing rather than the self-serving thing has always been a necessary exercise — and it is one battle we fail to fight until we are led to do it. Those who dare to speak out against the sins of our greed, our indifference and our intolerance are often the objects of public scorn. In today's toxic environment of swaggering American arrogance and the co-opting of religious faith by narrow fundamentalism, any criticism of this country is regarded as heresy. The Rev. Jeremiah Wright may have been inflammatory in his rhetoric but an examination of the entirety of his

"... God damn America!" and post-9/11 sermons bears witness to this fundamental truth: He was not entirely wrong, nor was he anti-American. He was speaking to the need for self-examination and for change. He was preaching the Social Justice Gospel from his own undeniable experience, from his own undeniable pain.

Calmer voices should — and will — prevail. The definition of "people of faith" is, at last, expanding. For the common good. For battling the true moral sins of poverty, starvation, disease, ignorance, inequality and wars without end. Whether we join a movement for social justice in the name of God, in the name of Christ, in the name of Allah, or in the name of secular morality, is irrelevant. What matters most is that we unite in fostering the credo shared by all major religions and by all good people: We are, indeed, our brothers' and our sisters' keeper. Their suffering is our suffering. We have the power, if we choose to follow those who speak to our hearts and our collective conscience, to heal a broken nation.

If we want to lead the world we must restore the world's faltering faith in American leadership. And that will happen only when we have courage enough look in the mirror, see what's really there, and find faith enough to make it right.

100 (or More) Reasons Dems Have to Kiss and Make Up

April 6, 2008

We just hate each other. Clinton supporters are screaming "I'd rather eat glass than vote for Obama!" Obama supporters are hollering "I'd rather hop right into that hell-bound

hand-basket than vote for Hillary!" There are rabid supporters on both sides who threaten to vote Republican if they
don't get their way. Or, they say, they won't vote at all.

We're going to have to declare peace, folks. Even if we
don't want to do it.

According to the most recent George Mason Universi-
ty/HNN poll, in which 109 historians were surveyed over a
three week period, 98.2% of the respondents agreed that the
George W. Bush administration is a failure. 61% of them rate
W's presidency as the worst in U.S. history. In 2004 GMU/
HNN surveyed 415 historians. At that time, 81% of them
rated the Bush White House an "overall failure." Clearly, the
number of presidential scholars who recognize the Bush
years as disastrous is growing.

Repeatedly, historians have cited the same reasons for their
low opinion of the current president's policies: "... a doctrine
of pre-emptive war, crony capitalism, bankruptcy/fiscal ir-
responsibility, military adventurism, trampling of civil liber-
ties and anti-environmental policies." And, as for the singular
argument that George W. Bush is the worst president in history: "Although previous presidents have led the nation into
ill-advised wars, no predecessor managed to turn America
into an unprovoked aggressor. No predecessor so thoroughly
managed to confirm the impressions of those who already
hated America. No predecessor so effectively convinced such
a wide range of world opinion that America is an imperialist
threat to world peace."

We cannot afford a "throw-away" vote come November
because we're pissed off at Clinton or Obama. There's too
much at stake. John McCain has fully embraced the Bush

Doctrine, adopting his hyper-aggressive militaristic approach to foreign policy in the Middle East. Trading a swaggering Jesse James Six-Shooter School of Diplomacy administration for a gamble on Bart Maverick's "I'll call your anti-American attitude and raise you one pre-emptive strike!" notion of sound policy in a volatile region is Wild Western lunacy.

Senator McCain has embraced the Bush financial scam — a Darwinian economic policy ensuring survival of the richest and taxes weighted at the wrong end of the economic scale. In the Bush economy the more you make, the more you take. A McCain presidency promises four more years of the same disastrous policies that have us stampeding like a herd of spooked, mindless cattle toward the edge of a cliff. The impetus, if we make another mistake, could result in a lethal plunge from the precipice.

Not so long ago we thought we had a little wiggle-room. We were on firmer ground both economically and in our relationships to one another and the rest of the world. We were a strong enough nation, many of us believed, to survive a sizable political misstep.

I got a sympathy card from a friend in D.C. after the Supremes handed Dubya the White House in 2000. She was well-connected, a former press secretary to a member of the House, her husband a former Capitol Hill producer for C-SPAN and past president of the Radio and Television Correspondents' Association. She wanted to make me feel better. Her message?

"You're being hysterical about a 'dangerous buffoon in the Oval Office.' Stop. Calm down. Stop. This is America. Stop. Really. Stop. How much damage can one man do? Stop."

Seven terrible years later, we know how much damage one man can do. We don't need hundreds of presidential scholars to tell us how high a price we've paid for bad leadership. 81% of us — ordinary Americans — have joined the ranks of the "I'm Worried Sick, Man!" Club. We know this nation is badly off-course. We've come to realize that the United States of America is not the inevitable, immutable, invincible force we've always believed it to be. We are not impervious to economic ruin, to defeat. We are not invulnerable to the consequences of poor judgment and poor policies. One man can, when we are already staggering, take us down for the count.

Unless we're willing to risk everything we hold dear, everything we believe in, we Democrats are going to have to make peace with one another and support either Candidate Obama or Candidate Clinton when the time comes. Whether we like it or not. The tantrum vote or non-vote is not an option. The alternative to the lesser Democratic candidate, the one whose tactics offended us, the one we don't want or never liked, is the Bush Doctrine, "100-Year-War" McCain style. And that's too high a price to pay to get even.

Women, Politics and Posturing: It Can Kill Ya

April 8, 2008

Don't think, for a skinny minute, this is an easy job. Writing politics is war. It's dangerous out here, what with bullets flying, incoming mortar rounds and all. I lost my flak jacket and helmet the other day and had to low-crawl to my computer. With my youngest grandbaby on my hip. But I did it.

I'm one tough woman, willing to go where few men are brave enough to...

Okay, okay. Maybe no one was shooting at me. I misspoke. Just Like Hillary.

She thrilled us all with her wild Bosnian tale, her near-miss as First Lady, landing at the airport in Tuzla, her plane having taken evasive maneuvers to avoid being shot down...then her mad dash across the tarmac, hunkered down and dodging bullets every step of the way. You don't forget a near-death experience like that one. This was a time, Hillary told us, that a trip was "too dangerous for the president," so they sent her instead. This is one woman who's ready to take command and, like John McCain, she's taken hostile fire and lived to tell about it. Barack Obama? Shoot! (No pun intended.) All he's got going for him is a fine mind, the capacity to engage ordinary people in the political process and some good ideas about civility in politics and humane governance. Nothing heroic about that. What we need is a macho/hero type, and Hillary Rodham Clinton qualifies.

If only it had been a true story. Turns out there was no danger involved. Hillary landed quite nicely in Tuzla with teen-aged daughter Chelsea in tow. They enjoyed a sweet little ceremony there after deplaning, Bosnian children on hand to welcome the First Lady and First Daughter with hugs and kisses.

Caught in telling a whopper, Ms. Clinton took the typical politician's way out. "I misspoke," she said. "I was sleep-deprived...I'm human..."

Really? She did not "misspeak" about running the gunfire gauntlet in Tuzla. Saying "I misspoke" implies a little slip of the tongue. A tiny lapse, like "I'm sure bought milk on Monday—no, make that Tuesday." She says she was sleep-deprived? I don't care how much sleep you've lost, you don't mistake hugging a Bosnian child on the tarmac with dodging bullets. She lied. She told a deliberate, fabricated story to get a leg-up in a faltering campaign for the Democratic nomination.

In doing so, she has betrayed every one of us who have argued for a woman in the White House. Worse, she's made more than a few American mothers furious. A good mama—a smart mama—does not take her child along on a trip "too dangerous for [Daddy] to make." If that's not lousy judgment, I don't know what is.

We women expect better than this from one of our own. We don't want just any woman in the White House, we want one who represents the best of what a woman has to offer—and that's plenty. We want feminist principles in a campaign and in the Oval Office. If we have to vote for a man to get them, we will.

What's Cookin' in the McCain Campaign?

April 22, 2008

Well, it sure ain't Cindy McCain.

And political silly season is in full swing. Or, maybe this time, it's political silly seasoning. Seems candidate McCain's wife had her own special section at the official McCain for President website: McCain Family Recipes. She's just like us. Just like many American women/wives/mothers, she's busy in the kitchen, creating yummy new dishes for her family.

And some of the recipes were mighty impressive. Farfalle Pasta with Turkey Sausage, Peas and Mushrooms. Passion Fruit Mousse. Ahi Tuna with Napa Cabbage Slaw.

The New York Sun ran an article about Cindy-the-chef, featuring her recipe for Passion Fruit Mousse. It's great when a truly creative home cook makes the big time.

Except for one little problem: The recipes were not original. They were not "McCain Family Recipes." They were Food Network concoctions; paragraph-for-paragraph, word-for-word, ingredient-for-ingredient, measurement-for-measurement copies of recipes lifted from the Food Network website. The sole difference was the substitution of the word "slaw" for "salad" in the Ahi Tuna recipe. Nowhere, on the McCain website or in the NY Sun article, was Food Network credited.

When some eagle-eyed writer who watches Giada De Laurentiis's Everyday Italian on Food Network recognized one of the recipes, checked the others and exposed the sham, the shitakes hit the fan. Cindy's recipe section was scrubbed from the McCain website.

Naturally, the McCain camp was forced to issue a statement about RecipeGate. Their response? The butler did it. A McCain spokesperson said the entire thing was "…a low-level unpaid staff debacle." In other words, some poor little old unpaid intern wound up on the grill for using the Food Network as a resource to plagiarize recipes. Certainly, it was not Cindy McCain's fault. It wasn't her responsibility to provide said intern with family recipes for publication.

Don't get me wrong. I don't blame Cindy McCain a bit for not being Julia Child. Or Giada De Laurentiis. Or Rachel Ray.

If, like Cindy, I'd been born heiress to a multi-million dollar beer fortune, I wouldn't be spending hours in the kitchen either. I've spent the better part of the last forty years with one leg shackled to the stove, and I'm not ashamed to admit that there are days I'd like nothing better than to gnaw my foot off at the ankle and head for Antoine's in New Orleans' French Quarter. I love their Oysters Rockefeller. Or Carrabba's Italian Grill for some Polla Rosa Maria. Or even Kentucky Fried Chicken.

On the scale of political lies, blaming some "low-level unpaid staff" member isn't nearly as bad as Hillary's bellying up to a bar in Indiana, chasing Crown Royal shots with beer, toting a six-shooter and a brace of dead ducks and telling war stories about a'runnin' and a'dodgin' them bullets in Tusla. But a lie is a lie. Plagiarism, even when it's silly, is still thievery. Passing the blame to a defenseless volunteer is reprehensible.

Bottom line: Take the blame for your own careless dishonesty and bad judgment. And Cindy, if you can't stand the heat, stay out of the kitchen.

A Storm of Double Standards: McCain, the Media and Religion

April 29, 2008

What's fair is fair? Maybe not.

Barack Obama takes a public beating because his pastor, Jeremiah Wright, preaches "hateful" messages from the pulpit. Wright dares to criticize his country in angry terms and drags God into it. Obama, pols and pundits hollered, should have abandoned his church family the minute he heard a discouraging word. It is not enough that the senator from Illinois does not agree with Wright's harsher sentiments; he should have rejected the man along with the message.

The same standards do not apply to John McCain. He gets a pass on matters of hateful religious rhetoric. He admits that he wooed and won the endorsement of Texas evangelist John Hagee—even though, candidate McCain insists, he does not agree with everything Hagee preaches. The GOP candidate needs that religious right voting bloc, so it's okay.

Hagee has a long career of hellfire and brimstone intolerance. Does he drag God into the middle of it? You bet. He preaches a "God'll Getcha!" doctrine like the pro he is. If you like Jeremiah Wright on a tear, you'll just love John Hagee.

Hagee's God has quite a temper. Ask survivors of Hurricane Katrina. God was really ticked off with New Orleans, Preacher John contends. That Louisiana city, he says, brought the wrath of God down on itself in major fashion. New Orleans was guilty of "a level of sin that was offensive to God." A stroll through the famous French Quarter could taint the soul of a saint. Bars where liquor flowed like a mighty river, exotic dancers prancing around half-nekkid. And, heaven help us, there were homosexuals everywhere. We all know how God feels about those guys.

In the Gospel According to John Hagee, God got fed up and hurled Hurricane Katrina at New Orleans in a raging act of divine retribution.

Trouble is, thousands of folks along the entire Gulf Coast suffered and died. Whole towns, innocent communities, were wiped out; folks who had nothing to do with Sin City, had never been there and never intended to go. Millions lost their homes, their schools, their jobs. Their families. Many of them are still suffering, still displaced.

Worse, if Hagee's right about God's direct and purposeful involvement, we have a real problem. God's aim was not so good. He hit the Ninth Ward, home of the city's poorest citizens, hard. Nothing much was left of it but debris and dead bodies. God got middle class neighborhoods, too. But He missed the French Quarter; the black heart of Louisiana's Sodom (or Gomorrah, take your pick) was left unscathed. And that makes no sense at all. Unless John Hagee's a hate-mongering hot-head who uses the pulpit unwisely … and God had nothing to do with the disaster that struck the Gulf Coast. Sometimes you just can't go along with every word you hear on Sunday morning. Pastors are human, they're flawed like the rest of us—and sometimes they're wrong.

John Hagee's "message" is every bit as ugly, angry and destructive as Jeremiah Wright's has ever been. Barack Obama denounced the message but remained loyal to his pastor, as a man, and to his church family. John McCain does not attend Hagee's Cornerstone Church in San Antonio. He has no connection with or love for the church body there. McCain sought Hagee's endorsement for purely political reasons: he needed the votes and he knew exactly who he was embracing.

If Obama is guilty of sin by association, so is McCain. For the media and the public to condemn one and pardon the other is grossly unfair. You might even say it's unChristian.

This year's elections continue: The Brass Tacks and the Gas Tax

May 6, 2008

It's political pandering. Stunts. Promises candidates make that sound like the kind of goodies the voting public, in hard times, wants to believe so badly we don't think it through. Or do the math.

Richard Nixon did it when he told a war weary nation he had a "secret plan" to end the endless debacle in Vietnam. We didn't think it through. We fell for it. What never occurred to any of us (including the press) to ask was this: "Mr. Nixon, if you have a foolproof plan for bringing our troops home and you won't share that plan with your government NOW, does that make you un-American? Do you have the best interests of our troops at heart if you withhold such a plan until and unless we vote you into the Oval Office? Does that mean you are willing to have the blood of every American soldier wounded or killed on your hands in the interim—while you're politicking?"

It was a stunt. It worked. And the truth was that he had no plan at all. Secret or otherwise. The war, the maiming and dying, went on for years after he took office.

We want to believe in these folks who run for president. We know darn well they lie to us, but we need to believe the political-speak, especially when we're suffering. They know the drill. Promises made are so seldom kept that conventional wisdom in non-election years is that all pols use the expedient, oily promise-'em-anything tactic. They count on our tendency to accept something shiny without scratching the surface.

Both Republicans and Democrats are at it again. It's John McCain's brainchild. He wants to "give us a holiday" from gas prices killing us at the pump. He'll suspend the gas tax from May through Labor Day, he tells us. That will save us somewhere near twenty cents on every gallon of gasoline. For argument's sake, let's say the savings at the pump is twenty cents. Say we use 80 gallons of gasoline every month. That would be twenty gallons a week. What kind of cash would we pocket without having to pay that gas tax? $16 a month. For three months. That would be $48. Do the math.

The gas tax is supposedly earmarked for repair and maintenance of our infrastructure. You know, roads; bridges— like the one in Minneapolis that collapsed during rush hour awhile back due to neglect. Seems we need every cent of the gas tax—and more—to "keep us safe."

Hillary Clinton, not to be outbid in the "Watch me being the pro-active Democrat!" category, sees McCain's hand, calls him and raises him one. She'll do the same thing for us and, add to that, she'll go after Big Oil's windfall profits to pay for it so we don't lose our ready cash for infrastructure.

What do we get? A quick hand-up-your-skirt cheap thrill. It just sounds so good. These folks mean to make our hard lives a heap easier this summer. We don't need much. $16 a month savings? Shoot! We can buy another few gallons of gas with that kind of money.

O Bubba, Where Art Thou?

May 10, 2008

Camp Clinton: It's not just for irritable feminists anymore. Or for skittish seniors, who want a little comfortable change — but are not sold on Change-with-a-capital-C (read: not equipped to gamble on the young black guy.) It's not just for her share of a struggling, disillusioned working- and middle class. Put 'em all together and whaddaya got? Not enough to win the nomination. Not enough, even when you try to scare them straight (the three a.m. phone call and Bin Laden lurking in your attack ads ...) or keep them mad as hell (He's a bitter elitist and the wrong kind of Christian!) Not enough, even when you cross your fingers behind your back, morph into Mighty Ms. McCain, and dangle the amorphous promise of a (really big?) gas tax break for a few months. Gas Tax PanderGate only works if the folks you want to woo and win are too damn dumb to do the math.

The North Carolina and Indiana primaries should have been the Hallelujah Chorus that ended the Democratic primary season's bloody, operatic second act. Not the campaign, perhaps; there is an argument to be made for letting the last few states have their say. Hillary has the right to stay in the race as long as she can pay the bills and garner a few more votes. But the time for oblique attacks on Barack Obama's character, on his church, on his judgment, is past. They didn't work on the majority of Democrats. The time for praying lightning will strike him or a scandal (like, say, a Bimbo Eruption) will hit like a tsunami and take him out, is surely over.

Or not. All is not lost, and this time Hillary Rodham Clinton has found more than her voice (for the umpteenth time). She has, at long last, found her constituency. The "Bubba Vote." Her best argument for herself after May 6th? That Barack Obama cannot win "... working, hard working, Americans ... [imagine pregnant pause here] ... WHITE Americans ... WHITES who [have] not attended college ..."

Oh, Lawd. Now she's really gone and done it. As a Southern woman, living Deep in the Heart of Bubba Country, I should have seen it coming. First South Carolina and Louisiana primaries are dissed as "Jesse Jackson Land" and "Ya know, there's a large black vote down there ..." A clue. I didn't get it. No 21st-century Democrat uses one race against the other. No way.

Next thing we know, Hillary's swaggerin' like Dubya, talkin' 'bout a'runnin' and a'dodgin' them bullets in Tuzla; she's tough as any GOP warrior (and as fast and loose with the facts). Then she's bellyin' up to the bar in Indiana, a shot of Crown Royal in one hand and a big ole beer in the other. Shee-it! That lil ole gal from upper-middle class white Chicago suburbia — who never worked an assembly line or cleaned office buildings or waited tables or pumped gas or changed bedpans or got laid off and depended on food stamps in her life ...

Hold on a minute here. This is not about feeling the pain of working class America. This is about winning. Whatever it takes.

Hillary Rodham Clinton is hankerin' to be a Good Ole Boy. She's redefining the criteria for a Democratic winner come November: The one who gets Bubba gets the nomination. Bubba's white, poor and uneducated. He don't like uppity folks. He's in a bad mood. He loves his beer bottles, his bullets and his bombs. And Bubba won't vote for a you-know-what.

O Bubba, Where Art Thou? Well, folks, he's not just in Ohio and Pennsylvania, West Virginia and Kentucky. He's not just Southern poor white trash. He's everywhere, in every socio-economic class. Scratch his politically correct veneer and have a look-see. He's stuck in the reptilian, lizard brain mindset about who's superior to whom, who's lazy, who's three-fifths human. As I write this, Good Ole Boy Bill is stumpin' rural West Virginia for all he's worth. He knows Bubbas everywhere will get the message. There is no grace in it, no respect, no hint of "Barack Obama is a fine candidate for president, but my wife is a better one and here's why ..." None of that lofty rhetoric stuff. Bill's triggering the primal "Us against them" mentality. The slick, reptilian underbelly of his oratory is this: "Obama and all them smart aleck media boys are lookin' down their noses and laughin' at you. They think you're dumb as dirt. Hill and Bill know you're smarter than ever'body else thinks you are — and we're the only ones who give a hoot in hell what happens to you ... Let's you and me show 'em! Sic 'em!"

This Bubba-pandering is not about empathy for an expanding underclass living in fear of what tomorrow will bring in a failing economy. Not when Candidate Clinton herself places such emphasis on the modifier "white ... white." Not while Bill is fanning the flames of class and color warfare.

This is the worst kind of divisive pandering. It's demeaning and manipulative, appealing to the basest instincts of voters; the old down and dirty GOP Southern Strategy resurrected by desperate Democrats.

The last thing we need is this kind of raging Bubba Vote determining which candidate best represents the Democratic Party's vision for America. Bubba's already had his say and he's done his worst. He gave us eight years of George W. Bush.

Sexism, Racism, Politics and Double Standards

May 13, 2008

We're ridden with them. Double standards. If nothing else, Campaign 2008 lays bare the hypocrite in all of us. Gender bias hurts the Clinton campaign, racial prejudice haunts the Obama campaign.

We deny it, but there are plenty of us who just can't get comfortable with the notion of a woman in the White House. She might be smart enough, but with PMS and menopause — well, you know. Women are too emotional. A man is a safer choice. Right? Wrong. Men get by with things that women don't. A tough-talking man is bold. He's assertive. A good thing. A tough-talking woman? She's a bitch. She's aggressive. Not a good thing. A man who won't keep his fly zipped? Honey, there's a real man. He's too much man for just one woman. "Boys will be boys…" There's your conventional wisdom at work. Boys are expected to be bad. There is no "Girls will be girls…" mantra to hide behind. A woman with a yen to stray isn't "too much woman for just one man." She's a tramp. There are no words like "tramp" or "slut" for a promiscuous male.

An equal number of us are skittish about electing an African American president. We white folks have been slow to accept the lofty idea that the color of a man's skin has no bearing on his worth, his character or his intellectual capacity. We don't like admitting to bigotry, but we're guilty nonetheless.

Racism can be a tough call. We've gotten clever about hiding our prejudices. We begin sentences with "I'm not prejudiced, but…," and what follows that "but" is generally a racially negative remark. In the case of an African American presidential candidate, we avoid responsibility for our bigotry in a number of ways. We project our own racism onto others, as in "I'm not prejudiced, but this country is not ready for a black president." Or we find another peg to hang our biases on. He doesn't wear the right lapel pin. His name's strange. He must be a Muslim — okay, he's a Christian — but he's not the right *kind* of Christian.

From the advent of slavery in America, whites held to the belief that Negroes were not quite fully human. They were, we decided, only 3/5 as human as we were. Since that made them 2/5 beasts (of the field), slavery was no sin. White folks were simply superior beings. There was even a "one drop" rule: whites were whites and blacks were blacks. One drop of "Negro" blood and you were one of them — not one of us. I suspect too many of us still cling to that old myth about "tainted" blood. Even liberals, we enlightened folk, are prone to saying "Well, sure Barack Obama is a black man — but his mama was white!" What we never hear is this: "Barack Obama is a white man — but his daddy was black!"

We're hypocrites. We're too often gender-biased. Well-adjusted men have tender, feminine character traits. Well-adjusted women have bold, assertive masculine traits. That's a blessing, and I figure God knew what he was doing.

We're too often racially biased. All of us are brothers and sisters, all of us human, all of us are equally valuable.

How should these simple truths impact our votes? We vote for the candidate who's smart enough, whose positions on the war, the economy, education, health care and the environment most closely represent our own priorities. If you're a bit sexist, but like Clinton's political stance, vote for her tough male half. If you're a tad racist, but you like Obama's vision, remember his mama. Vote for the white half.

Hell's Belles! NARAL Enrages
The Clinton-Or-Die Contingent

May 15, 2008

NARAL, just because you're officially Pro-Choice America doesn't mean you have one. A choice, that is. Just because you've served as a powerful voice for the reproductive rights of American women for forty years doesn't mean you deserve a little respect from your membership. Or that, just maybe, you know what you're doing. Sheesh.

What were you thinking?

Well ... NARAL's political action committee chose to endorse pro-choice Barack Obama. Nancy Keenan made the pro-choice choice public and then came the blowback — well, let's call it Hurricane Hillary and have done with it. No matter that the announcement praises both Clinton and Obama. No matter that Ms. Keenan makes clear how valuable both Clinton and Obama are to NARAL and to American women. No matter that Ms. Keenan quotes Barack Obama on choice:

A woman's ability to decide how many children to have

and when, without interference from the government, is one of the most fundamental rights we possess. It is not just an issue of choice, but equality and opportunity for all women.

No matter that Obama supports and defends Roe v. Wade.

It's not enough. The fact that both Democratic candidates are adamantly pro-choice is not enough. Raging Clinton-backers stormed NARAL's Blog for Choice site in droves. Bottom line? NARAL is a traitorous organization which betrayed Hillary Clinton — and all women, for God's sake, are Hillary Clinton. And Barack Obama is a MAN.

Hell hath no fury and all that. Hundreds and hundreds of women (and not a few men) blasted NARAL on-line. The Clinton-Or-Else bloc is canceling their membership in droves. To be fair, there were comments from rational women on both sides of the primary fence. But there were too many she-wolves, fangs bared, howling at the moon. A sampling of the feral fury:

"Senator Clinton, is a woman for pete's sake ... [sic]"

"... an insulting slap in the face to [Hillary's] career and to all women ..."

"... women support women!"

"You made your bed — now go sleep in it with B Hussein O."

"... are you a bunch of stupid ignorant women ... a bunch of rich bitches ..."

"You'll be remembered as part of the howling mob who tried to tear apart the woman who dared reach for the highest office in the land."

"Since when did Barack Obama get a uterus and ovaries? NARAL SUCKS! I will vote for McCain if Obama is nominated, we might as well get used to being barefoot and pregnant right away ..."

"You guys suck. Obama sucks. I'm so pissed off."

"An local astrologer [sic] did a current-trend chart on Obama & it was very similar to HITLER'S chart. This is scary!"

"The liar is not even black! He's half black! Hillary is not half woman!"

Obama, according to this Clinton faction, can't prove he's really pro-choice. In New Hampshire the Clinton camp proved he's soft on women's reproductive rights — because they said so. And she's a woman. So what if he is pro-choice? Hillary's been pro-choice longer. And she's a woman. NARAL should have waited it out until HRC says it's over. And she's a woman. How could they — especially after the Clinton landslide in West Virginia changes everything? And she's a woman. Good Lord! As West Virginia goes, so goes the nation! And 70 percent of women in WVA voted Hillary! Because she's a woman. And they know a real woman when they see one.

There are nut cases involved in every campaign, supporting every candidate. Certainly, there are flakes among Obama supporters. But let's be honest: Barack Obama does not fuel that fire. He doesn't write an "I'm a victim because ..." script for them. He is who he is — and neither the man nor his message has changed since that first February day of his candidacy in Springfield. He hasn't had his surrogates whine that "those other guys are ganging up on me" following debates.

He hasn't claimed his spouse's experience as (miraculously) entirely his own. He hasn't wept for the camera when "It's hard ..." He hasn't embellished his history with tales of gunfire. He hasn't belted down Canadian whiskey with a beer chaser or hugged his gun and waxed sentimental about his huntin' days. He hasn't said something like, say, she's unelectable because reports show "Her support is weakening among working — hardworking Americans — *black* Americans ..."

NARAL endorsed a candidate based on his character, his record and, I suspect, to signal us — we women who have been conflicted about this primary — that Obama is most likely to win this nomination and it's okay. He's one of us. Being a staunch advocate for women's reproductive rights is a matter of character and of spirit. No uterus required.

In the Rough? Bush's Extreme Wartime Sacrifice

May 20, 2008

The Iraq War has cost us more than we ever dreamed we'd pay back in the "We are 100% sure Saddam has WMD, he's going to nuke us into the middle of next week, he's in like Flint with al Qaeda, Iraqi oil will pay for all this, it won't take longer than six months and the people of Iraq will greet us a liberators!" days. I've been Bush-bashing about that disastrous invasion for years. Every American soldier maimed or killed made me angrier. Every military family asked to sacrifice their loved ones again and again, through multiple deployments, to the meat grinder made me madder still. And I blasted George W. every time the news got worse, the war got bloodier, more costly and there was still no way out of his Grand Old Plan war strategy.

Honestly, it never occurred to me that Dubya has been sacrificing, too. I mean, he's almost always grinning or dancing or joking around when I see him on TV, for Pete's sake. My bad. I should have asked the poor fella how hard he's had it. Since I didn't, how could I have known the depth of his wartime despair and what he was willing to surrender for the war effort? Thank heaven he's cleared that up for me.

In a solemn interview last week our Commander in Chief finally 'fessed up. Our troops and their families aren't the only ones giving up whole chunks of their happy lives for Iraq. George W. Bush has given up...golf. It was tough, but it was the right thing to do. It didn't seem fittin' that he was puttin' around on the golf course while American families mourned their dead. Didn't look good.

He even remembered the day — the exact, terrible moment — he packed up his little putter. He was on the golf course in central Texas, just a'drivin' and a'puttin' away when "...they [some of his staff or the secret service] pulled me off the course..." They told him that U.N. diplomat Sergio Viera de Mello had been killed in Baghdad. Bush was crushed. "...they pulled me off the golf course and I said '[Golf's] just not worth it anymore to do.'" So he quit. Cold turkey.

That's enough to bring tears to the eyes of even a hardened, Bush-bashing liberal like me. Except that it seems as if old George got himself a good lie on the fairway. And, when you want to sink a killer shot, a good lie is really important

— or it's bye-bye birdie. So to speak.

De Mello's death, the traumatic event that triggered the end of Bush's golf game, happened on August 19, 2003. In the CBS archives there's at least one photo of Dubya happily playing another round — in October of 2003.

At the end of the day, whether it's a good lie or a lousy memory, is irrelevant. What's relevant here is the outrageous comparison of giving up a game — any game — to the sacrifices made by those whose lives are ravaged, ruined, by an endless, futile war. Some years ago, when the truth about the war in Iraq finally dawned on both the press and the public, someone asked George W. Bush if he had trouble sleeping at night. Nope. Not one little bit. He said he slept fine. But since then he's had to give up his playtime, and maybe that's rough enough for a golf lovin' guy.

No. It's not enough. I don't know about you, but I reckon a lot of our troops and their families might feel a little better about Dubya if he said he's been losing sleep. Sorta like they're doing.

Kamikaze Kittens, Faux-Feminism and All-Or-Nothing Politics

May 22, 2008

Smart, progressive women, where are you? We've got to stop this prolonged, gender-driven tantrum. Shrieking "I wanna woman in the White House. Now! Or else!" solves nothing. And it could cost us more than the election.

In light of a probable Obama nomination, Clinton supporters, some of them writers, are saying the damnedest things:

"The Democratic Party has sent a signal to women that Hillary's candidacy is not historic ... Try winning in November without them!"

"Obama supporters are sexist ..."

"He called a woman 'Sweetie'!"

"If they cheat Hillary out of this nomination, I'll never vote for Obama! He's a MAN!"

And, in response to a plea from Barack Obama for his supporters to be nicer to Clinton supporters: "This is one Hillary supporter who will NEVER vote for the most Liberal Nut Job in Training Pants ... I'll let you know BO if a black kisses my butt today! I still won't be voting for you!"

Irate women for Hillary threaten to organize. Nationwide. If Obama wins the nomination, they say they'll do far worse than simply refusing to vote for him, they'll start a new women's movement to keep him out of the White House. Clinton Supporters Count Too and Operation Turndown are revving their engines like wild-eyed NASCAR drivers on a Sunday afternoon at Talladega.

To be fair, there are Obama women prattling like menopausal nutcases, too:

"All you: sore, losing bigotted [sic], ignorant butt holes can kick the biggest rocks you can find!"

"We don't need you [Geraldine Ferraro] adding to the divide in the party. If you are not going to support the democratic nominee and feel McCain better represents your values, then leave the party and shut the hell up!"

Obama women are angry about the tone Clinton supporters have taken, outraged to find themselves accused of being "traitors to the cause" and "betrayers of all women" because they support a man for president. But there are far fewer of them screaming and they are more likely to support whichever Democrat wins the nod. They're more apt to see ending the war, having access to affordable health care, education, the economy, the environment and civility in political discourse as primary objectives. Since Clinton and Obama are equally committed to women's reproductive rights as a private matter — between a woman, her husband, her doctor and her God — they don't see why the woman in the race must, absolutely and irrevocably, trump the man. Obama women, in the main, are not gender-driven. They didn't choose to support the senator from Illinois because he's a man, and they won't support Hillary Clinton because she's a woman.

I'm an Obama supporter. This Women's War worries me. The attention given the most vitriolic women on either side of the Clinton/Obama debate worries me. Those are not the women I know. These are:

Betty, eighty year old retired newspaper editor; South Carolina:

"I'll tell you what I told [a journalist] who came to interview me fifty years ago because I was the only woman editor in the state at that time: She asked me how I felt competing against men, and I told her that's just what the job had me doing. She asked if I was a feminist and I said, 'Listen, I love my husband and I love my son. I am in no way against men. I'm against women being underpaid when compared to men, being held down instead of being promoted to executive positions. So, that makes me a feminist, doesn't it?'

"I think what a lot of us were hoping for is that Hillary could become president. But that doesn't make me 'against' Obama ... I'm a Democrat ... both candidates are so much better than McCain, there's just no contest in my mind. I'll vote for the Democrat."

Lynne, 38-year-old college administrator, wife and mother; Florida:

"Am I a woman first, or an American first? ... the reason I am allowed to vote is because I am an American citizen and, presumably, because I want what is best for my country ... in every election it is my responsibility to vote for the candidate I believe will best lead our nation. If I fail to do so — regardless of the gender of the candidate — then I betray myself, my beliefs, and the other citizens of my country by failing ... to make what I believe to be the best choice.

"I do not deny that it is because of feminists that women have made such great strides in the past fifty years. At this point, though, it has been proven that women can compete quite well with men. It is only a matter of time before a woman becomes president ... and I'd rather wait for the right one than jump for the first one ... I'm a woman with a mind of my own. I acknowledge that the actions of others made it possible for me to be where I am ... I am grateful, but I don't feel beholden to push past progress into reverse discrimination. In any arena."

Tananarive, novelist, screenwriter, wife and mother; California:

"I'm a black woman — so I'm in a different position. I have attributed the greatest hurts and slights in my life to my race, not my gender ... while the significance of Hillary's gender has never been lost on me, and I definitely felt pride in Geraldine Ferraro when she was on the 1984 ticket — I am not torn about Obama's nomination. Quite the opposite: I'm thrilled by it. I'm thrilled for all the aging civil rights activists of all races and genders who literally ducked gunfire — like my mother, Patricia Stephens Due — for causes like voting and gaining access to jobs, public restaurants and bathrooms only a generation ago ... the same decade Barack Obama was born.

"However firm the glass ceiling may be fixed in place for women, the fight against racism has been so dominant in my experience that I am a little perplexed at the way some Hillary supporters seem convinced that a black man would get a fairer shake at the nomination than a white woman. Still, I know full well that if the candidates' positions were reversed, many blacks all over the country would be saying, 'See! A black man never had a chance.' I might well be one of them.

"These were two extraordinary candidates during an extraordinary time. The reasons for the outcome are many, and seem to have much more to do with organization and a generation gap than sexism. One won, one lost.

"What if there's no deeper significance than that?"

Gail, mid-fifties; Illinois:

"It's the message, not the messenger! All I want are issues important to me to be addressed, and my viewpoint represented fairly. I don't care about the face of the person who does that. Unfortunately, I would expect Clinton to give more weight to the interests of big business than mine. I like business, I even like big business, but I don't like them getting government bail-outs and corporate welfare ... [welfare]

which, we're told, [is] a really Bad Idea for everyone else. I want a level playing field.

"Someone who sees herself to be the victim of gender bias may be (too) quick to see gender bias in others. [The] same with religious bias, race bias, age bias, education bias, working mother bias, occupation bias ... it's not just the lens we see others though, it's a magnifying lens."

Laura, 37, mid-level corporate executive, grad student, wife and mother; Washington, D.C.:

"I grew up in post-modern feminist society. I enjoyed the benefits of Title Nine, Affirmative Action, increased gender parity in the home and workplace.

"While I have experienced my share of sexism in and out of the office, I know that my experiences are not the same as my mother's generation, or even women 10-15 years older than I. As Senator Obama said in his speech on MLK Day, 'I stand on the shoulders of giants!' As true as his words were for a progress we've made in race issues, the same is certainly true for the benefits I reap as a woman.

"... I believe I am typical of my generation in that I do not feel a compulsory loyalty to the female trailblazers of the past. I am grateful for what they've done, but they do not have the right, nor will I give them the power, to dictate my vote."

Carol, late forties, respiratory therapist; Illinois:

"My basic nature is that of strategist. Challenges present me with the opportunity to review the content of my personal 'tool box', accessed for fixing things. Given that our nation's challenges are vast and often high-level, I examine the perceived 'tool boxes' of those running for the office of

POTUS.

"POTUS is not a gender-driven issue for me. Neither is judge, doctor, carpenter or auto mechanic. MSM is emboldened in fanning the flames of gender divide while race talk is tippy-toed and 'white-gloved' as a risky venture with potential loss of advertising dollars and viewership. MSM's current blow-up of gender-divide amounts to we, as women, being safely 'had' as water cooler fodder. I'm an Obama volunteer, still feminist, and especially love Michelle Obama's example of being a contemporary empowered female.

"Any Clinton supporter who vows to support McCain over Obama is misplacing her anger. It's 'safer' to be angry at the DNC or the ... primary opponent. The harder task is to self-analyze their own campaign's strategic errors.

"It would be the greatest betrayal [of] all women to demand an all-or-none loyalty with an all-or-none strategy, giving an all-or-none result. Coercion through threat of emotional meltdown and 'October surprise' is not a true feminist trait, is it?"

These are the women I know; they're bright, thoughtful, reasonable. They are representative of thousands, millions, of us who are strong women, feminists, hard working citizens, daughters, wives and mothers. Surely we outnumber the either/or crowd?

I raised three kids back in the day. I know a temper tantrum when I see one. I've seen my share of toddlers, furious because they've been told they can't have that ice cream cone they covet right this minute go kiddie-crazy with wild rage and batter their own faces or bang their wee little heads against the wall. Or hold their breath until they turn blue. The message? "If I can't have what I want I'll show you! I'll kill myself! Then you'll be sorry!"

Too many women, on both sides of the Democratic gender divide, are falling prey to the Bush/Rove "You're either with us or you're with the terrorists!" mindset. It smacks of a threat; the suicide bombing of the Democratic Party at the worst possible moment. Sadly, Clinton women seem to be the most willing to blow up the entire building if they can't have the front office.

This Kamikaze approach is nothing if not a disaster in the making. Feminism is about equality, about equal opportunity, equal respect, equal pay for performance in the workplace. The devolution of equal rights for women into a nasty, fist-flinging, name-calling temper tantrum is not feminism. It's self-destructive. It's an embarrassment. Worse, it may be indicative of a level of ugly immaturity that makes a mockery of a long, noble struggle for the rights of all women. And that's the worst kind of sexism.

Third Party Blues: Libertarian Convention 2008

June 3, 2008

Libertarians are fed up. They're fed up with a self-propagating two-party-only America. They're fed up with taxes, with big government and all those pesky federal agencies. Like NASA, the FDA, the CIA. They're fed up with the war in Iraq — they were against it from day one. Libertarians stand for Liberty in America. And Liberty means no interference from Washington.

They're pro-choice. They're pro-gay rights. They're pro-medical marijuana. They're anti-war, anti-Patriot Act.

I watched the Libertarian Convention, broadcast from Denver, Colorado, over Memorial Day weekend. It was fascinating.

Seven candidates vied for the Libertarian presidential nomination. All of them were given time on the dais to speak to the delegates, asking for their support. Of that seven, five were candidates you wouldn't know unless you were a member of the party — but they were, it appeared, veteran Libertarians. There were two noticeable exceptions, long time Georgia GOP uber-conservative Bob Barr and former Democratic Alaskan senator, Mike Gravel.

As a Republican member of the U.S. House of Representatives (1995-2003,) Barr was a leader in the effort to impeach Bill Clinton. He was an author of the Defense of Marriage Act (no homosexual marriages allowed;) he authored the Barr Amendment in '98, prohibiting the District of Columbia from voting to permit medical marijuana use. Barr voted for the Iraq War Resolution in 2002 and for the Patriot Act. And, in 2002, Barr was dumped by the GOP in the Georgia primary. He's a born again Libertarian, joining the party in 2006.

His "please nominate me" speech was a very long mea culpa, apologizing for all those GOP votes, all those Barr Bills which so offend the sensibilities of Libertarians... Elect me and I'll repair all the damage I did.

Mike Gravel, the veteran Democrat who failed to get enough support among fellow Democrats to stay in the race for their 2008 presidential nomination, joined the ranks of

Libertarian converts, too. He was, at least, anti-war, pro-choice and sick of government business as usual. The leap to Libertarianism was not such a torturous, Herculean feat for Gravel. But he got little more traction with Libertarians than he did with Democrats. It may have been his speech. The poor guy verbally meandered all over the map, lecturing Libertarian delegates as if there were something really important he meant that they didn't get, then trying to explain what he meant by what he meant. I didn't get it, and apparently they didn't either.

Real Libertarians spoke, too. One candidate, Steve Kubby, admitted he had no experience. Not a bad thing because, he said, it also meant he had no experience "talking out of both sides of my mouth." And, he went on, unlike Republicans and Democrats, "I have no experience pointing the finger [of blame]." He did have some experience, Kubby added, "giving the finger." The delegates loved that.

True Libertarians, like candidate Christine Smith, were incensed that "a neocon can come in here, announce he's a Libertarian and run for the nomination…" Barr was welcome to join the party, Smith said, but he should earn his way to leadership by proving his Libertarian mettle. That meant being one for more than two years. He might actually win the nomination, she fretted, not because he was the best candidate — or even a Libertarian — but because he's famous. The press might break with tradition and pay attention to a Barr-led party. Faithful Libertarians, she said, should not compromise what they've always stood for only because some new guy has name recognition.

At the end of the day, just as Christine Smith feared, Libertarians proved more weary of being ignored than true to the purity of their party's core beliefs. They gambled on fame and the sudden conversion of a disgruntled Republican. Bob Barr won the nomination.

Senator Clinton, Tear Down This Wall!

June 5, 2008

Twenty-one years ago President Ronald Reagan delivered the greatest speech of his political life. He stood before the Brandenburg Gate in West Berlin, before the obscenity that was the Berlin Wall, and challenged Mikhail Gorbachev:

"... If you seek peace, if you seek prosperity ... Mr. Gorbachev, tear down this wall!"

This nation of ours has suffered our own divisive walls for far too long. The one between races; the one between genders; the one between the haves and the have-nots; the one between red states and blue states; the one between lies and the truth.

If we lose the White House in 2008, there will be a strengthening of the old walls and the creation of terrible new ones: the wall between women and their reproductive rights; the wall between those who would have an end to the bloody debacle in Iraq and those who insist an ill-conceived war without end is worth more bloodshed, more loss of lives; the wall between those who promote war as the answer to international differences and those who want a diplomacy first government; the wall between those who revere the Constitution and the Bill of Rights and those who have been — and will continue to be — dismantling those fundamental freedoms which have ensured a strong, vibrant democracy.

We have walls enough to tear down, walls enough to guard against. We cannot afford the divisive wall constructed by Democrats against Democrats during Campaign 2008 to stand. It is the wall of sexism; racism; I'm the best one; you're naïve, irresponsible and inexperienced; my church is better than your church. It is the wall of rage: "I will never vote for ... !" It is the wall Harriet Christian typified on Saturday, May 31, when she shrieked, "God damn the Democrats!" She promised us John McCain would be our next president — and she'd help him win.

We look to you, Senator Clinton, to do your part. You are the only person who has the power to begin bringing down the wall that words built. Words spoken in anger or in desperation built it and words can remove it. It begins with you. It begins when you say to a bruised Democratic Party that politics can be tough — even ugly. When you tell us the truths we need to hear: Barack Obama is not, and has never been a sexist, a racist, less patriotic or capable than you or John McCain. It begins when you tell us no one robbed you of the nomination; that you did your best, fought hard, served as an example to women and came up a little short. It begins when you speak the truth without qualification and with all the passion you invested in your own campaign for the nomination.

We cannot afford another four years of the Bush Doctrine because supporters of any candidate have been whipped into such a frenzy they no longer see past their own pain and anger, because they lose sight of the larger picture. Not even if they're yours — and you love them. Our country is at stake. Ours. Theirs. Yours.

Ronald Reagan said of that Soviet wall dividing parents from children and brothers from sisters, "... This wall will fall, for it cannot withstand faith; it cannot withstand truth ..."

Those words in West Berlin proved to be a remarkable measure of his legacy. Now it's your turn, Hillary, to look ahead, to decide what the measure of your legacy will be. It can be a small one, a defiant, destructive, divisive end to the primary season. Or it can be a great one which rises above disappointment and personal ambition for the sake of your party and your country. We need the best of you now in support of a new Democratic administration that will bring us the change we desperately need, one which will unite us again. The choice is yours to make.

Senator Clinton, tear down this wall!

Little Women: A Sad Story of Stereotypes

June 10, 2008

"For Gawd's sake — Y'all don't tell mama her parakeet is dead! When she finds out, that woman won't be fit to live with for a week!"
— Southern sexist wit and wisdom

Hillary Clinton's loss is a tough one for those women who identified so completely with her candidacy that anything other than a win is both unimaginable and unbearable It's especially tough for baby boomer feminists, who grew up hearing our mothers referred to as "the little woman" or "the weaker sex." God, we hated that! So, from the moment "sexism" was adopted as the root word in the Clinton Camp's political lexicon, Little Women from coast to coast put up their dukes. This was no ordinary race for the Democratic nomination.

This was war. Surrender was not an option.

An army of Clinton women seems to have forgotten the difference between a fight to the finish and a fight to the death.

Hillary's defiance on the evening of Tuesday, June 3rd made matters worse. Her refusal to offer any sort of concession speech, her "You can't make me ..." attitude and the tacit threat of what she might do with "eighteen million votes" was self-centered, self-serving self-promotion. It wasn't pretty. The blowback hasn't been any prettier.

Clinton surrogates defended her non-concession speech to a fare-thee-well. They redefined campaign etiquette:

"This should be Hillary's night ..." New rule: The nominee has not earned the right to a night of his/her own..

"She knows she lost ... she will concede ... she will help unify the party, endorse Obama and work her little heart out ... BUT ... This is really, really hard; Hillary needs time to get used to the idea of losing ... She needs to decompress. We owe her that time ... and kindness ... and understanding ... and patience ... so she'll feel better ..." New rule: It's a different world now that Democrats of both genders are equally viable candidates. But the woman only has to concede if and when she feels up to it.

It ain't over until HRC says it's over. Under pressure from the NY Delegation and others to get this Democratic show on the road, Hillary finally says she'll give up the ghost. On Friday, June 6th. No. Make that Friday, June 6th and Saturday, June 7th. This is really, really hard, remember? It takes days and days and days ...

Meanwhile, Mother Nature does abhor a vacuum. In the

space between non-concession and concession, Little Women by the thousands are rallying the troops. This ain't over yet. No Way We'll Vote For That Man! websites are springing up like Republican men at an Anti-Choice Convention.

One woman offered this pearl of wisdom to the rest of them: "We can tolerate four years of John McCain — then Hillary can run again and win in 2012!"

Ah. Little Women. Here's what they're willing to do:

Little Women will sacrifice the reproductive rights of their sisters, daughters and granddaughters for a generation.

Little Women will sacrifice 47 million uninsured Americans for at least another four years.

Little Women will tolerate corporate welfare at the expense of the working poor.

Little Women will tolerate a minimum wage that guarantees poverty, hunger, homelessness.

And worse, Little Women will sacrifice the blood of thousands more of our husbands, wives, mothers, fathers, brothers, sisters, sons and daughters to the Bush/McCain vision of "winning the war" in Iraq.

This is feminism? This is what Hillary Rodham Clinton's amazing race inspires women to do? At the end of the day, then, what has Senator Clinton done for the Women's Movement? How did we get here?

I'm sixty years old. I've been around the political block more times than I care to admit. I can't recall a time — ever — that any man who lost a close election demanded "time to adjust to the pain of losing" before conceding. Hillary lost a close one and got a case of the vapors. Little Women responded in like manner. Senator Clinton needs to roll up her sleeves and get this cart out of the ditch — in no uncertain terms.

Damn. Can't you hear it? Every red-blooded, gen-yoo-ine, knuckle-draggin' sexist in America is snickering, "Now, ain't that just like a woman?"

The Audacity Of Hope: South Carolina Is Obama Country

June 12, 2008

Imagine my surprise. The shock. I check my in-box and there it is, big and bold and all caps: An e-mail from the South Carolina Democratic Party. Subject: SC IS OBAMA COUN-TRY.

I opened the thing and began to read.

"This is truly Barack Obama's moment — will you help us elect him? In January, South Carolina Democrats showed the world we could get behind Barack Obama's message of change ..."

Damn right. On January 26, 2008, I was — to paraphrase Michelle Obama — really, really proud of my state. For the first time in my long, politically engaged life. I was foot-stompin', "Hallelujah!" shoutin', tears-a-flyin' proud. I cried like a baby and hugged folks I barely knew. Honey, this South Carolinian's balloon didn't land for a week.

I gotta tell you, as much as I love my home state, last fall I would rather have had Florida or Michigan get the early primary date. South Carolina has glorious beaches, aristocratic Old South Charleston, the fabulous foothills of the Upstate. We have Southern cuisine to die for (you haven't lived until you've had a heaping plate full of Low Country shrimp and grits). We have some fine colleges and universities. We have class and culture, gentle manners, soft accents, wonderful people.

But we have Bob Jones U, a wide swath of the fundamentalist Bible Belt and a long, ugly history of the KKK, Strom and the Dixiecrats and Jim Crow. Clearly, we still don't know which flag to fly high over the state capitol, which to salute first. We have loved Bush, bullets, bombs, beer bottles and Biblical bombast. We're hard-wired somewhere to the right of Attila the Hun. As a liberal and a supporter of Barack Obama, an empowered South Carolina scared the bejesus out of me.

Oh, ye of little faith.

The SC primary statistics speak for themselves: Over 532,000 Democrats voted — that's about twice the number who voted in 2004. It's around 100,000 more than the number of Republicans who voted in their primary. Obama netted 55% of the vote to Clinton's 27% and Edwards' 18%. Among Palmetto State Dems, Obama carried 54% of women, 81% of African Americans, 49% of white Democrats between the ages of 18-35. In exit polling, 55% of South Carolina Democrats said Barack Obama was the candidate most likely to unite the country.

In the final days before our primary a number of polls, including the McClatchy/MSNBC survey, told us Obama could expect to win no more than 10% of the white vote. They were wrong. When the voting booth curtain closed behind them, 25% of white Democrats voted for Barack Obama. While not the majority of us, two and a half times more white folks than expected chose Obama.

The statistics, the two-to-one rout that spelled the end of the Edwards campaign and exposed the vulnerable underbelly of the Clinton campaign, became the Big Story.

It was the wrong story.

As early as September 2007, when Hillary Clinton was still "inevitable," Brad Warthen (editorial page editor of The State — South Carolina's largest newspaper) wrote:

"... on Saturday the [Obama] campaign is going to try to knock on 50,000 doors in South Carolina. Every county is organized, hundreds of volunteers are ready in-state and hundreds more are expected ... from elsewhere to help. Should be quite an impressive feat if they can pull it off — and if any campaign can, it's Obama's.

"... I overheard somebody at another table at breakfast talking about Obama, and I find myself wondering if the guy is taking over South Carolina ..."

No less a veteran journalist than Lee Bandy, who covered SC politics for forty years, said he'd never seen anything like it. The grass roots movement surprised everyone, as did the momentum, the enthusiasm of the Obama campaign which had brought the principles of community organizing to a state where the Democratic Party had become little more than a political cypher. The party of the also-rans.

It was clear months before the primary, despite conventional wisdom and poll numbers, that something was happening on the ground in South Carolina. Something different. Something new. Obama field organizers moved to the Palmetto State for the duration. They lived among us, ate meals with us, attended church with us. They met with us in small groups, in our homes and our churches. They discussed issues with us — Iraq, education, health care, jobs, poverty and how the widening gap between the haves and the have-nots impacts us all. They shared their stories with us: How they'd come to believe in Barack Obama's vision, his plan for the nation. If we had questions, they provided answers.

And they asked us to share our own stories. Our own problems, our concerns, our needs. They listened. They took note of what we said. The information would be shared with Obama HQ in Chicago.

The Obama campaign in South Carolina became a personal one. "Each one reach one" was central to the effort here. We were, at the end of the day, responsible for our own campaign — house by house, neighborhood by neighborhood, town by town ... It was an exercise in empowerment and individual responsibility. Such a bottom-up campaign defied reason. Defied political logic. Barack Obama, as Democratic nominee, was a long shot.

Oh, ye of little faith.

On January 26th, South Carolina voters upset the political apple cart. In major fashion.

Now the state Democratic Party declares we are Obama Country. It's a lifelong Southern liberal's dream. But the vaunted media-map of red states/blue states still shows us scarlet. As red, I am prone to complaining, as a ripe tomato.

There's hope. Democrats outvoted Republicans at our primaries. There are more women than men who vote in South Carolina. Younger voters are fully engaged. African Americans are energized and committed. We are, in increasing numbers, fed up with George W. and the war. We're fed up with being lied to, with politics trumping sound, humane public policy. We're overworked and underpaid. Too many of us have seen our jobs outsourced. We need health insurance. We're tired of an educational system that leaves our children on the bottom rung of the ladder. We're poorer than much of the rest of the country. Too many South Carolinians are desperately poor. We're sick of promises made and broken. We may well be sick and tired of Lee Atwater-style 527s and dishonest, dishonorable smear-mongering. He was one of us, after all, and on his deathbed he deeply regretted the sins he'd committed in the name of winning-at-any-cost.

As red as a ripe tomato. Maybe so. But sometimes "ripe" is too close to "rotten" for consumption. The grass roots movement is gearing up again. Maybe, on Election Day 2008, South Carolina Democrats — from the bottom up — will lead a statewide revolution. We'll refuse to take one more over-ripe bite; we've been mindlessly red for far too long. This is Obama Country.

The McCain Myth: "Clinton Ladies, I'm Your Man!"

June 17, 2008

22 percent of women — "feminists" all — who supported Hillary Clinton swear they will not vote for Barack Obama. Why? They're angry at sexist pundits and a sexist media, none of whom gave Hillary a fair shake. She lost the nomination, they insist, only because she is a woman. Barack Obama, they declare, is a sexist, too; part of a vast, left-wing conspiracy

against a woman running for POTUS. If not for him …

John McCain is stepping into the Democratic feminist void, wooing these disaffected women like a randy suitor after an invite to the Sadie Hawkins' Day Dance.

What's scary is that some of these women are ready to do-si-do with him.

John McCain is a war hero. No doubt about it. But he is no great friend to women. In a 2000 interview with Tim Russert, McCain said he would support a constitutional amendment to ban all abortions. All abortions. That would mean no exceptions for rape, incest or the life of the mother. Russert asked repeatedly if he understood the issue in question — that it meant all abortions, even therapeutic ones. McCain answered, "Yes, sir." The man means what he says.

In 2003, Sen. McCain voted against legislation that would have required insurance companies to provide coverage for prescribed contraceptives. For birth control. This hit home with me. One of my daughters was paying a hefty full retail price for birth control pills because her husband's health insurance provider would not cover contraceptives. They would, however, cover Viagra. Erectile dysfunction was clearly a priority. Preventing an unplanned, unaffordable pregnancy? Not so much.

An argument, in that case, could be made for abstinence. If you don't want to risk a pregnancy, be a good girl. Don't have sex. That dog won't hunt. When the provider is footing a chunk of the cost for Viagra so men can perform in bed, they're sure not selling celibacy. They're selling a good time for the good ole boy and expecting women to pay the piper.

McCain voted to terminate Title X family planning programs. Title X provides low income women with both birth control and cancer screenings. The old "ounce of prevention" theory for the have-nots.

On the issue of a woman's reproductive rights, he's got us coming and going. He's not willing to keep us covered for contraceptives to prevent pregnancies and he's not willing to consider any abortion as necessary.

He's such a man. Does he have much respect for women? How does this man treat the woman who's been his partner for decades, given birth to his children, kept the home fires burning?

In 1992 John McCain hit the campaign trail in Arizona, seeking re-election to his senate seat. On a campaign stop, in the presence of three Arizona reporters, his own aide Doug Cole and consultant Wes Gullet, husband McCain surfaced publicly:

Cindy McCain playfully twirled John's hair. "You're getting a little thin up there," she teased. Candidate John's face went scarlet. "At least I don't plaster on the makeup like a trollop, you c#t!" he snapped. c#t, for those of you who don't get it, rhymes with runt. It's one of the most vulgar terms that can be used when speaking to or about a woman. A "trollop" is a disreputable woman, a promiscuous woman, a streetwalker.

McCain's explanation for the obscene rant against his wife? He'd "had a long day." That's tough. Apparently he thought it was reason enough to humiliate his wife.

Whatever his virtues, this guy has little to offer American women. No understanding, no protective or preventive health care benefits and, by any measurable standard, no respect.

War Without End ... Amen, Amen

June 24, 2008

Time magazine cover, June 16, 2008: A Prozac capsule, half of it military camouflage green. Under it: "The Military's Secret Weapon. For the first time in history, thousands of U.S. troops are being given antidepressant drugs to deal with battlefield stress ... Is this any way to win a war?"

Deanie Mills loves the military. Hers is a military family. She's a Texan, a writer, wife of a career Marine, mother of a Marine and an aunt to two more. Her son and her nephews have served a total of seven tours in Iraq and Afghanistan.

"...they tell me how much harder it is to go back each successive time," Deanie writes. "I can see for myself the problems they have readjusting.

"Understand that this is not a criticism of the military or the troops. I want to make [that] perfectly clear. [But] there is a terrible toll under repeated demands of redeployment... Our troops are exhausted, their families unraveling [25,000 military divorces last year] ... suicides in-county have sky-rocketed [115 in 2007] ... for the first time in history, soldiers and marines are heading off to combat situations with up to a third of them taking [antidepressant] drugs while deployed.

"Our military is doing the best it can, under impossible conditions, to maintain a groaning level of troops without a national draft that could replenish the forces that are con-stantly demanded by our civilian commander-in-chief to fight this war the way he wants it fought.

"Did you know that, in order to shield Americans from dead troops, the flag-draped caskets, which are often flown in the cargo holds of commercial airlines from Dover to their homes, are hidden [from sight] in cardboard boxes?"

Deanie — and her military men — are supporting Sen. Barack Obama for president. They've been Obama supporters from day one. They want the war their Marines and their country were misled into fighting over. Sooner rather than later. They like Obama's policy of a measured, deliberate withdrawal. Because they have lived the military life, serving in Vietnam and in the Middle East, they could not support John Edwards' or Dennis Kucinich's "pull 'em all out immediately" position on Iraq. Care must be taken, we must protect our own.

What the military Mills family does not want is another four years of the Bush Doctrine. They do not want John McCain's Iraq policy, one adopting Bush's prolonged war "strategy." They do not want the Bush/McCain vision of an endless occupation of an Arab nation. The Mills' combined seven tours of Iraq have covered the entire duration of this war — and they will tell you that Sunnis, Shias and Kurds will never accept American occupation without bloodshed. U.S. casualties will not end until the American military presence in Iraq ends.

Deanie writes: "So, from one mother to another, I am begging you.

"I am begging you.

"BEGGING YOU.

"Please do not hand the reins of power over to a man under whose watch more and more flag-draped caskets will be flown home in cardboard boxes…"

There's little of value I can add to this testimony from

a woman whose military life has spanned over forty years. Forty years of loyalty, of sacrifice — in Vietnam, in Iraq and Afghanistan. So I'll end this column the way Deanie Mills ends all her correspondence:

"Love — and Semper Fi."

The Gas Menagerie: McCain and Graham Join the Drill Team

July 1, 2008

Both John McCain and South Carolina's Lindsey Graham have long supported the moratorium on expanding Big Oil's offshore leases beyond the millions and millions of acres they've already secured for exploration, drilling and production. There had to be some protected coastline, for Pete's sake. We Americans love our beaches, our seafood — and we don't want either one blackened. Unless we're talking New Orleans style, iron skillet-seared fish and shrimp.

Any notion of lifting the ban that kept South Carolina's coastline pristine worried Graham. He said, "I feel terrible about that. The worst thing we can do as a nation is take the easy way out ... If you start opening up offshore drilling, then you are buying time and you are not addressing the fundamental problem with fossil fuels ... All of our coastal communities I've talked with believe offshore drilling would be a detriment to our economy along the coast. I tend to agree with that."

You go, Lindsey! South Carolina has poverty problems, but we've also been blessed with a coastline to die for. Or fight for, as the case might be. Our beaches are the base for what is, arguably, this state's largest industry: Tourism. On the national list of America's top ten beaches, our Myrtle Beach ranks second. Over 30 million people travel to Palmetto State beaches every year, pumping $16.7 billion into our economy. According to S.C. Congressman James Clyburn, we expect that figure to grow to $25.5 billion by 2010.

In 2000, more than 201,100 South Carolinians were employed by the tourism industry. It is projected that, by 2010, an additional 52,500 travel and tourism related jobs will be pumping money into the state's economy. In a state with a population of just over 4 million, a quarter of a million folks working in travel and tourism jobs is a mighty big chunk of the workforce. We need the jobs. And we can't afford to risk the beaches that provide those jobs.

John McCain has flipped on honoring the moratorium on expanded offshore drilling. On the June 22 edition of Meet the Press, Lindsey Graham officially joined him. When McCain flips, Graham flops. Brian Williams challenged Lindsey to explain the dramatic turnaround.

"Four dollars a gallon!" Lindsey exclaimed. He and John McCain are feeling our pain at the pump and, dadgum it, they're coming to the rescue. South Carolina, Graham lamented, is full of poor folks who drive gas-guzzling cars and can't afford four dollars a gallon.

He's absolutely right. They're driving big, energy inefficient vehicles — lots of very old second-, third- and fourth-hand cars and trucks they cannot afford to replace with newer, higher-gas-mileage models. Four dollars a gallon is rough on any middle- or working-class American. For the working poor, struggling at or below the poverty line, the cost of gas is devastating. South Carolina has more than its share of the working poor. They're vulnerable to expedient campaign rhetoric.

Promise them — promise the burgeoning struggling class anywhere in America — some relief at the pump and you've struck oil at the polls come November. They're scared to death. Terrorism in America is thriving at every gas station from Myrtle Beach to Marina Del Ray. How can we afford the spiraling costs of food, medical care, insurance and the like if the cost of a gallon of gasoline means we can't afford to get to the workplace?

The GOP has mastered the fine art of scaring us into voting their way. The McCain/Graham cure for the common man (and woman) is selling the public GOP gas relief. Lift the moratorium, they tell us, open up more OCS acreage for Big Oil, and the four dollars a gallon terrorist will be defeated. We'll all be safe. It's mighty comforting to hear that. We'll turn the corner. Mission Accomplished (just like total victory in Iraq).

Except that it's not true.

Joe Biden challenged Lindsey on Meet the Press: "This [lifting the moratorium] is a gift to the oil companies by John McCain! They [already] have 41 million ... acres of offshore leases. They're only pumping in 10.2 million of those acres. 79% of the offshore oil available ... lies within those acres that they now have. Why are they not pumping?"

Graham had no answer for that.

Neither he nor John McCain have a ready answer for this, either:

The Minerals Management Service, a bureau in the U.S.

Department of the Interior which manages the nation's natural gas, oil and other mineral resources on the outer continental shelf, reports that access to these new Pacific, Atlantic and eastern Gulf regions "... would not have a significant impact on domestic crude oil and natural gas production or prices before 2030."

Leasing would not even begin before 2012 and production would not be expected to start before 2017. Further, at America's current consumption rate (20.8 million barrels per day), the oil reserves made available from lifting the moratorium would last this country less than 2 ½ years.

So. We allow Big Oil to lay claim to more of our precious coastline before they've drilled 75% of the offshore acreage they already have available. Then we wait 22 years for "significant impact" on the price-per-gallon we're paying. And we trust that, if all goes well, after 22 years we'll enjoy the benefits of this new source of our very own domestic oil for a couple of years? Hello?

John McCain, caught in this truth- and time-warp of actual facts, now tells us that lifting the moratorium would have a "psychological" impact on us. He says that's "beneficial." Handing Big Oil ready access to more offshore acreage is a good thing. It'll make us feel better.

Lindsay Graham? He warns us about Barack Obama, a flip-flopping candidate who will say anything to win the election. Anything. Ya just can't trust that guy.

The McCain/Graham drill team? They're giving us the same old hand-up-your-skirt political pandering and the same old oily, empty promise: "Just give me a little bit, honey ... Trust me, trust me ... I'll still respect you in the morning."

Mm-mmm. Every four years there's some guy trying to get at us in the steamy back seat of his gas-guzzling muscle car. I say we keep our skirts down. You know the drill: Just say no.

You Might be Patriotic if...

July 8, 2008

If there's a moment in time that every American is an American, it is surely on Independence Day. The annual fireworks fest, the celebration of a new nation's grand experiment in modern democracy. No matter our personal politics, our disagreements over public policy, we are one nation, one people. Something wonderful was born along with the conception of the Declaration, the Constitution: a vision; a government "by the people, for the people;" the birth of a free nation in a world still held in thrall by the Divine Right of Kings.

We forget that the birth of our free society was not one without labor pains. It began with disgruntled citizens, with open dissent, with protests in the streets, with fiery anti-government-as-usual rhetoric, and ended with a revolution to overthrow that oppressive government. None of it was easy, much of it was a messy business. There were two American factions: Loyalists who believed government was government, the King's Law was the law, and right-minded citizens should honor that government and obey that law. Then there were the other guys: Those rebellious ones who would not settle for living under the yoke of a monarchical government they believed to be abusing their human rights. Neighbor turned against neighbor, brother against brother.

In the current American climate, we forget there was — and still is — honor in the dissenting opinion. Honor in opposition to the status quo. The definition of patriotism has been narrowed to include only those who march in lock-step with one party, with one notion of what is truly American. The "You don't support our troops...You're either with us — or against us" mentality has extended to United States citizens who don't toe the current policy line. It's unfair and it is fundamentally unAmerican.

So. You might be patriotic (and a decent human being) if:

● You supported the invasion of Afghanistan, but opposed the war in Iraq.

● You do not support the U.S. occupation of another country.

● You do not accept the defense that torture ("enhanced interrogation") of prisoners held by the United States, in violation of the Geneva Conventions, is okay "because they might be terrorists."

● You believe that black sites and extraordinary rendition of prisoners for the sole purpose of torture is illegal, immoral and unAmerican.

● You believe there is a need for some rational form of gun control — well short of "Taking away my Second Amendment rights and all my guns!"

● You believe abortion as a casual means of birth control is immoral, but...

● You believe the government has no business interfering in the very painful, private matter of women's reproductive rights. Anti-choice laws didn't work in the past and they won't work now. Wealthy women, as before, will have access to safe procedures. Poor women will pay the ultimate price …

● You believe in comprehensive sex education and the availability of birth control.

● You believe gays and lesbians are people, too. With rights.

● You are extremely uneasy with additional offshore drilling, oil spills, water, land and air pollution. You are incensed that Exxon-Mobile, last quarter, had the highest earnings of any corporation in history and you are convinced your government is in bed with Big Oil. At our expense.

● You believe alleviating poverty must become a national priority. You believe universal health care, like that enjoyed by, say, your own family in Norway and Denmark, is not only a good idea but a moral imperative (See Matthew 25:40).

● As a member of the loyal opposition, you love your country. Even when you oppose its policies.

Gas Pains: How America's Wealthy Get Theirs...

July 15, 2008

Ouch. Like most Americans, I'm suffering a severe case of gastric distress. At the pump. It's painful when half a tank — for a small car — costs over $30. We watch, horrified, as the price per gallon escalates and we are powerless to do a thing about it. We don't know if we're coming or going…I take that back…ordinary folks aren't doing either one. We're staying home, plotting forays like military strategists: How many stops can I make on my way to or from work to save gas? What's open early and how can I keep frozen foods or meats from spoiling in the trunk for nine hours? If I shop after work I won't be cooking before 7 p.m. or out of the kitchen before 10 p.m. and I'm too tired to shop and cook anyway...Taco Bell's cheap enough...fat fast food, carbs and empty calories never looked so good...

Makes you wonder what other folks are doing with their time and money. $4 per gallon doesn't have much impact on the well-to-do. According to economists, the richest 10% of Americans own nearly 80% of all wealth. Like Exxon CEO Lee Raymond, who retired a couple of years ago with a $400 million "Golden Parachute." He's one of that 10% — even if he'd swear he's a retiree living on a "fixed" income. John and Cindy McCain, with a net worth of $40 million, are members of the Ten Percent Club. So are Romney ($202 million,) Clinton ($34.9 million,) Dubya ($21 million) and Dick Cheney ($80 million.) The Obama family, whose net worth is a paltry $1.1 million, isn't among the elite.

If the uber-rich aren't spending the bulk of their cash on gas, grits and gravy, where is their money going? I did a little on-line shopping. Topic? New fad consumables for those who can afford them. The best of the best took me right back to gastric distress:

It's coffee. Kopi luwak; the rarest beverage in the world. Seems that civets, cat-like mammals, climb coffee trees in the jungles of Indonesia and gobble up the ripest beans they can find. In short order, they ingest, digest and produce some fine, fermented coffee beans. The rare beans are crapped out in cat-poop. Indonesian villagers hastily harvest the feline fertilizer, by the lump, for export. It's gotta be fresh, mind you, and it's gotta be in its original cat-poop lump form so that buyers know it's authentic kopi luwak. Enzymes (and waste) in the civets' digestive tract add something extra special to the ordinary coffee bean.

Purveyors (and happy consumers) swear by it. It's "…the best I've ever tasted…smells musty and jungle-like green, but roasts up real nice…a little funky…almost syrupy…not your average coffee aroma…"

Animal Coffee, a prime distributor, sells regular kopi luwak for $75. a pound. For the coffee connoisseur, however, Animal Coffee offers a premium Arabica kopi luwak in a two ounce pouch…for $40. That would be $320, for a pound of coffee. With a musky, fresh-roasted manure bouquet…

Maybe only the very rich have the stomach for it. And with a gastric gap like that between the haves and the have-nots, it's little wonder that wealthy Washington has done nothing, for decades, to promote alternative energy and protect the rest of us from a looming oil crisis. They'll suffer gas pains at the pump only if they pay the price at the polls.

Hard Times? It's All in Your Head

July 22, 2008

"You've heard of mental depression; this is a mental recession…We have sort of become a nation of whiners. You just hear this constant whining, complaining…"

— *McCain economic advisor Phil Gramm, July 2008*

"I would imagine that we are [in a recession], but a lot of our problems today are psychological."

— *John McCain, April 2008*

There you have it. Expert economic analysis. Right from the top.

Gas may be $4 a gallon, the cost of groceries might be rising faster than Grandma's best biscuits, our 401Ks and IRAs may be tanking with the market, foreclosures are all over the news, IndyMac Bancorp just went belly-up and analysts warn us that as many as 150 more banks may fail in the coming 12-18 months...but any problems we have with the state of the U.S. economy are mental problems. If we'd just stop whining and complaining, we'd feel a heckuva lot better. And our money would go a lot farther, too.

Now, John McCain was real quick to denounce Phil Gramm's "You're nuts" assessment of our money woes mania. He doesn't agree with old Phil. "He doesn't speak for me," McCain snapped. "I speak for me." But note, if you will, the dates on which the McCain/Gramm diagnoses of our national manic depression were made. McCain was the first to play the crazy card. Way back in April. Besides, if your hand-picked top economic advisor doesn't sorta speak for you on matters, well, economic, then what's he doing with the job?

And who is Phil Gramm, anyway? He's the ultimate D.C. insider. He served in the House and then the Senate from 1978-2002. Twenty four years on Capitol Hill. It was old Phil who led the fight to shove through the kind of deregulation and no-oversight legislation that freed up Ken Lay & Jeff Skilling at Enron to cook the books, commit fraud, loot their own corporation and leave their loyal employees — who'd been urged to invest in "their own company" — with no jobs, no stock, no 401Ks, no pensions.

Whose wife was on the Enron board of directors, serving on their audit committee? Phil Gramm's wife, Wendy. For that service, the company paid Ms. Gramm as much as $1.85 million in stocks and dividends, as much as $50 thousand in annual salary and $176,000 in fees for attending meetings. Enron was Phil Gramm's largest corporate contributor.

Phil resigned from the U.S. Senate in January, 2002. He'd worked his way up the legislative ladder, becoming chairman of the Senate Banking Committee. That experience proved handy. Gramm's been a lobbyist since, until April 2008. And not just any lobbyist. His client was UBS, a Swiss international banking and sub-prime mortgage giant. Recently UBS executives have been cautioned against making any trips here to the States. Crossing U.S. borders, it seems, might result in criminal prosecution.

Enron was George W.'s top corporate contributor, too, from his '94 Texas campaign right up to January 2004. Big money, free rides on Enron jets. At one time Ken Lay was on Dubya's short list to become energy secretary. Mmm, mm, mm. What's that old song? "There ain't nothing surer — the rich get rich and the poor get poorer…"

Or maybe Phil and John are right. It's not our checkbooks that are unbalanced. It's us.

Faith, Hope, and the Courtship of South Carolina

July 10, 2008

Always a bridesmaid.

That's the sad story of the Palmetto State. We are wooed

and won during primary season by progressive and conservative suitors alike. They love us then. We are Scarlett O'Hara to a dance card full of dashing beaux who promise us commitment in such gallant terms we're shopping for something diaphanous and white before you can say "Where's the ring?" Mm-mmm. Hoops and crinolines, buttons 'n' bows, tiny little ole pearls and yards and yards of tulle is what I'm talking about, sugah.

We get ourselves all gussied up for the ceremony, and then find out it's a shotgun weddin' to the rascal Big Daddy picked for us way back in the day. We don't even have to get out of the pick-up. We might hum "O Promise Me" and swoon over the young fella who really loves us and wants what is best for us, but we always end up hitched to the man who, like Big Daddy, has a God, guns, guts and glory fetish. It's a bad marriage, and we spend a mighty long time wondering why it is we're still doin' poorly, and why we're lonesome and miserable. Where's the romance — or the future — in that?

Truth to tell, we South Carolinians have been jilted before we got to the altar so many times we don't bother with trousseau shoppin' any more. We've lost faith. Abandoned hope. The Dems gave up on us long ago and the GOP knows we can be had, cheap.

John McCain is Big Daddy's dream, his ultimate nocturnal emission. Ole John is the uber-Dubya with a chest full of service medals, an itchy trigger finger, and an attitude. We can stay in Iraq until Kingdom Come. We can either "Bomb-bomb-bomb, bomb-bomb Iran!" or kill 'em all off with gen-yoo-ine, made in the US of A cigarettes. Either way, he's the 21st century Marlboro man. He's that lone maverick on a stallion, silhouetted on a garish western sunset, who might just do anything.

Rasmussen says he's nine percentage points ahead of Barack Obama in South Carolina.

Above all, McCain is a hero. He's got a sweet, reluctant sort of "Aw, shucks" way of sharing his "I went through hell for you" experience in Vietnam, but a visit to the South Carolina for John McCain website puts the lie to all that false modesty. Prominent on the page is a video. One of those compare and contrast masterworks that warms the cockles of the American heart. It's an either/or thing. Shots of young, virile, handsome McCain suffering for the greater good at the hands of the enemy ... juxtaposed with footage of the "Summer of Love" and all those filthy, high-on-God-knows-what hippies with their tongues down each others' throats. You were either for him or against him; you were either a red, white and true blue AMERICAN or you were one of those vulgar traitors to God and country. And he hasn't changed a bit. He's still living the heroic higher purpose. And you can't touch that.

We Southerners, even those who had family clout and avoided the Vietnam draft like a raging case of Southeast Asian STD, do love us some war hero.

There are two McCain-lovin' posts on the front page of the website, both written in June. "Welcome Clinton Supporters!" is the message in both pieces. The McCain-Clinton union, it seems, is a match made in GOP heaven. Y'all come right on over here where Big John will make you feel all better.

What you won't find on the South Carolina website is any sense of urgency, of energy. What you won't find are any events scheduled in the Palmetto State. None. John's right cocky. He knows the pick-up carrying his Carolina bride is on the way. She's his for the taking. Shoot, he won't even have to shave first.

History, as they say, always repeats itself.

Unless that truck's passenger seat is as empty as W's cranium when Big Daddy pulls over for the cursory nuptials.

It could happen.

Romance is in the air. Unlike our progressive suitors in the past, Barack Obama won't give us up without a fight. In April Obama HQ quietly began decorating the church for a real wedding. State Field Desk Organizers went to work. South Carolina had her very own partner in Chicago and the grass roots movement was rebooted. Mission: Help bring in the North Carolina primary for Barack. And bring it in big. Phone banks sprang up statewide to call our North Carolina cousins. On May 6 Obama won a commanding double-digit victory in the Tar Heel State.

Meet-ups are on again. Platform Parties are in the works for the third week in July. Phone bank and canvassing teams are reorganizing. A statewide voter registration drive is underway. Phones are ringing again. Charleston for Obama called the rural Pee Dee Region offering help and volunteers if needed. Groups from all over the state are talking a mass meeting in Columbia soon.

Obama for President paid staff are on the way back to South Carolina. The same kind of professional staff that birthed a grass roots effort in the run-up to our primary; one that had veteran Carolina media saying they'd "never seen anything like it." The same kind of staff that organized a loose, defeatist confederation of Southern liberals into a powerhouse that delivered an Obama rout on January 26th.

Always a bridesmaid. Never a bride. Not a real one.

But this time the Carolina story may have a happy ending. We're being courted right up to the church doors. And the music is playing. Maybe this time we'll make it all the way to the altar. What a thought. It's enough to get us thinking diaphanous and white again ... yards and yards of tulle ... and tiny little pearls ...

GOP Co-Star: South Carolina's Sanford Wants It So Bad He's ... Speechless

July 13, 2008

South Carolina Governor Mark Sanford wants the veep spot. He wants it so badly he salivates at the very thought of four years living at Number One Observatory Circle — the big, Queen Anne style Victorian residence of the Vice President of the United States of America.

The former U. S. Congressman's chances of moving back to D.C. aren't so hot. Two reasons: South Carolina isn't as risky or as valuable for the GOP as, say, Florida; and Sanford really blew his own shot when he balked at endorsing McCain during the week before the S.C. primary. Bad move. Lousy timing. Some folks say he was being a really smart, savvy pol, keeping his options open in a state where Mike Huckabee could have preached his way to a win. McCain supporters? They're not so generous about where Sanford's loyalties should lie when it counts most. It was, at best, a bad audition.

Now Governor Mark, seeking a spotlight somewhere, is

tap-dancing as fast as he can to make up for lost momentum. How do you prove yourself months after the main act has left the stage? Well, duh? You go for the lead in the Sunday Morning Talking Head Show Line-up. Sanford performed on Sunday's Late Edition with Wolf Blitzer. Oh, my. It was not an Emmy-level debut as Best Supporting Actor in a Drama Series. A comedy? Maybe.

Like I said, he's salivating for the veep role. Face it, swallowing all that drooling ambition can hamper the best of soliloquies.

Poor Mark. He looked so good. Casual and tan as always, effortlessly pseudo-rumpled upper class. All those white teeth. That captivating Southern grin. Gawd. He was practically Rhett Butler. What could possibly go wrong?

Wolf Blitzer. He ruined everything. One question — like the bad apple — can spoil the whole bunch. Given John McCain's new propensity to embrace all things Dubya, Blitzer recklessly asked Mark Sanford if there would be any real difference between McCain's economic policy and the Bush fiasco.

Sanford bared his pearly whites in pure-T South Carolina rapture.

"Yeah!" he declared.

And then the script failed him. There was a pregnant pause, folks — and you know how the GOP feels about unsanctified pregnancies. Sanford looked in every direction but the camera's while he groped for a line. "Yeah ... I mean ... for instance ... take ... you know ... umm ... ahhh ... take for instance the issue of ... uhh ..." Governor Mark Sanford, vice presidential hopeful, rap-tap-taps his knuckles on Wolf's table.

"... I'm drawing a blank," he says, grinning, trying to Southern-charm his way out of the hole he's in. "I hate it when I do that ... Oh — yeah! Earmarks!"

Sanford launches into a spiel on Maverick John at the Pork Barrel Corral. It almost works. We can see McCain, both six-shooters drawn, bullets a'flyin', mowin' down the Earmark Gang at high noon and God Bless America!

But Blitzer cuts and runs. Cut: NAFTA. Run: Okay, Obama may have nuanced his policy for NAFTA reform a la general election mode, but as far as NAFTA is concerned, aren't Bush and McCain on the same page?

Sanford hangs down his head like Tom Dooley. "They are ..." he admits, pauses. "... For free trade."

Not one to give up the economic ghost, Sanford goes on to say how John McCain is solidly behind the demise of pork barrel spending — like that awful farm subsidy stuff. McCain, he declares, was all for limiting subsidies like the ones given farmers who earn more than $250K a year. Times are hard. We've got to cut spending. We can count on McCain.

Sanford went off-script. Truth to tell, there were two Senate votes in December, 2007 about farm subsidies. One, S AMDT 3695, was to limit subsidies. The other, S AMDT 3810, was a vote to adopt an amendment that grants subsidies only to part-time farmers, ranchers or foresters with an average adjusted income that DOES NOT exceed $250K and to full-time farmers, ranchers and foresters with an average adjusted income that DOES NOT exceed $750K.

McCain did not vote. No vote. None. Either time. For or against either amendment. Hardly a testament to a dedicated, do-or-die foe of both the pork and the barrel it came in.

If there's such a thing as guilt by association (see GOP rule as it applies to Barack Obama and Jeremiah Wright), McCain is guilty as sin. His pet lapdog Lindsey Graham voted against both subsidy amendments. No limits on this man's pork. Pay up to that rich farmer, buddy boy. Here's your constituency.

Mark Sanford just doesn't get it. Can't blame him. His personal script was crafted to win elections in South Carolina, where we have the highest high school drop-out rate in the nation and are ranked 49th in ACT/SAT scores. We don't expect much. We like a Good Ole Boy in office, and we'll vote for him almost every time. Mark Sanford sold us on his Po' Boy creds. He understood all about hard work, long hours and sacrifice, he told us. He learned those earthy values growin' up, workin' hard on his daddy's South Carolina farm. We could practically smell the rancid sweat of hard labor wafting all around Sanford as he talked about the bad old days.

But Mark did not grow up working on daddy's Carolina farm. Daddy wasn't a farmer. He was a cardiologist and Mark was born in Ft. Lauderdale, Florida. Mark was born to privilege. He and his family came to South Carolina to spend summers and holidays on daddy's property. A farm? Sorta.

There's nothing inherently wrong with Sanford's real history. We're born to the families we're born to — we don't get a vote. But it gets mighty tiresome hearing all these overgrown children of the upper-middle class and the wealthy lying about how they really, really understand us because they, too, have struggled to live the American Dream.

It's the worst kind of elitism. Sanford floundering, then pandering as usual — lying to the poor American unwashed like we're too dumb to dig up the truth.

This South Carolinian reckons Mark Sanford did more than shoot himself in the foot on Sunday with Wolf Blitzer. He blew his lines. His foot? He blew the whole thing right off at the ankle. It's his own fault for trying to bluff his way out of a bad script.

And it's partly John McCain's fault as well. He gave Sanford damn little to work with.

A Matter of Character: McCain's Conspicuous Consumption

July 28, 2008

John McCain's new and improved campaign strategy, pundits say, is character assassination. There's only one way to beat Barack Obama, a popular candidate who is as likable as McCain is abrasive, as ready with facts as McCain is goof-prone and as rhetorically eloquent as McCain is the robotic bombast. And that's a GOP duel to the death. Dirty words at thirty paces. Shoot that uppity young Democrat right through his moral center. Snatch up a few big guns from the old Righteous Right Arsenal: "I'm more honorable than you, I love America, our troops and God better than you." Add some brand-spankin' new, tailor-made subliminal weaponry: "I'm safe (heroic, white and Christian), you're dangerous (never a POW, black and maybe even a Muslim.) Clearly Senator Obama lacks the moral, ethical gravitas to lead the nation in troubled times.

In matters of personal and professional character, let there be no doubt John McCain has it all over Barack Obama.

John McCain has no shame.

Social Security, he says, "is an absolute disgrace." The system, he declares, "is broken." He's absolutely right. The United States government has been borrowing money from the Social Security Trust Fund for decades, snatching the surplus to help "balance" the budget or to fund other programs. Our futures have been mortgaged for federal quick fixes — and the debt owed the Trust Fund has never been repaid. Estimates of that debt range from hundreds of billions to $2 trillion to "The government doesn't really know what it owes ..."

It is what it is. The money's gone, the Boomer Generation looms and we're left with a moral dilemma: What do we do to salvage the system for folks who really need it?

One proposal, made more than once in the past, is that those who are fortunate enough to have reached retirement age with inherited wealth, accumulated wealth from successful careers or hefty pensions, make the choice to forgo cashing in on their Social Security benefits. Face it, if your net worth means your annual income is, say, $100,000, $200,000 or more, you own your own home and you have health care benefits, do you really need Social Security? Where is the moral compass pointing when we say "I don't need it — but it's mine and I'm damn sure not letting someone else touch my money?"

B.J. Jarrett, spokesperson with the Social Security Administration, says no one is required to take Social Security payments. Anyone is free to decline benefits for a higher purpose. On moral grounds. Because he is a man of character.

I know. It's a lot to ask. Personal character does not come

cheap.

John and Cindy McCain are worth millions. It's reported that her inherited Budweiser distributorship is worth more than $100 million. She and hubby John keep their finances neatly separate, file their taxes separately. Cindy's reported total income, for 2006, was more than $6 million. That's right: More than $6 million dollars for a single year. She's requested — and received — an extension on her 2007 taxes.

Senator McCain reported a total income in 2007 of $405,409.

Of that nearly half-million dollar income, $23,157 was the senator's Social Security benefits. Yep. He draws his Social Security. He'll be 72 soon and says he started receiving those payments "... whenever I was eligible."

The McCains don't live like you and I live. Between 2004 and last year they spent $11 million buying five condominiums for their own family's use. Two of the family condos are in the same exclusive Coronado, California building. Nice and close to the Pacific. They needed two, Cindy says: "When I bought the first one [John], who is not a beach person, said, 'Oh, this is such a waste of money; the kids will never go.' Then it got to the point where they used it so much I couldn't get in the place. So I bought another one."

Between January 2007 and May 2008, Mrs. McCain charged as much as $500,000 on a single credit card — in one month. Concurrently, she charged $250,000 on another card. To be fair, it's their money — and she pays off her charges every month.

One professional wealth manager says the recent hike in the McCain family's credit card charges "could stem from furnishing, decorating and moving into" all those new condos. Lord knows it takes real money to provide your family with truly tasteful surroundings in multiple homes. And, of course, there are incidentals. Like clothes. Cindy told interviewers at Vogue magazine that she's partial to suits by German designer Escada. At $3,000. each. If John's elected president, she went on, she may switch loyalties to American designer Carolina Herrera — whose clothing line is every bit as pricey. It's the least one can do. For America.

Unlike millions and millions of Americans, the McCain family is in no danger of unemployment, loss of health insurance or foreclosure on any of their homes. They're solvent. In the extreme.

But surely the issue of character comes into play here. There is a cogent argument to be made that there is moral bankruptcy in a lifestyle so luxuriously self-indulgent during war time, during a recession. While Social Security staggers under the weight of strain and drain, John McCain is cashing in on a "broken" system. And that, to use his own words, "Is an absolute disgrace."

The Untouchable Hero McCain

Aug. 5, 2008

Anyone who really believes the Vietnam War ended in 1975 is, well, *dinky-dao* (Americanized Vietnamese for "crazy"). That misbegotten conflict, a war we never should have fought and the only war we ever "lost," cost us the respect of much of the world, polluted U.S. policy, spurred a national identity crisis and scarred the American psyche. Vietnam remains unfinished business.

33 years later, that unfinished business is the elephant in the room. It's still poisoning the well of American politics.

The press and the public, the vast majority of whom never served in any war, are seized with a belated paroxysm of Mass Mea Culpa. We're beating our chests, heaping ash on our heads, wallowing in collective guilt; because we failed miserably, decades ago, to "support our troops." We sent them off to an endless war of questionable origin and purpose, then treated them like shit when they came home. We called them war criminals. Baby killers. Neither they nor their families were offered counseling of any kind to ease the difficult transition back into civilian life.

We had not yet learned to hate the war — not the warrior. Bad government, not a bad military, condemned 2,709,918 Americans to the misery of Vietnam. Bad government, not a bad military, cost us 58,226 American lives, 61% of them under the age of 21.

33 years later, having served in that war and having survived a nightmarish stint in the Hanoi Hilton make John McCain — no matter what he says or does — untouchable. He's become America's sacred cow. He's the war hero du jour and, with the tacit approval of a bedazzled press, his honorable war record inoculates him against responsibility for dishonorable actions. Criticism smacks of anti-Americanism; we've got to be damned careful what we say and how we say it when referencing any problems we might have with John McCain's politics.

Or his nasty temper, which includes foul language directed, in public, at his own wife. Another candidate, say, Barack

Obama, would have been pilloried by press and public alike for calling his wife a trollop and the C-word (which does not bear repeating.) What man of moral character would say such a thing? Obama's political career would have been blighted. Beyond repair.

How about what appears to be McCain's shaky grasp of the difference between Shia and Sunni; between Iraqi insurgents who want us out of their country and al Qaeda?

Or his deep concern about punitive Russian policy directed toward Czechoslovakia — when there has been no Czechoslovakia since 1993?

Or his equally deep concern about the "serious problem" our military faces "along the Iraq/Pakistan border" — when the two nations share not one inch of adjoining territory?

Or his insisting, despite the facts, that Bush's surge pre-dated the Anbar Awakening?.

Mistakes like these have crippled more than one presidential hopeful's campaign. Gerald Ford's 1976 foreign policy gaffe, "There is no Soviet domination of Eastern Europe ..." was "The Blooper Heard 'Round the World" (Time, October 18, 1976.) Echoing worldwide media response, Time said Ford's blooper was an amazing gaffe, "... Especially for one who is running partly on a campaign theme of experience in foreign policy ..."

Unlike Ford, John McCain has gotten an "Aw, shucks! We all know that's not what he really meant ..." media pass. We can't call a string of foreign policy bloopers serious reason for re-examining a candidacy. Go there and we're attacking a war hero who suffered for his country; we are waging a media campaign without honor.

YES, WE DID

Let's be clear: There is no doubt Senator McCain's service to his country was both honorable and admirable. There is no doubt he suffered terribly during five and a half years as a POW. No one — not Senator Barack Obama, not General Wesley Clark, not any other Democratic surrogate — has questioned the value of McCain's service, his patriotism or his honor during wartime. Everyone conceded, long ago, that John McCain is a hero.

Going to Vietnam made McCain no more heroic than over two million other Americans. By enlistment or by the draft, a member of the military knows that going to war is a matter of duty, not heroism.

Getting shot down while flying a mission is not an act of heroism. It is a tragic consequence of war. Being captured by the enemy is not an act of heroism. It's rotten luck. Time spent as a POW is not an act of heroism; it is certainly time spent in hell, against your will. Surviving it, living by the military Code of Conduct, is not so easy to do. But McCain and over 1,200 other men did it. According to the Code, a POW is to refuse "parole or special favors." McCain was offered his freedom because his father was Navy brass. He declined. He was doing his duty. That was undeniably the tough choice; it undeniably epitomizes honorable military conduct.

Clearly, John McCain had the courage and the determination to do his duty, to survive, and to do it with honor.

Honor is the cornerstone of the McCain campaign. Honor is his brand, his mantra. Honor.

But there is precious little honor in John McCain's strategy to win the White House. His attacks, which include pronouncements like Barack Obama "would rather lose the war than lose the election," his intimation that Obama does not support American troops, are dishonest and are deliberately crafted to brand the Democratic candidate "unpatriotic." The message? Unlike the honorable Vietnam war hero, Barack Obama is unAmerican. He is a coward and a danger to American safety, democracy and values. McCain knows better. Where is the honor in this?

Given the popularity Senator Obama enjoys both here and (especially) abroad, the honorable John McCain approved the Britney/Paris/Obama-as-celebrity video. If he can't compete with the articulate, visionary message or the likeable messenger on equal terms, he'll make something cheap, something suggestive of it. Confronted with the sleazy nature of the ad, McCain dubbed it "campaign humor." It's a joke. He's proud of it and there's more to come. Where's the honor?

And there's "The One." An Obama-as-phony-Moses piece of work. This one, which hints at a messianic complex, hints at the advent of the anti-Christ, hints at mass mania, is an insult to God, to the church, to people of faith, to every American citizen who believes four more years of the Bush Doctrine is a bad idea. This McCain-approved video says a great deal about his contempt for all of us.

There is no honor in this kind of campaign. There is no honor left in the man who would countenance it. There is certainly nothing heroic about smear- and fear-tactics.

The Vietnam War is over. It's time for John McCain to do the honorable thing in 2008. It's time he acts the hero. It's time he stops resting on the laurels of his Vietnam saga and relying on the collective guilt of a nation to shield him from his gaffes, his flaws, his nose-dive into the deep end of the politics-as-usual cesspool. It's John McCain's turn to be "The One." The One courageous enough to pull his own campaign out of the gutter and run for the presidency on nothing more — or less — than his own vision, his own proposed policies for the country's future.

It's time for John McCain to be The One. The One who has some honor left.

Politics and Religion, Heart and Soul

Aug. 5, 2008

"Lord, protect my family and me. Forgive me my sins and help me guard against pride and despair. Give me the wisdom to do what is right and just. And make me an instrument of your will." — Senator Barack Obama's prayer at Jerusalem's Western Wall

It's tradition. For believers, both Christian and Jewish, a trip to Judaism's holiest site is a matter of faith. That faith, made visible, is in the form of private prayers committed to paper and tucked into the crevices of Jerusalem's Western Wall. More than a million such prayers annually are left between those massive stones; stones hewn over 2,000 years ago. Twice a year those communications with God are collected and buried on the Mount of Olives.

It is also tradition that prayers left in the Wall are sacrosanct; they are meant to remain messages from the heart of the believer to the Almighty. For God's eyes only.

In the pre-dawn hours of Thursday, July 24, Senator Barack Obama made his pilgrimage to the Wall and left his prayer. That should have been the end of the story. What the senator from Illinois prayed for was nobody's business.

But moments after Obama and his entourage left the Western Wall, a young Orthodox Jewish student, who should have known better, ignored tradition and violated the sanctity of a believer's privacy. He fished out Barack Obama's prayer and took it to the Maariv newspaper — which promptly published it. The young man has since owned up to his actions and has apologized to Senator Obama, saying he "hoped he hasn't hurt him."

Had this happened here in the States, we wouldn't be too terribly shocked. In a country where paparazzi and unethical reporters routinely trample the rights and privacy of others for a media all too willing to pay cash on the line, we're no longer surprised. Coming from Jerusalem, the holiest of cities and one steeped in religious tradition, it's an aberration. A shocking one.

Obama's plea to his Lord has become the prayer heard 'round the world. Every news service has carried the story and the text of the prayer. I'm as guilty now as any other writer who's passed along a story that should never have been published. I tell myself, as I hover here over the keyboard, that I'm doing nothing wrong. The news is already out there, everybody already knows all about this. So, I'm not violating Senator Obama's privacy. Not really. But I keep pausing as I write, still wondering where the honor is in jumping onto this particular bandwagon. Wondering why I feel compelled to write it anyway.

Because I've read and reread this prayer a hundred times. Because it has moved me to tears. Because I want you to realize where this candidate's heart is.

YES, WE DID

Whether or not you and I agree with Senator Obama's stand on the war, on the economy, on universal health care, on taxation, on the direction our nation should take in January, we can agree on this:

In Jerusalem Barack Obama prayed to God for what mattered most to him. He didn't pray that John McCain would keep confusing Sunni and Shia, al Qaeda and Iraqi extremists. Or that we'd all notice McCain's policy concerns about Czechoslovakia — when there hasn't been a Czechoslovakia since 1993. Obama didn't pray the press would make a big deal over McCain's memory lapse about his voting against a bill that would have had the same insurance companies who pay for men's Viagra cover birth control for women. He didn't pray that folks would listen up and get a little alarmed when McCain refers to "the Iraq/Pakistan border" as a "serious problem" since the two countries do not share a single inch of border.

In his most private moments with God, Barack Obama did not pray to win an election.

In a time when many of us pray for our high school football team to win Friday's game, that says a great deal about character. And about faith.

Bikers, Booze, Bare Babes, Bananas ... and Cindy McCain

Aug. 5, 2008

For those of you who don't live, breathe, eat, sleep politics: No serious candidate for office campaigns in any state, at any event, without fully understanding where it is he's going. Who it is he's speaking to. The message is always tailor-made for the crowd. Always. It is, admittedly, pandering. Know your audience. It's how you win hearts and minds. And votes. In a race for the White House, neither party, neither candidate, is innocent of the facts on the ground. Ignorance is political suicide.

John McCain is no novice to politics. He's been around the block a few times, running for national office — and for the presidency — since 1982. That's 26 years, folks. This guy knows the ropes.

This GOP candidate, the unchallenged man-of-unquestionable-honor, just did a nifty stint in Sturgis, South Dakota. He spoke to a wildly enthusiastic crowd, thousands of McCain fans, at the Sturgis Rally 2008.

They loved him.

The annual Sturgis event is a biker rally. Bikers, booze, biker babes. Certainly, there is no democratic way to fault McCain's appearance there. American bikers are, well, American. They have rights. They vote, too. Judge not, you know?

But John McCain's performance was beyond the pale.

Every year the Sturgis rally features a beauty contest. The "Miss Buffalo Chip" pageant is notorious (a buffalo chip, if you aren't familiar with the term, is buffalo poop). No modest "I'm competing in this ladylike bathing suit, in this ladylike pageant, for a scholarship to college" rule applies in Sturgis. Miss Buffalo Chip contestants bare as much as possible, with a tattooed, long-haired biker emcee shouting encouragement like, "Drop your pants! Do something!" At which point these scantily clad young women remove a few more articles of clothing, hike their butts in the air, emulate the act of sex onstage with bananas. Or with each other. It's how you win the title. ESPN reporter Jim Caple writes, "…it is essentially a topless beauty pageant. And, occasionally, bottomless, too."

It's a vulgar display by any standards.

McCain has already called his wife a trollop and worse in the presence of the press. He's a war hero. He got a pass. If Barack Obama had said the same things to Michelle, you can bet your Sturgis-bared, banana-strokin' butt he'd have been drummed right out of any political hopes at all. Maybe that pass emboldened McCain. Maybe, in Sturgis, he went too far.

In his speech, before these hard drinking, testosterone-driven bikers, John McCain made a little he-man joke. At Cindy McCain's expense.

Referring to their sexually steamy beauty romp, McCain told a laughing crowd he'd encouraged his wife to compete for the Miss Buffalo Chip title. "I told her," McCain crowed, "with a little luck, she could be the only woman ever to serve as both the first lady and Miss Buffalo Chip."

Decades ago, we older folks remember a comedian named Henny Youngman who was famous for his one-liners. His wife was often the butt of his jokes, some of which began: "Take my wife — Please!"

John McCain, the presidential hopeful who runs on the name brand of "honor," said much the same thing to a rowdy, sexed-up, hard-drinking crowd in South Dakota. Take my wife... He made a sick, suggestive joke of the woman he's supposed to "honor and cherish." He did it for votes. He thinks it's funny.

Lust is a nasty, soul-deep infection. Lust for power drove McCain to insult his wife in true gutter fashion. Again. How presidential.

Makes ya proud to be an American, doesn't it?

Sexus Perplexus: Prurience, Politics and Piety

Aug. 9, 2008

Poor John Edwards. He should have known better. Illicit sex is the ultimate American no-no. It's the "black act" we love to hate; visions of all that sneaky, naked panting and groping dance in our little heads like sugar plums. It's all so deliciously obscene.

It's also the ultimate political "Gotcha!" And it's the ultimate national exercise in sheer hypocrisy. We American moralists are highly offended by sex. We can't stomach filth like sexually explicit song lyrics. Or frontal nudity on the big screen — or the small one. We'll condemn, boycott and Triple X that immorality every chance we get. It's nasty. We're decent folks who do not tolerate obscenity.

Sometimes.

But we tolerate gore. We like our bloody slasher flicks, action movies with heroes decapitating bad guys, fantasies with dripping arms and legs flying off the torsos of enemies everywhere. Eyes wide with the stunned expression of sudden, violent death; bullet holes through the forehead, scarlet splatter on white walls. Bring it on. That's exciting. That's not nasty, like sex.

And wars. Even illegal wars, immoral wars fought for an ideology of supremacy or for profit. For oil. We tolerate them just fine. We sanitize the language of bloody violence perpetrated en masse on innocent women, on the elderly. On babies and children. They become collateral damage. That's not obscene. It's war, it's our war — and it's always justifiable.

We turn on our dirty little corporate war only when it drags on too long and we have to pay a personal price. Like sacrificing our own kids — over and over and over again. Or finding we're in debt up to our sanctimonious necks, the Iraq War didn't pay for itself as promised, money's really tight and we're paying $4 a gallon for gas.

We tolerate the obscenity that is poverty in a nation of great wealth. The American homeless, the hungry, the uninsured. We tolerate rape and genocide. In Rwanda. In Darfur. Poverty, disease, malnutrition, gang rape and genocide aren't nasty. Like sex.

List, if you will, the political leaders in America who've done pretty much what John Edwards did. John McCain. Rudy Giuliani. Bill Clinton. Newt Gingrich. Larry Craig. David Vitter. Eliot Spitzer. Want to take an historic look at the personally morally-challenged? Thomas Jefferson. FDR. JFK. LBJ. There are plenty of flawed men to add to your roster.

List those who've done worse. Like Mark Foley, crusading publicly for abused and exploited children while preying on young congressional pages.

Now list the crimes committed by the Bush administration. The lies that led us into war. Black sites, Abu Ghraib, Guantanamo, all of which violated morality, American democratic values, federal and international law. The suspension of habeas corpus. War profiteering through no-bid contracts for crony corporations in Iraq. Warrantless wiretapping. Outing a CIA operative. Corrupting the DOJ for political purposes. This president might have been an intellectually barren candidate, a wastrel, a substance abuser, but he was no wayward Bill Clinton; he may have violated the law, trampled over the Bill of Rights, made a mockery of the constitution ... but he never cheated on his wife. Ask any moralist. He's one righteous dude.

What's obscene here? What moral and ethical failures actually threaten this country?

We need to get off our pious high horse. We have our national panties in a wad (at least for the present news cycle) because a presidential wannabe had dirty sex. What defines the tainted soul of John Edwards? Not Rielle Hunter. Two things should bother us far more than his antics with a blonde in a hotel room.

One (and this one has bothered me since the advent of primary season): His 21,000 square foot home in North Carolina. Twenty one thousand square feet. Why, that's as big as my local Walmart — and wa-a-ay more elegant. How much cushy space does a family of five need? What do you say when the kitchen's dirty — "Clean-up on aisle four"? When you've grown up as poor as Edwards did and you run an eloquent campaign on the issue of a "Two Americas" war on poverty, where's your social conscience? How do you justify that kind of self-indulgence?

Two: John Edwards' own words about his infidelity. "I did have an affair. But I did not love her." I did not love her. Well, as long as he didn't get emotionally involved ... that makes it all better! Doesn't it?

"I-did-not-love-her" Edwards, meet "My-wife's-a-trollop-worthy-of-the-Miss-Buffalo-Chip-title" McCain. You guys have a lot in common: the shameless objectification of women. Use 'em as the target for your vile temper, use 'em as the butt of your vulgar jokes, use 'em for no-commitment sexual gratification. The violation of a gender for convenience — of any kind — is a tad obscene.

Too bad for John Edwards that he couldn't just pull the plug on his inflatable gal pal, let the air out and forget the whole thing.

America, we need to re-examine our sexually-based standards for what's obscene and what's not. We have the power to change the definition of true obscenity. The act of illicit sex? That's the least of John Edwards' problems.

And it's the least of ours.

John McCain, War Games And The Draft

Aug. 22, 2008

John McCain has it on good authority (George W.) that The Hundred Years' War is more than a boring chapter in European history. It's Chapter One in the Bush/Cheney foreign policy crisis handbook, War Games: The Pre-emptive Punch Power Play.

Yes, We Did

The Bush/McCain doctrine is clear: It is imperative to strike the first blow when we have a notion someone out there means to hurt America. Or even piss us off. Especially if they've got oil. Or a pipeline. We hit first and we hit hard. Any perceived enemy is fair game. No verifiable evidence of evil intent required. These Grand Ole Pugilists know evil when they see it. Dubya has sixth sense enough to look into the eyes of another power player and see right into the guy's soul (a skill, one can hope, he will share with McCain should November bring us a GOP victory.)

Bellicose, saber-rattlin' War Games. That's what Bush/McCain foreign policy is all about. America is not alarmed.

Our role, as defined by the current administration, is to go to the mall. We are the Shop-for-Freedom Fighters. The vast majority of us are non-military families. And it's just fine to play the War Game when the "pieces" — the toy soldiers — belong to somebody else. But what do you do when the troops are worn slap out?

My friends, John McCain feels a draft.

And I'm with you all the way, good buddy. We Southerners are famous for firing the first shot when we're in a snit. I'm with you when you say the new draft should not be like the old one. You did not, of course, offer us any idea as to how you would amend the Selective Service. So, liberal or not, I'm going to do my patriotic duty. If we're going to fight the good fight for the next hundred years, we need some damn rules.

We need a draft again. A shiny new one. The old Selective Service was just that — selective. There were easy deferments for those who had the money to stay in college. Lots of Vietnam-era privileged guys got a sudden yen for graduate degrees. And others, like George W. and Dan Quayle, could avoid the draft altogether because daddy had money, had power, had influence. Daddy just pulled a few strings and got you bumped ahead of every other poor guy on the National Guard waiting list, or got you into grad school even when your academic record put you so low on the list of applicants you left skid marks.

Nope. We can't have that. We're going to play fair this time. No matter whose keester winds up in a sling.

Look to games to define the rules of fair play for games. Let's do it like, say, the NBA. You know, first round draft picks, second round, third round and so on. And no deferments. None. Here's how it goes:

First Round: The kids, nieces, nephews and/or grandchildren of every member of the executive branch who supports the war. The president and vice-president are the first Americans to send all of their family's kids off to war. Every last one of them.

Second Round: Legislative branch kids. Legislators who vote to authorize war send their own children. Along with executive branch kids, they are the first wave to the front lines.

Third Round: DOD, Pentagon and war-mongering think tank policy makers/writers. All their young'uns are gone.

Fourth Round: Hit up corporate America. Kids of defense contractors, oil company execs and the like.

If you love the notion of a war, if you promote it, vote for it or stand to make a profit from it — then you are certainly happy to do your patriotic duty. You'll want to share, to the fullest extent, the power and glory of your righteous war. You've earned the privilege. Kiss your kids goodbye. For the duration.

Senator McCain, I am so with you on this new draft.

And it'll work wonders. I'm sure of it. You can bet we'll see some serious talking going on in Washington. We'll see a veritable renaissance of diplomacy and intelligent, thoughtful discourse in solving our problems. There won't be another Vietnam or Iraq in our future — not with the kids of the powerful at risk first. Talk about your checks and balances! No more manipulative, lying, pre-emptive rush to war without consequences. Like impeachment.

War Games will be rare indeed when the children of the powerful and privileged are the first to play. The cost of war, our leaders will tell us then, is too damned high.

The Press and the 'Low Information Voter'

Aug. 26, 2008

You gotta love the mainstream media — those entrenched, reliable news sources who define the news rather than reporting it. A common complaint among serious journalists, many of them veterans of decades in the industry, is that the lines have been blurred between "news" and "commentary."

News is straightforward "who, what, where, when, how" reportage. Just the facts, unvarnished and right up front. It's a tough job. Hard digging for the true story, commitment to sourcing every detail, getting it right. Real news is a treasure. Real news informs the public. Unbiased information makes us all smarter.

Commentary? That's a different animal altogether. Commentary is not news. It's one writer's opinion about the news.

And that writer's opinion is colored by his/her personal biases: Liberal, conservative, secularist, pro-religion in public policy. We all write observations rooted firmly in our own take on the issues at hand. Unlike the newsman/woman, we are entirely selective in what we write. If we don't like the news about our side we can debunk it, ridicule it — or ignore it altogether.

Too many news folks now tend toward editorializing on the spot because they want to "help us understand" what's happening and who's making it happen. Under the guise of reporting they tell us what they think we ought to think. And we like it. We don't have to read much or think too hard when the pro at the news desk or at the keyboard gives us the easy 30 second sound-bite. This non-news approach has dumbed-down the public.

The same news professionals who've sound-bit us into a national stupor have given us a nifty new label: The Low Information Voter. That would be millions of Americans. The Low-Info types do not read multiple newspapers or news magazines. They do not watch (or read) in-depth analyses of foreign and domestic affairs offered by actual experts in the fields. All that takes time. Lots of it. Much of it is boring (no Paris, no Britney, no sex, no "He's-a-troop-hatin'-traitor.") The Low Information Voter ingests the hyped sound-bites, many of them created by right wing or left wing talking heads. Low-Infos never read the post-headline investigative journalism which proves the sound-bite was all wrong.

Examples:

● Despite investigation and debunking by every major worldwide news service, over 30 million Americans still believe Barack Obama is a Muslim.

● Despite the Pentagon's March 2008 report that there was no connection between Saddam Hussein/Iraq and the attacks on 9/11 — a report based upon 600,000 official Iraqi documents seized by U.S. forces following the invasion — about 90 million Americans still believe Saddam/Iraq were responsible.

Why? Because we were sold misinformation by politicians — and by a press too quick to go for the "grabber" headline. It's hard to put that genie back into the bottle.

● The latest irony? The Olympics. Rumors were rife that the Chinese women's gymnastic team violated the rules, having at least one gymnast under the age of 16 competing in Beijing. And they whipped the Americans. Within hours the New York Times was on the story. They did some serious digging — and managed to get their hands on a number of Chinese documents proving three members of their gymnastics team were underage. Chinese documents. From a secretive country not open to American media.

The NYT dug up that story in a heartbeat. But the run-up to the invasion of Iraq? They couldn't find a thing. Except Dick Cheney swearing he knew where the WMD were, Saddam was behind 9/11, we'd be greeted at liberators and we'd be out within six months.

The truth is out there. We just have to dig it.

What Hillary Didn't Say

Aug. 27, 2008

"[I am] a proud supporter of Barack Obama!" and "No way. No how. No McCain!" were surely stellar moments in Hillary Rodham Clinton's Denver speech. She asked THE challenging question of her PUMAs and other fractious supporters: "Were you in this campaign just for me?" And she made it clear that "Hillary or else!" won't do when "Nothing less than the fate of our nation and the future of our children hang in the balance."

It was good. Real good. It was Hillary Clinton at her very best, calling for the unity we Democrats must have to win this election. Pols and pundits raved. She'd hit one right out of the ballpark.

I have admired this woman for years. I have loved her for her strength, her grace in the face of terrible personal pain. I've loved her fierce intelligence. I was beaming at the screen while she spoke at the Pepsi Center. But, at the end of the evening, I was left wanting something. The impossible something. I want that bell unrung and, if I could have written part of Hillary's speech, here's what she'd have said to us:

"You know, politics is a nasty business. In the midst of a heated campaign, we candidates say, or imply, things about one another — even when we share the very same ideals — that we later regret having said. I'm no different, and tonight I'd like to take this opportunity to set the record straight.

Barack Obama is no sexist. At no time in this campaign did he denigrate women, nor did he imply that I, as a woman, was unfit to lead this country.

His record on women's reproductive rights is just as solid as mine.

I called him irresponsible. I called him naïve. I said he was all speeches and no solutions. I said he was not ready to lead, that he lacked the 'experience' to be our commander-in-chief. I approved the 3:00 a.m. ad to put the fear of God into any Democrat, Independent or disillusioned Republican who was seriously considering voting for Barack Obama. It was less than honest; it was a mistake made in the heat of a campaign I was losing. That mistake, along with comments I made to undercut his successful campaign during primary season, has played right into the hands of the GOP. They are using my words, my ads, against my party. Against my candidate. Against the change I know is best for my country.

I want to say this to all Democrats, to all Independent voters and those Republicans who recognize the danger of four more years of the Bush/McCain Doctrine:

I said what I felt I had to say to win. I did what I felt I had to do to win. That's politics and we all know it."

To John McCain and his minions:

If you insist upon using my words now, hoping to manipulate my 18 million supporters, then use the words my campaign adopted when I said I was open to having Barack Obama as my choice for vice president. We said, quite clearly, that while we believed he was not ready for the White House during primary season, that he would be ready by August to serve as vice president, to ascend to the Oval Office in the event it became necessary. And that means that I knew then what I know now: Barack Obama is ready to lead this nation — I would not be here tonight, endorsing his candidacy with all my heart, if I believed otherwise.

Senator McCain, I will not sit idly by and allow you to exploit this woman for your own negative campaigning. I'm a fighter. I will fight for what I know to be right — and that means you will have me to deal with from now until election day.

And, finally, to my 'Sisterhood of the Traveling Pants Suit':

It's tough being a woman in a world still weighted toward the best interests of men. There is that glass ceiling holding us down. We all know it, and we all know we have to finish the job of breaking through those 18 million cracks we made in it.

But it is a disservice to you, to myself, to all women, to believe that the reason I did not win the Democratic nomination is sexism or that the DNC conspired to rob the first woman presidential candidate of her rightful victory.

We all know, when we're honest, that my staff and I made serious financial and tactical errors during my campaign. Those mistakes cost us the nomination. We cannot allow our personal feelings of gender loyalty or outrage to supersede what we all know to the fundamental truth of this election: John McCain is every woman's worst nightmare. He is harmful to women and other living things. Voting for him makes a mockery of everything you and I have fought for.

Not voting is every bit as bad. Such an abdication is petulant and harmful to our country, our families, our future, ourselves. The time has come to rise above petty politics and our personal ambitions or agendas. There is too much at stake.

The choice has never been so clear. It is not a choice between bad or worse. It is a choice between right and wrong.

Barack Obama is the right choice. I know it and you know it."

McSame's McVeep: A Token of His Esteem ...

Aug. 30, 2008

John McCain's choice of Sarah Palin for vice president says more about the character of the man at the top of the ticket than it does about the woman in the number two spot.

His lust for power overrides both his common sense and his Country First meme.

A candidate who is a veteran of more than two decades on Capitol Hill and is a career-long member of the Republican Party certainly knows where the talent and capability lie within his own ranks. McCain could have chosen Olympia Snowe or Christine Todd-Whitman or Kay Bailey Hutchison as a running mate. He could have chosen any one of these women and made the case that, should he succumb to yet another recurrence of melanoma, his second-in-command would be qualified to serve as POTUS. On day one.

But he didn't.

I won't waste words parodying Sarah Palin, although the cheap shot is mighty tempting. I've seen the dismissive jetsam and flotsam online, the Vogue shots, the references to "the beauty queen." It's tasteless and counterproductive. I've seen the photo of Palin scantily clad with cleavage down-to-there and a tight skirt up-to-here and shoes that would do credit to any madame's paid escort. I won't Palin-bash over that picture, either. If I had a body like Sarah Palin, honey, I'd strut my stuff in private and have one very happy husband.

I won't list the ways this poor woman is tragically underqualified for such high office in unimaginably tough, dangerous times. Plenty of bloggers and reporters are doing that chore. I won't write a scenario of what might happen in the White House, at 3:00 a.m., should old John need hospitalization and Sarah Palin answers the damned red phone. Nor will I concoct a scene where VP Palin actually tries to tell "Stormy" McCain he's wrong about something.

I won't yell and scream (although really, really I want to) about a Veep — that heartbeat away from the Oval Office Veep — who believes her feminist sisters should be denied the choice to terminate a pregnancy even in the case of rape. Or incest.

I won't publicly agonize over her love affair with weapons and big oil drilling-for-dollars, her denial of human responsibility for global warming, for her blind refusal to recognize that the endangered polar bear is the canary in the coal mine. I won't rant about her unbelievable affinity for Pat Buchanan and Ted Stevens. Or over her pending problems with the Alaskan legislature about abuse of power (God knows we've gotten used to that dynamic in the White House.)

I won't launch into a tantrum because John McCain only met the woman one time, choosing a running mate he clearly did not, and does not, really know.

And I won't hate her because she's beautiful. Although that's a tough call for an old warhorse my age.

I won't. Because none of that matters as much as this simple, terrible fact:

There is something seriously off-kilter about John McCain. We all know his history with women's rights is, to put it kindly, unenlightened. We all know his treatment of the women in his own life, from infidelity and desertion to Miss Buffalo Chip, is mighty tawdry. That's his personal life. Unsavory as his behavior has been, a good, Clintonian argument can be made that a lack of character (and of respect for his wives) in his personal life does not disqualify him for the presidency.

But this time John McCain's tin ear for — and lack of commitment to — the true worth of women invades the public sphere. This is serious business. The man had choices here. There are experienced, qualified Republican women. He refused to choose one of them and, in doing so, his contempt for women is showing like a dingy, oversized slip beneath a mini-skirt. He has made a joke of every highly qualified woman's right to climb to the top of the ladder. He's made a mockery of the vice presidency in the process. And he's risking the security of the nation he swears only war hero McCain has the judgment to lead.

Sarah Palin is, very likely, a nice enough woman. But she's no Hillary Clinton; she's the anti-Clinton. John McCain has cynically trivialized Ms. Palin as a token candidate. This is an ill-conceived maneuver, pandering to American women he clearly believes are so lame-brained that we can be fooled by tokenism. It's downright abusive. It typifies the mindset of a man who simply doesn't get it. Not about smart women and not about national security.

We're not stupid, Senator McCain. We don't want any woman who says yes on either ticket. We want the best woman for the job.

How Many Houses Do You Own?

Sept. 2, 2008

John McCain said it himself: "I don't know as much about the economy as I should."

How a bright man can serve over 25 years on Capitol Hill, including a stint as chairman of the Senate Commerce Committee, without learning "much" about the U.S. economy is a puzzlement. How he can run a campaign based upon all that "experience" while pleading ignorance about economic issues should concern every voter.

John McCain doesn't get it about regular folks, hard earned money and hard times. He doesn't have to.

When asked by the press "How many houses do you own?" McCain could not — or would not — give a straight answer. He faltered, stammered, then told reporters his staff "would have to get back to them on that." Smart move. With millions of Americans facing foreclosure and millions more finding the homes they've worked so hard to own are now worth less money than when they were purchased, no sly politician wants to admit to owning at least 8 luxury homes — or that he pays more money in a single year for household help for all those houses than many of us earn in a decade.

Excuses have been made for McCain's memory lapse and for his personal Lifestyle of the Rich and Famous. His brother, Joe McCain, explains it this way:

It is McCain family tradition that their wives handle all the money. John and Cindy, Joe contends, have an arrangement similar to the one the McCain brothers' parents had. "The person who took care of all the business was my mother," he told reporters. "My father had no idea about the family business, what oil leases he owned in Oklahoma…one time, she bought a house to remodel [in Southeast Washington] while he was at sea."

John McCain has not been "at sea" since the '60s. He's lived right here in the States since his return from North Vietnam.

He grew up the son of military brass — and, unlike the regular GI family who now struggle to make ends meet, officer's families do not suffer severe financial hardship. Certainly, they did not suffer real financial hardships at all when the McCain boys were growing up, nor when John McCain served as a naval officer. I know. I was an Army wife from 1967 thru 1970. An NCO's wife. Back then we had decent housing provided by the military, all our medical was covered by the military and we enjoyed discount shopping on post at a commissary and the post exchange. The Hansen family lived off-post in a government leased home in South Miami. We had four bedrooms and two full baths. Our only expense? The phone bill. Our first child was born at Homestead Air Force Base Hospital. We had complications and were in the hospital for over a week. Total cost? $8.

Today's military should have it so good. They don't.

An angry McCain staffer offered his own two cents' worth on the issue of multiple homes and a "Champagne wishes and caviar dreams…" lifestyle enjoyed by John and Cindy for the last quarter century: Senator McCain was a prisoner of war! He was a POW! He lived in a Hanoi cell for five years!

So he did. And he suffered there. But that was forty years ago and a "remedial riches" argument is one dog that won't hunt.

John McCain hasn't got a clue about regular folks' current anxieties about jobs, housing, health insurance, groceries, gas, prescription drugs, surviving a recession.

He's voted with Bush economics more than 90% of the time. Enough said.

Palin's Terrible 'Executive' Family Decision

Sept. 3, 2008

Barack Obama's response to the news that GOP vice presidential nominee Sarah Palin's 17 year old daughter is five months pregnant is crystal clear: The families of candidates, especially the children, are off-limits. Period.

It's the right position to take. The fact that Alaska Governor Palin's teenaged daughter made the tragic mistake of having pre-marital sex at such a young age — and got pregnant in the process — has nothing whatever to do with her mother's qualifications (or the lack of them) for public office. Nor do the mistakes our kids make always define the caliber of our parenting skills. At a certain age, our kids do what they will no matter how carefully, how lovingly they were raised. They may break the rules and break our hearts, but their lapses are no reflection upon our judgment as parents or as people.

None of us has the right to judge and condemn Sarah Palin because Bristol Palin failed the "abstinence only" test.

There are, however, issues of judgment involved.

First: Governor Palin slashed Alaska's legislative funding for social programs, including Passage House, a transitional home for teenage moms. The mission statement for Passage

House: "To provide young mothers a place to live with their babies for up to 18 months while they gain necessary skills and resources to ... create and provide a stable environment for themselves and their families." In other words, a pro-family safe haven for kids whose parents aren't as accepting as the Palins of an unwed mother and her baby. When, like Palin, your pro-life stance extends to banning abortions even in the cases of rape and incest, there is an undeniable judgment gap here. Pro-life agenda should not stop the moment a baby draws its first breath. Pro-life means adequate services for that child and the mother who chose to keep it.

Second: Palin says her daughter will marry the father of the baby. She's fine with that.

Meet Daddy: 18 year old Levi Johnston. Like millions of other high school kids, Levi had a MySpace page. Here are his own words about who he is:

"I'm a fuckin' redneck who likes to snowboard and ride dirt bikes ... But I live to play hockey. I like to go camping and hang out with the boys, do some fishing, shoot some shit and just fuckin' chillin' I guess ... Ya fuck with me I'll kick [your] ass."

Levi goes on to say he's "in a relationship" but "I don't want kids."

Pro-life. Absolutely, no exceptions, take-no-prisoners pro-life. If that's your core belief, then you protect that baby's life. You protect your own child, the one who is already paying a very high price for passion in the back seat of a car. You fail to protect either one when you compound one costly mistake with another. Marriage is a sacrament, no? Marriage is a bond, for life, of love and faith and commitment.

None of us knows whether or not Bristol Palin is equipped for such a sacred responsibility. But clearly, Levi Johnston has some growing up to do — and that painful process is not one that should be inflicted on a child bride and an innocent baby.

Marriage is not a convenient solution to a parental pride problem. It is not punishment for doing the "nasty." It is not a morality bandage we slap on the wounds of "sin" or "shame" to make them publicly acceptable.

And any parent, Ms. Palin, who thinks marriage is any of the above lacks judgment. Good judgment: The criteria for a credible candidacy and for sound governance.

A Heartbeat Away From that 3 a.m. Phone Call

Sept. 16, 2008

It matters.

In the event of the illness or, heaven forbid, the death of the president, the vice president must be qualified to step into some mighty big shoes.

When the candidate seeking the highest office in the land — and that of leader of the free world — chooses a running mate, we have the right to expect he'll make that choice with utmost care.

Especially if, like John McCain, he's 72 and has had recurring bouts of cancer.

Word among political insiders is that McCain very much wanted Joe Lieberman for the No. 2 spot.

Or former Pennsylvania Governor (and former head of Homeland Security) Tom Ridge.

There's a strong case to be made for either candidate's qualifications to "…serve as president from day one…," and that is the criteria McCain, himself, set for his vice presidential pick.

But that was before he picked one.

Maverick McCain had to face political reality.

He couldn't have Lieberman or Ridge, no matter how qualified they were to serve.

The far Right base wasn't buying.

Both Lieberman and Ridge are pro-choice. In the contest between national security and abortion, well, McCain chose Sarah Palin. She's so "pro-life" she wants abortions outlawed — even in the cases of rape or incest.

Score? Anti-choice: 1, National Security: 0.

What an odd choice from the guy who swears "We're in danger! Experience is everything!"

Only weeks ago, when Virginia Governor Tim Kaine was on Barack Obama's short list for Veep, McCain advisor Karl Rove was quick to condemn the very idea. Kaine, Rove said, just wasn't qualified.

"Tim Kaine has been governor of Virginia," Rove lamented, "for only three years."

Before that, Karl complained, Kaine had been, what?

Mayor of Richmond! And Richmond, Virginia, Rove went on, is no big city.

With a population of only 200,000 — well, you know.

You just don't make the leap from mayor of Richmond to

governor of Virginia to the vice presidency!

Such an Obama choice, he said, would be "…intensely political" and "would not be first and foremost concerned with 'Is this person capable of serving [as president from day one]…'"

Then ole John picks Sarah Palin.

Two terms as mayor of Wasilla, Alaska, and 20 months as governor of the state.

Rove waxed ecstatic in his interview about the pick of this governor. She's got loads of experience!

After all, Wasilla, Rove said, is "the second largest city in Alaska!"

And Alaska, Rove et al will tell you, is the largest state in the union! In square miles, anyway.

Facts:

Kaine: 4 terms Richmond City Council. 2 terms mayor of Richmond. Lt. Governor of Virginia for 4 years, governor for three.

Population of Richmond city: about 200,000.

Population of Greater Richmond area : 1.2 million.

Population of Virginia, 2006: 7,642,884

Virginia in population/responsibilities-based size: 12th largest of 50 states.

Palin: 2 terms mayor of Wasilla (part-time). Under two years a governor of Alaska.

Population of Wasilla: about 8,000

Population of Alaska, 2006: 670,053

Alaska in population/responsibilities-based size: 47th

largest out of 50 states.

Bush/Rove/McCain logic: Tim Kaine? A risk to national security, a cynical political pick, not enough experience. Sarah Palin? This gal's got all the experience she needs to become President of the United States and Commander-in-Chief. From day one.

If that flip-flopping nonsense doesn't scare you, you're not paying attention.

Praying For Pipelines Not My Kind Of Religion

Sept. 22, 2008

I am a person of faith. A believer. Prayer is a part of my daily life. And I've had a rough week.

After my regular column ran in the paper down here in South Carolina last week all hell broke loose. It was a column in which I wrote that Sarah Palin should not be judged, as a person or as a parent, by her very young daughter's poor choices — but that Palin's poor judgment was fair game. The compounding of one terrible mistake (teenage pregnancy) by another (marriage to a vulgar kid who's clearly not yet husband/father material) is not the kind of rational thinking we need in a vice president who's too close to the Oval Office for comfort. I also called into question Palin's slashing funds for pro-family, keep-your-baby services in Alaska. Pro-life, if that's your core belief, does not end the moment the accidental kid draws breath.

Irate Southern Christians had a field day with my phone number. I won't bore you with a string of individual quotes.

Here's a "composite call." Comments in brackets are mine:

"Happy birthday, Linda! [Yes, it was my birthday]. How's your poor husband? I know his long illness has been just awful for you folks [My husband has been seriously ill with cardiomyopathy, and severely deficit-impaired from two major strokes, for the past five years]. I want you to know I'm praying for you to get what you deserve ...

"... and you folks deserve to get sick and die [Yes, my husband is dying] after all the trash you've printed [sic] in the paper! Who do you think you are to say terrible things about good Christian people like sweet little Senator Palin [sic] and our president, who is a praying man [Jim Jones was a praying man right up to the minute he ordered his followers to force that poison-laced Kool-aid down their children's throats] and a genuine hero from Vietnam [sic]? And what do you have against rich people, anyway?" [Greed trumping human need? Other than that, I'm fine with wealth]

God is good. But not all Christians are — well, Christian. If you get my drift.

I'm a believer. I'm a progressive Christian, which means the divine messages that sing inside my head are these:

"The last shall be first and the first shall be last ..."

"Blessed are the meek, for they shall inherit the earth."

"Blessed are the peacemakers, for they shall be called children of God."

"It is easier for a camel to go through the eye of a needle, than for a rich man to enter the Kingdom of God."

I'm a person of faith and I've had a rough decade. One during which "the last" and "the least," "the meek" and "the peacemakers," have been rolled over by a trivialized right-wing God and the politicians that God serves. That God is an irate, petty fellow who is obsessed with political sexual lapses, but doesn't worry much about lies and the innocent casualties of a bad, greed-based war. He's a "Prosperity Gospel" deity who rewards the really, really good Christian with bigger houses, bigger cars, better parking spaces and plenty of cash, but doesn't worry much about poverty, homelessness, disease and needless death worldwide. He sure isn't fretting over nearly 50 million uninsured Americans who have no access to health care — other than the McCain vaunted emergency-room-as-proof-no-American-is-really-uninsured excuse for ignoring the sick

Poor, sick folks wouldn't be poor, sick folks if they lived right. Good Christians, you know, want not.

Clearly, the right-wing God and liberal folks have been at odds about what's important for a decade or more.

I should have felt better when John McCain chose Sarah Palin as his soul mate. Jeeze. She's a self-proclaimed Bible Babe. We Southerners do, Lord, love our Bible. The Beatitudes — all those "Blessed ares ..." — must be the cantata of Palin's conscience, the liturgy of her legislative agenda. This is a woman who knows the power of prayer.

She blew it. The Iraq war, she claims, is a "task from God." That's bad religion. But there's worse: She encouraged a crowd of fellow believers to pray for her pipeline project.

That's not just bad religion. That smacks of apostasy.

Mea culpa. Maybe it's me. I don't pray for pipelines. I don't pray for a raise or a better house. I don't pray for God to "Make a way, Lord, make a way!" for me to get what I want in life. Or what I want in politics.

Not when there's Darfur, where, a few short years ago, a two year old baby girl was gang raped by members of the Janjaweed. A two year old. A toddler. Gang raped by big, strapping, evil men who did it because they are evil and because they could. She was left with fistulas — open, seeping holes — from her tiny little female parts to her rectum. God only knows what other kind of permanent damage was done to that baby's heart, to her mind and to her spirit.

I never knew her name. I don't know what's become of her; whether she's dead or alive. But I pray for that child every day of my life. Every day. She is the focus of my prayers and has come to symbolize every child in pain, in want. She's come to symbolize every suffering soul on this earth; every man, woman and child who is victimized or cheated or ignored or hungry or sick or homeless or lost.

More people of faith than not pray for peace, for an end to poverty, disease and human suffering. Sarah Palin prays for pipelines. Others pray that those who do not agree with them will "get what they deserve." They deify war and wealth. They justify greed. Their God wants the good guys to have the big bomb, most of the world's oil and plenty of cash.

That's a mighty good reason to vote for the other guy; to vote Obama/Biden and know you're doing the best thing for your country, for yourself, for humankind. And it's a good reason to make a rational choice: Vote to separate cynical, self-serving, rancorous religiosity from good governance.

McCain as economic reformer? That's loose change

Sept. 23, 2008

Fannie Mae. Freddie Mac. Lehman Brothers. Merrill Lynch. AIG.

Wall Street teeters on the brink as banks, brokerages and insurers collapse. Billions of dollars — some estimates say a trillion dollars — of wealth is gone within days. The Wall Street Fat Cats have pocketed their speculative, shady millions and left the rest of us, struggling, ordinary taxpayers, to foot the bail-out bill.

And that's what happens when the voter is sold this bill of goods: The pure profit-driven free market is always good. Government rules (regulations) about their methods, about how much they risk to make their free market profit, are always bad.

Avid proponents of deregulating the market have promised us that, if we only trust corporate America to do the right thing with minimal — or no — oversight, we'll all be wealthier because of it. It's the old Trickle Down economic game. Let the Fat Cats rake in the cash and they'll take real good care of the little guy.

John McCain has been an avid supporter of deregulation for over twenty years. He was still a deregulating free market lover the first week of this month. September. In St Paul, at the Republican National Convention. Government, get out of the way. No rules. Just profit.

We've watched, horrified, as our economy has badly faltered in the past few months. John McCain insisted "We've done pretty well" under George W. Bush. John McCain insisted "Our economy is fundamentally strong…" He has said those magic words over and over again. On Monday, September 15th, despite the failures of Fannie and Freddie, Lehman and Merrill Lynch, he kept swearing the economy was strong. He began Tuesday, September 16th with the same message. Then AIG crashed.

We were a strong economy on Monday. By Tuesday afternoon, McCain had flipped. We are now an economy "in crisis."

On Tuesday, Straight-talking McCain said he was against a government bail-out of AIG. And we all know that man means what he says.

On Wednesday, McCain flopped. He's now for the bail-out.

He's Maverick McCain, who, after two decades, is suddenly sick and tired of the greed and dirty dealings of deregulated business. He's got the experience to clean up the filth on Wall Street. He wants some accountability! We need some dadgummed rules! And that, folks, means regulations.

John McCain was against regulations before he was for them.

Now he asks us to believe he's the populist reformer who'll take on all those financial lobbyists who've created this economic disaster. He'll take 'em on alright. 83 of them are on the McCain for President team. Among them:

Chief political adviser Charlie Black (Freddie Mac)

National finance chairman Wayne Berman (AIG, Fannie Mae, Freddie Mac)

Campaign congressional liaison John Green (Fannie

Mae)

McCain vice-presidential vetter Arthur Culverhouse (Fannie Mae)

McCain's transition planning chief William Timmons (Freddie Mac — and the American Petroleum Institute, to boot).

McCain adviser and good buddy "This mental recession is all in your head and you're a nation of whiners" Phil Gramm remains in the McCain ranks. Good old Phil. He's the one who co-authored the Gramm-Leach-Bliley Act in 1999. You know — the one that took the teeth out of federal regulations which had protected us, since the banks failed and the Great Depression ravaged us, in the '30s.

John McCain has been a career long advocate for no rules corporate pandering. He's toed the George W. Bush economic line and has defended Bush economic policy.

John McCain is not the solution to Wall Street greed. He's a longtime part of the problem.

Presidential campaign 2008 in Black and White

Sept. 30, 2008

There are some words so loaded with negative meaning we just don't use 'em. But, face it, politics brings out the beast in most of us. Georgia GOP congressman Lynn Westmoreland recently said presidential candidate Barack Obama is "uppity." That word is hyper-loaded. We've all grown up here in the South; we all know what word follows uppity.

And anyone who thinks race and racism aren't a part of

this election is being willfully disingenuous. Westmoreland didn't use "uppity" by accident. He meant to paint a word-picture, and he did.

The double standard here is breathtaking.

When Obama's pastor, the Rev. Jeremiah Wright, railed against America for genocide (Native Americans,) slavery (African Americans) and a bad war, he said "God damn America!" Terrible words. Terrible. There's no arguing that those words were the wrong ones. Wright was absolutely right about social injustice — but his words were awful and inflammatory. A video clip of only the very worst of that sermon made national news, fed to us over and over again in a continuous loop. Wright is unAmerican. Unpatriotic. Dangerous. The myth that Barack Obama is — or ever was — Muslim has been totally debunked. But clearly he is a bad Christian. He should have condemned Wright and walked out of that church.

Obama paid a price. Fair enough — if the same price is demanded of the other side.

How do these words strike you?

"I'm an Alaskan — not an American! I've got no use for America and her damned institutions! The fires of hell are frozen glaciers compared to my hatred for the American government ... I won't be buried under that damn flag ... you say, 'The hell with them!' and you renounce allegiance and you pledge your efforts, your effects, your honor, your life, to Alaska!"

— Joe Vogler founder, Alaska Independence Party, 1991

If those words aren't anti-American, what is? If that sentiment and that party's core belief, secession from the U.S. and independence for a sovereign Alaska, aren't unpatriotic, what is? The Alaska Independence Party (AIP) is alive, well, and hating the United States of America today. The mission of the AIP has not changed.

And Alaska Governor Sarah Palin opened their 2008 convention with these words: "I'm delighted to welcome you to the 2008 Alaska Independence Party convention...Keep up the good work!"

Todd Palin, the good governor's husband, was a card carrying member of the AIP from 1995-2002.

He remained a member through her tenure as mayor of Wasilla. In 2002 — when Palin made an unsuccessful bid for the GOP nomination for Lt. Governor of Alaska, Todd Palin left his secessionist party. How convenient.

One thing's sure: While hubby Todd was a bona fide member of a political party whose credo is "We Hate America," Sarah Palin did not condemn his activities. Nor did she "get up and walk out."

Quite the contrary. Governor Palin, in 2008, tells the AIP to "Keep up the good work!"

So where's the continuous, inflammatory news loop now? Where's the red, white and blue outrage now?

Anti-American is anti-American, isn't it?

Maybe not. Maybe it's no big deal. If you're white.

Tag Team Terrorism:
The Bush, McCain, Palin Soap Opera

Oct. 7, 2008

Be afraid. Be ver-r-r-ry afraid.

Barack Hussein Obama does not see the same 99 $^{44/1000}$% pure Ivory Soap America you and I know and love. Really. The McCain/Palin America is pristine; its shiny neo-conservative principles fit neatly in the palm of your hand. It never sinks. Ever. It floats.

There's a reason Barack Obama can't see that floating moral American certitude (or stop harping on the sinking of the USS Economy along with the working- and middle-classes): He's too busy "palling around with domestic terrorists." And he's not like you and me; he doesn't love America enough. And he's a liar. Boo! He is one dangerous dude.

Prior to their freshly frenetic pursuit of the White House, John McCain swore he had the corner on the Truth, Honor and the American Way market. Palin? She had the Cute, Sassy Six-Pack 'n' Soccer Mom market sewed up tighter than a tick on a hound's back. It just wasn't enough. So they've sunk to whipping up a foaming anti-Obama rage on the stump and they're trying to tell us it's soap.

Not everything that foams is Ivory, honey. Sometimes it's nothing more than that stinking stuff we see bubbling from the mouth of a dying, rabid dog. We'd be well advised to learn to tell the difference.

Be afraid. Be very afraid. This is the GOP sales-pitch we've been buying ever since "Hunt him down, smoke him out!" Dubya & Co. declared Osama bin Laden's Afghanistan-based al Qaeda wasn't nearly as scary as Saddam's Iraq. Those damned nationalized oil fields ... all that wealth ... cheap gas ... the notion of establishing a permanent, menacing American military presence in the Middle East ... We had to get over there and clean up! Surely a mushroom cloud was headed for the American heartland. Or for D.C. Or Altanta, Tampa, Dallas, Fargo, Cheyenne, Boise ... Yourtown, USA was next. The meme? No doubt. No questions. No criticism. Invade Iraq or die.

By Campaign 2004, the fear factor meme was more of the same — with a nifty twist: "Vote GOP or die." When Vietnam War hero John Kerry appeared to be a threat, the GOP swift boated him right to the bottom of the political pond. It's hard to stay afloat when you're weighted down with all that bubbling slime.

John McCain decried such tactics then. He was one clean military guy/statesman, a product of Ivory Soap America. He was 99 $^{44/1000}$% pure and he'd never sink to a smear and fear campaign. Not like George W. v. Kerry. Not like that. Never like the rabid filth-mongering Dubya campaign that crushed McCain in South Carolina. John Sidney McCain was too honest for that. Too honorable.

Until now. Until the going gets tough, the issues and the public's confidence aren't falling his way. Joe Biden was absolutely right when, during the vice presidential debate, he said: "The past is prologue."

We have an eight-year-long past of domestic terrorism in America. The Bush/Cheney/Rumsfeld cabal have successfully terrorized an entire nation into silence. Into voting as we're told.

Terror of all Muslims, of any nation or culture which isn't wholly "on our side."

Terror of a fair, affordable health care program for every American.

Terror of immigrants.

Terror of gay and lesbian human rights.

Terror of women's reproductive rights.

Terror of real diplomacy.

Terror of admitting errors or correcting our course.

Terror of speaking out for fear of being labeled "unpatriotic."

Terror of the truth when it belies our squeaky clean self-image.

We hardly need to worry overmuch about imported terrorism. Like Mary Shelley's Frankenstein, we have created our own monsters. They are our very own home-grown domestic terrorists. We have elected too many of them to seats of power and have allowed them to scare us into submission.

John McCain and Sarah Palin are the new GOP Tag Team Terrorists. It's the George W. Bush Fear Game all over again.

If we've got a lick of sense left, a scintilla of decency, we'll rise up and tell these folks a simple truth about their methods: This time it just won't wash.

The Veep Debate? The Bridge to Nowhere

Oct. 7, 2008

It was the Expectations Game, Deluxe Edition.

Sarah Palin's interviews with Fox's Britt Hume, ABC's Charlie Gibson and CBS's Katie Couric were so disastrous that even long-time conservative columnists were panicked. Such lofty Republican writers as George Will, David Brooks and Kathleen Parker were begging her to do the right thing for her party and her country: Drop out of the race to "spend more time with her family," give McCain a chance to choose a qualified candidate.

Palin's foreign policy experience? She's governor of Alaska — and you can see Russia from there; when Putin "rears his head" and Russia "invades U.S. airspace, where do they come? Alaska!" (Russia has never invaded Alaska's airspace.) Palin couldn't remember what newspapers she reads. She couldn't think of a single Supreme Court case except Roe v. Wade. She swore to Couric that McCain had certainly voted for the regulation of U.S. banks and business. When Couric asked her (very politely, I might add) to give a single example of any time John McCain ever voted in favor of regulations ... Palin said she couldn't think of one, but "I'll find one and get it back to ya!"

These were not profound, elitist questions. Governor Palin was not victimized. She was not tricked. She was asked questions any candidate for the second highest office in the land should be able to answer. With ease.

But she's been cute and sparkly, and heaven knows most Americans like shiny things. But gaffe after gaffe has even the

GOP faithful demanding a repair job. So Palin disappeared to one of McCain's Arizona spreads with two McC strategists and buckled down for a week long cram session. How many talking points could she memorize before facing Biden?

It didn't matter. The bar was set so low by Thursday night all Palin had to do was remain upright and breathing for 90 minutes and she'd win the debate.

She did remain standing. She had her talking points fixed in her head, she informed moderator Gwen Ifill she had no intention of answering a question "the way you want me to" or at all if she didn't want to. She made a few bloopers. There is nothing in the U.S. Constitution which gives a vice president "more legislative power" than is already being wielded on Capitol Hill. The commander of U.S. forces in Afghanistan is General David Kiernan — not "General McClellan." And you can't say your running mate is the born-again Regulator-in-Chief who'll lay down the law to big business and then keep saying "Government, get out of the way of families AND get out of the way of business" in the same debate and make a lot of sense.

Polls and pundits say Joe Biden won the debate. Conservative pundits say "At least she didn't do any further damage." Folks who loved her on Wednesday still loved her on Thursday night. It's the "I'm not sure about her" Republicans and Independents who are still not enchanted by the Palin charm. Bush was charming, too. He was "the kind of president you could have a beer with." Palin is selling herself as "the Joe Six-Pack vice president." I think we've had quite enough Budweiser.

At the end of the campaign day, she is who she is and she

knows what she knows. Which is not enough. The "executive experience as governor" won't wash. George W. was the "executive" of much larger Texas for much longer — and look where that's gotten us.

McCain/Palin Political Party Dance: The Limbo

Oct. 14, 2008

This dance was all the rage years ago. Catchy Caribbean music throbbed, a couple of folks held up a long pole and dancers took turns prancing under it. It wasn't easy. The dancer had to bend backward from the waist, body contorted and bobbing in time to the music. There was one rule: Fall down or touch the pole and you're out. 'Round and 'round the line of eager dancers went — and each time you reached the pole it was lower than before; to keep dancing, you had to bend farther and farther backward, go lower and lower to get under the pole. One after another, dancers were eliminated. There could be only one winner: The champ was the lowest of the low.

It's great entertainment at a party, particularly if you're belting back a few beers or some Pumphouse Rum Punch.

As a political jig, it ain't so funny. In Campaign 2000, the George W. camp danced the Limbo all over South Carolina. John McCain had "fathered and illegitimate black baby," was "a liar and a cheat," had "betrayed his country while a POW," had come back from Vietnam one watermelon shy of a truckload. You couldn't trust this guy anywhere near the Oval Office. The beat went on until McCain's character was so tainted he didn't stand a chance. His candidacy ended right here. It was a dirty, dishonest campaign. And it worked.

In 2008 McCain pledged he'd never stoop to such tactics. No smears. The American voter wanted an issues-based campaign and he would deliver.

Then the economy tanked and his poll numbers sank along with it.

When the issues turned toxic for the GOP, honorable John's campaign manager Rick Davis hinted at what was coming: "This election is not about issues," he declared. "This election is about a composite view of what people take away from these candidates."

The Wall Street crisis deepened. It was clear John McCain's career-long "No government regulations for business! Let the free market police itself!" mantra had been responsible for the corporate raider mentality which first corrupted then bankrupted our financial institutions. A McCain aide told the press their camp had to change the subject. "If we keep talking about the economy, we're going to lose."

The GOP couldn't have the attention of the American voter focused on all that issue stuff — like McCain's own words in the Sept/Oct edition of Contingencies, the magazine of the American Academy of [insurance] Actuaries. His plan for solving the nation's health care problems:

"Opening the health insurance market to vigorous nationwide competition, as we have done over the last decade in banking, would provide more choices of innovative products less burdened by the worst excesses of state-based regulation."

There's your presidential sound judgment. Deregulate insurance companies. Like we did banks. We can't be talking about that.

So it's time to dance. Time to lower the Limbo bar. Barack Obama — "That one" — is labeled a terrorist for serving on the Annenberg Challenge Board with former Weather Underground member William Ayers. About 40 years ago, when Obama was eight years old, Ayers was, indeed, one of many college-aged anti-war agitators. They did, indeed, demonstrate, rail against their government and bomb empty government and university offices. Some of their activities were despicable. Obama has publicly condemned the violence. Ayers never maimed or killed anyone. He was guilty of extreme vandalism. Guilty. But for the last few decades Ayers has been a teacher at the U of Chicago and an activist for better education for kids living in poverty. That was the focus of the board on which both men were asked to serve. The funding for that board? From former Republican Ambassador Walter Annenberg's foundation.

No matter. This is down and dirty Limbo time. Barack Obama is a terrorist sympathizer, a Muslim with a radical agenda, he hates America and apple pie and babies. Not a word of it is true. The horrific theme which resonates under all of this smacks of pure and simple racism. "That one." "He's not like you and me." "WHO IS BARACK OBAMA?"

The dance will only get dirtier between now and election day. There can be only one winner. And the chorus of the Limbo Song says everything we need to know about the McCain/Palin campaign: "How low can you go? How low can you go? How lo-o-ow can you go?"

It's tragic. There was a time John McCain would not stoop to this.

Inboxes in South Filled With Warnings About Aliens, Commies and Schizophrenia

Oct. 21, 2008

It's getting right crazy down here in Dixie. When we're not talking to ourselves, we're talking to everybody else — whether they want to listen or not. Yada-yada-Muslim, yada-yada-antichrist, yada-yada-doesn't-want-America-to-win, yada-yada-he's-a-commie-socialist! Yada-yada-God-hates-him. And more.

I'm drowning in it. Get involved covering a campaign and you'll find your name gets on e-mail lists you never dreamed existed. You get mail, everybody's hollerin' and it's noisy as hell. I got some doozies last week from deeply offended progressives who're worried about the tenor of Team McPalin's dark "path to a narrow margin of victory." And I got more than a few from avid McCain supporters. They're mighty anxious to change my mind.

One of the uber-conservative messages in my inbox was a trip down Alien Invasion Memory Lane. The compelling reason to vote Republican in 2008? Well, honey, this oughta knock your Democrat-lovin' socks right off your feet: Way back in July 1947 a space ship crashed on a cattle ranch just outside Roswell, New Mexico with five little aliens on board. Apparently, they got loose, felt amorous and proceeded to wreak devilish havoc nationwide. That's scary. But what's scarier? The fact, the writer said, that exactly nine months later, in April, a slew of liberal elitists just happened to be born — among them Al Gore, Bill and Hillary Clinton, John Kerry, Nancy Pelosi and Howard Dean. No wonder they're all so sympathetic to illegal aliens. It's in their DNA.

On fact-checking the story, I found that none of the above arrived in April 1948 and that, in fact, Pelosi was born in 1940, Kerry in '43, Bill Clinton in '46. Only poor old Al Gore was suspect. He was born on March 31, 1948. Since I wasn't present when Gore was conceived, I can't swear to his being fully human. He has always been a right stiff-looking feller, but I like him anyway.

The final days of campaign 2008? It sounds like Silly Season.

Maybe not. Maybe it's more than that: It may be the Mean White Christian Silly Season.

Another conservative e-mail was a soul-saving warning: You can't be a Democrat if you're a Christian. No way in (pardon the expression) hell. All Christians are hard-wired Republicans. Democrats, after all, are the Abortion Party. No values, just free-wheeling, whoo-boy! sex for everybody and birth control by scraper and scalpel. Republicans are the True Believers. The GOP is the sole God-fearing party of life. So vote McCain/Palin. Or else. Got Life? The hallmark of John McCain's party is reverence for all that good life stuff.

Not to belabor the point, but we all know how valuable conservative columnist Kathleen Parker's life was to God's Own Party when she dared suggest Sarah Palin as Veep might not have been such a smart move on John McCain's part. One of the GOP faithful wrote: "Your mother should have aborted you and tossed the fetus in a Dumpster ..."

So much for the McCain/Palin camp's simplistic absolute good v. absolute evil meme.

An e-mail campaign originating in Tennessee hit South

Carolina over the weekend. This one's slicker than a slimy swamp-frog's belly: An American flag, big and bold as brass, is the first thing you see. It's a great looking flag, too, and ought to be enough to get any voter's heart revving, get the conservative mind in gear. But it gets better: God has something to say about your vote. In large, lurid font:

"In a world that's rushing toward the end times prophecy, God will bless the true Christian leader, if we choose wisely. The Prince of Darkness' blood runs through the veins of the evildoer ... Vote for McCain ... Always remember one thing — GOD WILL HAVE THE LAST WORD."

Lord have mercy. The end's a'comin' and who does this guy think the evildoer is? Oh. That One. And maybe me. The Other One who's voting for him

Another bona fide lover of the Lord, one who also has an inside track to exactly what God is thinking about Campaign 2008 (and everything else), had this warning for us:

"God is not schizophrenic, he would not tell one person to vote for Obama and another to vote for McCain ... For all my friends who are voting for Obama, can you really look God in the face and say; Father, based on your works I am voting for Obama even though ... abortion ... liberal judges making laws that are against you ... homosexual rights, even though you destroyed Sodom and Gomorrah for this."

I kid you not, the South is awash in an evil aliens, hellfire and brimstone e-mail campaign.. If election day was scheduled for the end of November, rather than the first week, we'd be looking at forty days and forty nights of this stuff. I'd be desperately seeking not Joe the Plumber, but Archie the Ark Maker. I'm a wreck. Two weeks left until election day and

I've got a raging case of inbox phobia. The mail is enough to give me toxic shock syndrome and I'm averaging dozens of these, or links to others like them, a day.

I'm not the only one suffering.

Poor William Friedkin is getting mail, too. Did he take to the stump and holler "I'm for Satan," "Traitor," "Kill 'em Both" or "Bomb McCain and Palin?" Nope. All the man did was make a contribution to the Obama campaign. $2300 to Obama for America. He anted up for the anti-you-know-what. He contributed to the commie. He supports the social-ist.

Friedkin got a letter from Howard Rich, chairman of the Americans for Limited Government Foundation: "... As a do-nor to one or more of these [radical agenda or leftist] organi-zations, you have been able to engage in these activities with-out notice ... I am writing to inform you this will no longer be the case ... Your name has been put in our database ..."

While Friedkin was not born nine months after Roswell's aliens began impregnating unsuspecting American women (he was born in 1935,) he's a suspicious dude and Right-Wing Big Brother is watching. William Friedkin's name is on the list. And, if you believe your e-mail (like too many Southern-ers are prone to do) the end's coming and if Howard Rich can't do the job on Friedman, God'll do it for him.

Unless he sees the light. Then he'll vote Right. And God bless (the real) America.

Sarah Palin: 'Ya Think This Six-Figure Wardrobe Makes Me Look Phat?'

Oct. 27, 2008

Not a chance, honey.

Phat: (Derivation: slang; deliberate misspelling of the word fat.) Meaning: Excellent. Prominent. Cool.

Leave it to the African American community to reinvent a negative word, turn it on its head and make it a powerfully good descriptive term. They've been making silk purses out of sows' ears for centuries, and not by choice. In an America ridden with too much racism and too few options, they've survived through positive thinking. You gotta love that dogged optimism through etymology. But it won't work in this case. No way is Sarah Palin phat.

"You can dress her up, but you cannot take her out ..."

Now there's a phrase heard often down here in the South that does apply in Palin's case. Clothes do not make the (wo)man. McCain & Co. can dress up that gal in a $2500 Valentino jacket, a clinging black skirt and a pair of Paris Hilton's favorite Naughty Monkey high heels (average price about $100,) wind her up and send her out on the campaign trail looking like $150,000 ... but they cannot restyle a woman who believes the core of geopolitical/national security experience is "seeing Russia" from her yard. Or one who says she is a "voracious reader" but can't remember what newspaper she read this morning. Or one who still believes Iraq was responsible for 9/11, that we need not grasp the causes for global warming before we can solve the problem, that the earth is 6000 years old and nu-cu-lar is a word.

YES, WE DID

The GOP certainly cannot fork over the big bucks for their Veep-in-Waiting's personal make-up artist and hair stylist and expect they'll pretty up what's inside the woman's head. Or what comes out of her mouth. Like her "Don't-I-Wish" interpretation of vice presidential powers:

"... they're in charge of the United States Senate, so if they want to, they can really get in there with the senators and make a lot of good policy changes."

No matter how you count it, the RNC/McCain Camp have invested one hundred fifty thousand dollars in making Sarah Palin "look the part." They've spent this much hard cash in eight weeks. That would be a clothing, hair and make-up budget of $18,750 a week. For a woman who swears she's just like us. Like you and me. Hockey moms. Soccer moms. "Attention, Wal Mart shoppers ..." moms who've never had a two thousand dollar jacket or a hundred dollar pair of shoes in their lives and never will.

No matter how you count it, this is gross economic mismanagement. This is piss-poor fiscal responsibility on the part of the party — and the candidates — who tell us they're the only ones who can turn around our failing economy.

Talk about your earmarks, your pork barrel spending! Hardworking Republicans donated money they couldn't afford to give because they believed John McCain's vaunted judgment, his experience and his professed loathing for wasteful spending meant he would surely be the most responsible POTUS. Now they find Sarah Palin and family are wearing a six-figure chunk of their money because her Alaska gubernatorial wardrobe (and that of the First Dude, to the tune of five thousand dollars) was not chic enough?

Let me point out that Barack Obama has had his presidential candidacy work shoes resoled. And he's still wearing them.

It begs the question: What on earth has happened to the Republican Party?

Peggy Noonan may have said it best:

"In the end the Palin candidacy is a symptom and the expression of a new vulgarization in American politics. It's no good, not for conservatism and not for the country. And yes, it is a mark against John McCain, against his judgment and idealism."

Vulgarization is right. And neither McCain nor Palin looks phat.

And, one can only hope that, on November 4th, Sarah Palin will put on her shiny red Naughty Monkey stilettos, click her heels together and make like Dorothy. Fly away home to Wasilla, where she'll be the best dressed Guber in Alaska's history. And more power to her.

Cyber-Wars: Hate-Mail And The Obama Internet Campaign

Oct. 27, 2008

With the end in sight, we're faced with an ever more outrageous barrage of nasty, negative, anti-Obama emails. Relief comes in the form of the other e-mail campaign, the one conducted by (we're real Americans, too) supporters of Barack Obama.

The difference in cyber-war tactics is as stark as is the difference in the candidates.

Compared to the scurrilous, name-calling internet attacks from McCain/Palin fanciers on the far right, a cyber-trip with the Obama faction is a Walk on the Mild Side.

Are they passionate? Yes. Are they fired up? Yes. Do they mean to win this thing? Absolutely. Are they making a practice of calling McCain a fascist? Do they call him a "convenient" Christian who aligns himself with the likes of Hagee and Parsley in a cynical attempt to attract the same pseudo-religious fringe — "Don't confuse us with the facts" fundamentalists — which narrowly propelled George W. back into the Oval Office in 2004? No way.

The fundamental difference between the internet left and the internet right? The cyber-right is not campaigning hard for a John McCain in whom they have great faith to bring about real change. They're not arguing for public policy or for humane governance. They're just fighting against the other guy. They're led in that direction by an increasingly desperate and angry McCain/Palin camp.

The cyber-left is campaigning hard for something. They are for Barack Obama. They are for an end to a belligerent, no-diplomacy, big gun foreign policy. For accessible health care for all Americans. For better public schools. For a fair tax code which doesn't spell the demise of the middle class. For a minimum wage which means your "minimum" is enough food to eat and a roof over your head. For a solution to abortion that keeps the predominantly rich old white guys in Washington out of a everywoman's uterus and gets them, instead, into programs which actually address the social problems that lead to unnecessary abortions. Internet Obama supporters are no saints; they bicker amongst themselves like nobody's business. But Campaign 2008, to all of them, means something more than an outlet for the anger they've been swallowing for the past eight years. These folks are four-square for something. They want change. Positive change. Humane change. And they are deeply committed to the candidate who best represents hope for that change. They've been led in that direction, from day one, by a steady, unflappable Obama/Biden camp.

Their e-mails ring like testimonies at an interfaith revival meeting. They do not scream "Satan!" or holler "Sinner!" No hellfire and damnation, no demonizing the opposition, no fear and loathing. Their message is as positive as their vision for this nation with Barack Obama and Joe Biden at the helm:

From a white, middle-class Florida voter:

"... I've got a wife and two kids. Because the kids had no school today, I took a vacation day from work and took the kids downtown to vote early. Fifty-nine minutes later, two smiling children and I proudly sported 'I Voted' stickers.

"But I didn't vote for Obama.

"I voted for my ancestors, who believed in the promise of this country and came with nothing as immigrants. I voted for my parents, who taught in the public schools for decades. I voted for Steve, an acquaintance of mine from Kentucky (killed by an IED two years ago in Iraq). I voted for Shawn, another who's been to Iraq twice and Afghanistan once, and who'll be going back to Afghanistan again soon — and whose family earned eleven bucks a month too much to qualify for food stamps when the war started. I voted for April, the only African American girl in my high school — it was years before it occurred to me how different her experience of our school must have been. I voted for my college friends

who are Christian, Jewish, Mormon, and yes — Muslim. I voted for my grandfathers, who worked hard in factories and died too young. I voted for the plumber who worked on my house, because I want him to get a REAL tax break. I voted for four little angels from Birmingham. I voted for a bunch of dead white men who, although personally flawed, were willing to pledge their lives, fortunes and sacred honor, and used a time of great crisis to expand freedom rather than suspend it. I voted for all those people and more, and I voted for all of you, too.

"But mostly, I voted selfishly: I voted for two little kids, one who has ballet in an hour and one who has baseball practice at the same time. I voted for a world where they can be confident that their government will represent the best that is in this country and that will, in turn, demand the best of them.

"I voted for a government that will be respected in the world. I voted for an economy that will reward work above guile. I voted for everything I believe in. Sure, I filled in the circle next to the name Obama, but it wasn't him I was voting for — it was every single one of us and [for] those I love most of all."

From PJ Locascio, a 16-year-old junior at Heritage High School in Lynchburg, VA. He's not old enough to vote yet but, apparently, he's old enough to have received an "Obama is the antichrist" e-mail. PJ chose to join the cyber-campaign and wrote, in response to that horrific e-mail:

"This is one of the most absurd and racist things I have ever seen. You would rather believe that he, Sen. Obama, is the 'antichrist' than believe he's simply the better candidate. It's definitely not funny because a lot of voting-eligible Americans actually do think he's Muslim or the antichrist ... This was all done by the Republican agenda that continues to try to make Americans ... believe that he's ... out to destroy America; or that he is a socialist [who] will ruin the fabric of democracy ... Any-

one who believes this or passes this along ... is terribly misinformed ... it's what's called running a 'Fear campaign' ... This kind of campaign is very dangerous ... Every single one of you is old enough to think for yourself ... Next election, when we are finally old enough to vote, I really hope and encourage you to examine both of the candidates meticulously, without partisanship and really check the facts ... be your own person."

Clearly, a Virginia teenager has a keener view of where the mature voter's responsibility lies than too many hot-tempered bloggers who set their fingers loose on the keyboard before their brains are fully engaged. Too bad PJ can't vote.

Whatever the outcome on November 4th, those of us who've been observing both sides in this long campaign and writing about it all have learned a great deal about "real" American values and the true worth of the American conscience. And much of what we've learned that's worth believing in, worth fighting for and worth keeping, we learned from everyday Americans who support Barack Obama.

Win or lose, that is no small lesson to have learned.

A Final Word Before You Vote: Who is John McCain?

Oct. 28, 2008

During the 2000 South Carolina primary there was a nationwide flap over our loyalty to our country. The Confederate Flag flew all over the Palmetto State, even over our Statehouse. That "symbol of slavery, secession and war" became a hot-button issue.

John McCain refused to say a discouraging word about that flag. It was, he said, up to South Carolina to decide which flags were appropriate for South Carolinians. On February 19, 2000, he lost our primary in one of the ugliest campaigns in history.

On April 20, 2000, only two months later, McCain apologized for not having condemned the Confederate Flag, for not calling publicly for its removal from the S.C. Statehouse:

"I feared if I answered honestly, I could not win the South Carolina primary. So I chose to compromise my principles. I broke my promise to always tell the truth."

John McCain lied to win. He was for the Confederate Flag before he called it "hateful."

Flash forward to 2001, to Dubya's infamous, weighted to benefit America's wealthiest citizens tax cuts. John McCain opposed them. He said:

"I cannot, in good conscience, support a tax cut in which so many of the benefits go to the most fortunate among us at the expense of middle-class Americans who need tax relief."

Now McCain supports Bush Economics and wants to make the same tax cuts he condemned permanent. What's changed? Is the deficit down? Has the Iraq War paid for itself? Are we better off than we were back then and no longer in need of a tax plan weighted in our favor rather than that of the wealthy and big business?

In 2000, George W's toxic campaign, dishonest and inflammatory robo-calls and push polling, robbed John McCain of the GOP nomination. McCain was victimized by half-truths and outright lies. He knew it. Here's what he had to say about that campaign:

"Sooner or later people are going to figure out if all you run is negative attack ads, you don't have much of a vision for the future or you're not ready to articulate it…[I'm trusting in] the good judgment of voters not to buy in to these negative attack ads…"

Now McCain's campaign admits they must avoid the real issues — especially the failing economy — and create new issues if they are to win the election. Robo-calls, push-polling, mailers, surrogates and team McCain/Palin spread words like "Muslim," "Terrorist," "Anti-American" and "Socialist/Communist." When McCain, himself, is confronted with these smears aimed at Barack Obama by his campaign, he backs down. Obama, he says, is "not an Arab." Obama is not a terrorist. He's not unAmerican. In fact, McCain says, Barack Obama is a man he respects and admires; a good man, a citizen, a good husband and father. And, no, Barack Obama is not a communist. There is nothing to fear, he tells us, from an Obama presidency. Nothing. But the robo-calls, push-polling, "Terrorist!" mailers and poisonous speeches go on.

Loyal Republicans nationwide are openly critical of Sarah Palin's qualifications to serve as vice president; they are deeply troubled about her lack of experience should a 72 year old McCain become incapacitated during his presidency. They question his judgment in having selected Palin; so many truly qualified Republican candidates were available.

McCain is offended. Palin, he declares, has all the experience necessary: Four years as mayor of Wasilla (pop. 7,000 during her tenure) and 18 months as governor of Alaska (pop. 650,000). She has, he says, vital executive experience and is qualified to serve as President of the United States. She is clearly the best choice he could have made for America.

In 2007, John McCain was fighting an uphill battle for the

GOP nomination. His toughest opponents? Rudy Giuliani (mayor of New York, pop. 8,250,567, for eight years); Mitt Romney (governor of Massachusetts, pop. 6,349,097, for four years). Both had far more executive experience than Sarah Palin ever dreamed of having. During an October Republican debate John McCain made his position clear about their kind of experience: They didn't have enough to serve.

"…I AM PREPARED. I need no on the job training [he looks at Romney and Giuliani]. I wasn't mayor for a short period of time. I wasn't governor for a short period of time."

John McCain clearly dismissed Giuliani and Romney as unqualified when he had no choice if he hoped to win the nomination. Now Palin, who can't touch the expertise of either of those GOP alternatives, is suddenly the best person for the job.

Who is John McCain? The guy who'll say anything, sanction any negative attack to win what he believes George W. Bush stole from him with lies. How will he do it? He'll endorse whatever lie it takes to stem the tide of change.

McCain, McCountry, McChristians and McBigots

Oct. 31, 2008

It may be November, the leaves may be fallin' off the trees and our sweaters feel mighty good of a mornin', but it's gettin' right hot down here in the Deep South.

We South Carolinians may be just a teensy bit confused about which flag it is we ought to be a'flyin' over our State House, but we're nothin' if not a passel of patriots. Mm-mm-

mmm. We love America.

Georgia's Senator Chambliss is warning white folks that "The Other Folks are voting ..." And we all know who those uppity folks are. We like them okay — as long as they stay in their places.

North Carolina's uber-belle, Liddy Dole, says opponent Kay Hagan is palling around with "Godless Americans." If there's anything we Southerners cannot abide, it is surely Satan.

Between the rampant, gun-totin' super-patriotism and hyper-right-wing Christianity in South Carolina, there's little doubt who'll win our Big 8 electoral votes on Tuesday. Unlike our neighbors, North Carolina and Georgia, where the race is tight enough to squeak, the Palmetto State is a GOP goner. Real Clear Politics, in its 9/28-10/20 poll averages, shows McCain up by 15 points here. The October 23rd Winthrop University/ETV poll paints a more dismal portrait of the Palmetto State voter: John McCain is up by 20 points. Twenty. Points.

I think we might be a little off-kilter down here. The Winthrop/ETV poll was a study in bi-poller politics:

● 55.2% of South Carolinians believe the Bush presidency is a failure. But we're more apt to vote for McSame.

● 66.8% of us say this country is on the wrong track. But we're more apt to vote for McMore of the McSame.

● 44.6% of us believe Obama "understands the problems Americans face in our daily lives." 42.3% believe McCain "understands." Whoa! The tide turns ...

Nope. While more of us believe Obama understands what we're going through than believe McCain does, we're still more apt to pull that GOP lever.

● It's values. 53.5 % of us say McCain shares our values. Only 34.9% believe Obama has the same values we do. Whatever they are.

● Values. We got 'em down here out the whazoo and we're not about to change now. Too many South Carolinians have been drinking the "You-Can't-Be-A-Christian-or-a-Patriot-Unless-You-Vote-Republican" Kool-Aid. It's sweet stuff and, in 2008, the McChristian and McCountry mantra masks McRacism behind code words we can be proud of: UnAmerican. Muslim. Terrorist. Socialist.

You gotta give the McCain/Plain camp credit: They've covered the poison they're dosing out with a sugary coat of "American values" that goes down easy in the South. But some of us are sick of the taste. Some of us still believe there are enough of us to matter on election day. We believe we really are better than this.

Then there are these polls. I hate polls. Too many times they're wrong, and as many times — like the South Carolina Winthrop/ETV poll — they give us more information than we really want to know about who we are.

Dr. Martin Luther King's Dream … and Ours

Nov. 4, 2008

After a very long, ugly, and too often brutal campaign season, it is election day. This is an election unlike any other in our history. This is a day in which we may well redefine who we are as a nation. In some ways, whatever the outcome, we already have.

Election day 2008 falls exactly forty-five years, two months and seven days after Dr. Martin Luther King, Jr. spoke these compelling, prophetic words:

"I have a dream that one day this nation will rise up and live out the true meaning of its creed, 'We hold these truths to be self-evident, that all men are created equal.'

"I have a dream that my four little children will one day live in a nation where they will not be judged by the color of their skin, but by the content of their character…"

Senator Barack Obama's candidacy alone has fulfilled Dr. King's dream of a better, more inclusive America, a nation in which racism no longer crushes the dream of any American child to grow up, make the most of his/her education, work hard for principles and become a successful public servant — one elected to office by voters of all creeds and colors.

An Obama victory today will mean more than a win for the Democratic Party. It will mean more than simply an end to the Bush Era of war, corporate cronyism, scandal and the near-death of the middle class.

An Obama win will mean there are far more Americans who respond to a message of positive change and humane governance than there are those who allow racism to determine their vote. We will have risen above the absolute, immutable black/white divide.

An Obama win will mean that most Americans, at long last, have the moral character — and the conscience — to reject the old Atwater/Rove politics of the hate- and fear-mongering campaign; the vicious, distorted name-calling campaign. It will mean we're no longer buying the dishonest, frenzied, win-at-any-cost sales pitch. It will mean idealism trumps ideology, that intelligence trumps invective.

And it will mean, overnight, that the entire world sees we are better than our behavior in the last eight years indicates we are. The Bush-era age of belligerent rhetoric, unilateralism, pre-emptive war, defiance of the U.S.-inspired Geneva Conventions, and the loss of our international moral standing, will be ended. We will still have much work to do in repairing our image abroad, but an Obama victory will jump-start the process in a way no other candidate's rise to the presidency could have done.

The path ahead won't be an easy one. We'll face more economic woes before things improve. We'll have to dig deep, sacrifice and have a little patience while a new administration begins hauling us out of the chasm dug by the previous one.

But we will have sent out a clear signal to each other and to the world about who we are. About who we want to be.

Dr. King would be proud. We have touched the dream. What remains to be seen, at the end of election day 2008, is whether or not we have grasped it.

Yes, We Did

Nov. 11, 2008

What a ride this has been. No matter which side of the political divide any of us is on, we all know that history has been made in the United States of America. There is not one of us — white, black, red, yellow or brown, rich or poor, male or female — who cannot look at our children, our grandchildren, and say, "Dream big. Make the most of your education. Work hard. In twenty-first century America, you can grow up to be anything your heart desires." And this time, unlike any other time in our history, we can — and will — mean exactly what we say.

It wasn't even close. Barack Obama won with 53% of the popular vote to John McCain's 46%; a 7% margin of victory. A 7,612,457 vote plurality. Obama won a staggering 364 electoral votes, more than twice as many as McCain's 163.

Nothing will ever be the same again. And that is a very good thing.

Some of us "met" Barack Obama, a young state senator in Illinois, back in the fall of 2002, when he delivered a moving speech on the floor of the Illinois Senate. At a time when the vast majority of Americans, pols, pundits and ordinary citizens, were clamoring for the invasion of Iraq, basing our judgment on the facts as presented us by the Bush White House, Senator Obama spoke out against the rush to war. The Bush administration, he said, had not made the case for Iraq's involvement in 9/11; nor had they made the case for WMD or the "mushroom cloud scenario." Obama felt the war that should be fought was in Afghanistan, the target Osama bin Laden and al Qaeda.

He was absolutely right.

After years of war, multiple thousands of deaths, a thorough military search of Iraq and a Pentagon study of over 600,000 documents seized after the invasion, the Bush administration was forced to admit Iraq had nothing to do with what happened to America on September 11th. There were no WMD. There had been no danger of their much touted "imminent mushroom cloud."

Contrary to Bush's "It'll be quick war and it'll pay for itself…" argument, Barack Obama's assessment that invading Iraq would mean "…a U.S. occupation of undetermined length, at undetermined cost and with undetermined consequences…without a clear rationale and…STRONG international support [this war] will only fan the flames of the Middle East and encourage the worst, rather than the best, impulses of the Arab world and strengthen the recruitment arm of al Qaeda" proved to be spot-on.

Which begs the question: Whose command of the facts, whose judgment, was better as early as October 2002?

During the nearly two year campaign for the White House, Obama has proven, over and again, that his judgment and his temperament are well-suited to this particularly difficult time in our history. He has run a disciplined, civilized, "No Drama" campaign. No name-calling. No smears, no "Vote for me or die!" fear-mongering. No stridency. No erratic behavior. His choice for vice president was a thoughtful, reasoned one; wisdom, experience and expertise defined the man who would be a heartbeat away from the Oval Office.

On November 4th, the better candidate for our time won

by a wide margin; a fine, principled, patriotic American with a vision most voters believe is the best for us and demands the best of us.

The whole world watched as Barack Obama became the 44th President of the United States of America. They watched as we proved, at long last, that we will elect our leader based upon the content of his character, not the color of his skin.

We have reason to be proud of who we are.

Post-Election Blues: A GOP Postmortem

Nov. 18, 2008

If there's anything we knew we could count on from this generation of the GOP, it's been the party's unique ability to protect its own. Unlike rowdy, loquacious, self-defeating Democrats, Republicans have successfully kept their infighting — when there was any — a private matter. They have their own Ronald Reagan authored Golden Rule: Do not attack your fellow conservatives. Republicans do not eat their young. That credo has made them powerfully monolithic.

Until Campaign 2008, when the intra-party sniping began even before the election was over. McCain aides needed to pin the blame for a looming defeat somewhere, so Sarah Palin was targeted. Early. And with rancor. She was, McCain's inner circle said, "going rogue," she was off the reservation, trying to build her own future political career at John McCain's expense. She was "a diva," a "whack job," a "shopaholic." Governor Palin and "The First Dude" were referred to as "Wasilla Hillbillies looting Neiman Marcus from coast to coast."

Multiple McCain camp insiders spilled the beans (and their

frustration) to the mainstream media and the media reported it. The tactic is not a new one. Campaigns, like administrations, leak what information they want made public. It's how the game is played. What made the GOP civil war worse was the simple fact that attacks on Palin went on for weeks before election day and John McCain did nothing to stop it. In fact, he exacerbated the problem. New Rule: Palin could no longer be interviewed on TV without Senator McCain sitting right next to her.

Palin has, since the loss on November 4th, been busy defending herself. She's called the unnamed GOP sources "cowardly" and "jerks." She has a point.

While most of the leaked dirt was either true or had an element of truth to it, Pin the Tail on Palin was a game played by insiders in a desperate attempt to spare themselves (and McCain) responsibility for a poorly run campaign. That's not fair. The buck stops with the candidate. He's the guy who sets the tone, makes the final decisions, runs the show. In McCain's case, he's the one who had the final say in choosing the vice presidential candidate. He wanted Joe Lieberman, but when his advisors said no go, that Lieberman's pro-choice position would cost him the social conservative right, McCain went along with Palin. He'd only met the woman once and the choice was made far too late for proper vetting. Sarah Palin was not ready for prime time.

And that fatal flaw was no fault of Palin's. She is who she is and it was the responsibility of the McCain camp to know that her weaknesses included some pretty serious gaps in basic knowledge. Like a shaky grasp of civics which led her to say "the vice president is in charge of the senate" and could "get in there and make...policy." The blame rests on the candidate and on the same aides who've been leaking like sieves since the poll numbers tanked.

While I was one of millions of voters who felt Palin was neither smart enough nor prepared enough to serve a heartbeat away from the Oval Office in perilous times, what's happened to her in the last few weeks is a shame.

John Sidney McCain should have been the maverick he claimed to be, told his advisors where to get off, and chosen Joe Lieberman as his running mate.

He didn't. And, like her or not, Sarah Palin shouldn't be paying for McCain's mistake.

Anti-elitism? The Rift That Keeps On Giving

Nov. 25, 2008

"Sitting here in these chairs that I'm going to be proposing but in working with these governors who again on the front lines are forced to and it's our privileged obligation to find solutions to the challenges facing our own states every day being held accountable, not being just one of many just casting votes or voting 'present' every once in a while, we don't get away with that."

— Sarah Palin, 2008 Governor's Conference

"I think — tide turning — see, as I remember — I was raised in the desert, but tides kind of — it's easy to see a tide turn — did I say those words?"

— George W. Bush, 2006, when asked if the tide was turning in Iraq.

YES, WE DID

"One of my concerns is that the health care not be as good as it can possibly be."

— *George W. Bush 2008*

"Millions of Americans who watched Mr Obama's appearance on CBS' 'Sixty Minutes'...witnessed the president-elect's unorthodox verbal tic, which had Mr. Obama employing grammatically correct sentences virtually every time he opened his mouth...his subjects and verbs are in agreement...he is running the risk of sounding like an elitist."

— *Satirist Andy Borowitz*

We've endured eight long years of mangled grammar, tortured English, irrational rhetoric and the GO-Party line that really smart folks — those who speak with clarity, even eloquence, are unfit for office because "They're not like you and me." They're "elitists" because they excelled in Ivy League colleges; because, in a monosyllabic world, they have command of a higher form of language. The last thing a real American wants is to have leaders who are intellectuals.

How elite came to mean "too smart" and "too smart" came to mean suspect or not-quite-American enough to hold public office is a study in the politics of polarization. How do you sell the voting public the notion that electing candidates who aren't too terribly bright is good for the country? You use a "Real American" trope. Most of us are intellectually average. That's not a bad thing. The average (real) American is middle-class, bright enough to have been the fuel that kept a nation's engine running smoothly for the better part of two and a half centuries, hardworking, productive, generous and optimistic.

YES, WE DID

What we're not, in the main, is a nation of serious, book-reading intellectuals or public policy wonks. The success of the grand democratic experiment which is the United States of America has been grounded in the fact that, more often than not, we've elected super-intelligent wonks to lead us. And, more often than not, our faith in those intellectual giants has paid off. We looked for the best of the best for leadership and voted for the one we believed was smart enough to do the job.

Until 2000. When Al Gore suffered the "He's too smart. He's a policy wonk — and that means boring" meme and George W. was "Not too smart, but he's a guy who won't bore you to death with a lecture on foreign policy, the economy or climate change." W. was a president any one of us could have "had a beer with." Gore? A pinot grigio guy.

Too many Americans have been misled, for over eight years, into voting for the "real American" candidate who's most like Joe the Plumber. The key word here is "misled." The McCain/Palin camp's ideal "average Joe" was neither "Joe" nor a licensed plumber. Not a bit like you and me — unless we're pretending to be someone we're not.

Seems we've spared ourselves another four years of minimal mentality either in or too near the Oval Office. Not that every one of the four candidates running for the #1 and #2 spots was smarter than what we've had in the White House for eight years. At least one of them gave W. a run for his grammatical goof-prone money.

Maybe, on election day 2008, we average folks were the smart ones.

Sweet.

Happy Holidays? Aw, Shoot!

Dec. 2, 2008

Thanksgiving ushers in that most wonderful time of the year — you know, love, friends and family, harmony and counting our blessings. Throw in a turkey and some pumpkin pie…it just doesn't get better than that.

Does it? Seems South Carolina state lawmakers, led by Rep. Mike Pitts (R-Greenwood) have found a sure-fire way to improve our holidays: Usher in the Season of Grace with a Glock. Celebrate the Holiest of Births with a Browning. Guys, get your guns! Tax free.

Pitts meant well. His bill was inspired by retailers who sell firearms. Why should there be a late summer sales tax holiday for South Carolina families who need back-to-school supplies and clothing — and not one for gun dealers, they asked him. Those poor store owners said they needed a little economic stimulus, too. If retailers catering to school kids get a break, so should they.

Representative Pitts went right to work. "… to help dealers," he said, adding, "and another point was to bring recognition to the 2nd amendment."

So. It's good for business and it's patriotic, too. The Second Amendment Recognition Act was born.

Beginning at 12:01 a.m. on Friday, November 28 and ending at midnight on Saturday, November 29, South Carolina has declared a sales and use tax holiday on purchases of handguns, rifles and shotguns. Apparently dealers don't mind opening in the wee, dark hours and staying open 48 hours — until 12:00

on Saturday night — to accommodate folks wanting a good deal on guns. Sadly, the tax break does not extend to accessories. If you need ammunition, black powder, holsters and the like, you're still taxed. If your hunting preference runs to a quieter kill — say, using a bow and arrow — too bad. Archery supplies will be taxed.

Lots of guys I know (including some in my family) tell me they don't buy guns to shoot at animals or people. They are collectors. They are arms afficianados who simply admire gun craftsmanship, artistry. The look of them, the feel of them. They purchase weaponry to add pieces to a sort of art(illery) collection. Valid point. In that case, the ultimate artsy weaponry would surely be antique and collectible handguns. But antiques and collectibles, any handguns that do not fire a fixed cartridge, are not included in the sales and use tax free category.

I don't like guns. It's a personal thing, and I do not impose my own deeply held belief in some sane form of gun control on others.

The 2nd amendment is what it is, and Americans have a constitutional right to own guns. Most gun owners are responsible, law-abiding citizens. They love guns, I love books. Each of us has the freedom to buy what we most enjoy owning.

But I have a problem with this particular tax holiday at this particular time. I stood behind an elderly gentleman at a drug store a few weeks ago while the pharmacist explained to him that he simply could not hope to control the disease ravaging his body by taking only ½ the prescribed dosage of his medications. The retiree's hands trembled as he told the druggist, "You don't understand, sir, I live on a fixed income. I can't afford to take more than half a pill every morning and every night..."

There are needs in this state, in this economy, which are far more urgent than the profit margin at gun stores or a lover of arms getting a tax break on his weapon of choice. Like affordable medications, food for families, fuel for home heating, warm winter clothing.

This tax holiday, especially during the Thanksgiving/Christmas season, is (if you'll pardon the pun) aimed at the wrong target.

White Christmas? Black Friday

Dec. 9, 2008

Djimytai Damour died very early in the morning on the day after Thanksgiving.

He was a real person. He was only thirty-four years old, and his death was unnecessary. He wasn't sick. He wasn't in a speeding car, drinking, or driving recklessly. He was at work, doing what was expected of him.

Djimytai had been an employee of a Walmart in Garden City. N.Y. for only a week. He was placed there, as a temporary worker, by an employment agency. Authorities suspect that, because Mr. Damour was a large man — 6'5" and 270 lbs — store management decided to place him at the main entrance on Black Friday. Surely a young fellow that size could handle crowd control on a day which is, arguably, the busiest (and the nastiest) shopping day of any year.

About two thousand frantic Walmart shoppers thronged the store's entrance for the much-hyped annual post-Thanksgiving sale. They wanted their Christmas loot, they wanted it cheap, and they wanted to get to electronics or toys or home furnishings before someone else got the last deal on an "As Advertised — Limited Supply" item.

Damour died of asphyxiation after being trampled; crushed by a crowd which broke down Walmart's electronic doors in a shopping frenzy and ran right over him. A broken body is not enough to curb the American urge to shop for bargains; sources say rabid shoppers literally stepped over, around and on his body in their haste to get into the store.

Worse, Walmart customers shouted angrily and refused to stop shopping when management announced they were closing the store due to the death of an employee.

Someone is responsible for the senseless death of a young man who was only doing his job.

Walmart enjoys a well-deserved reputation for putting store profit (and very high corporate management salaries) above the welfare of ordinary folks who work in their stores. Management has elevated the avoidance of offering employee benefits — like group health insurance — to an art form. It's all about money. Making as much as possible, spending (on employees) as little as the law allows. Garden City law enforcement says Walmart failed to provide adequate security for the crowds they knew were coming on Black Friday.

The Damour family is suing Walmart — and the county — for wrongful death. Walmart refused to hire enough security and, apparently, local government did nothing to force the issue after warning store management their arrangements were inadequate.

Djimytai Damour was the sacrificial lamb to Walmart's greed.

There is, however, plenty of greed and guilt to go around

here. Authorities are reviewing store videos, but say it's unlikely anyone in the shopping mob will be prosecuted. And that's a crime; a moral and ethical disgrace.

What kind of people are we when the traditional family Thanksgiving becomes little more than prelude to the consumer gluttony that characterizes Black Friday? What kind of people are we when we break down doors to grab what we think we have a right to own? What kind of folks stampede like wild animals, crushing another human being to death, stepping over or on top of his body for greed's sake?

And what kind of people are we when we rage against the closing of the store after we've been complicit in the death of an employee?

There's been a lot of loud, morally superior talk in this country about "American values." Black Friday, with its consumer-crazed pushing and shoving, fighting for the last Wii, puts the lie to our values meme.

We love to tout American family values, too. But the Damour family, who have lost a loved one to American greed, might argue we ought to re-examine what constitutes "family values." The only values in evidence on Black Friday are "Get out of my way!", "Me first!" and "Mine, mine, mine!"

Joe the Plumber as historian, policy wonk...

Dec. 16, 2008

...and Maverick McCain turncoat. He's no longer John McCain's BFF. No lie.

Sam Wurzelbacher, aka "Joe the Plumber," doesn't like his American Hero anymore. In fact, Sam/Joe says he stopped liking John McCain while he was riding the campaign trail with him.

In an interview with right-wing radio jock Glenn Beck, Sam/Joe said, "I honestly felt even more dirty after I had been on the campaign trail with McCain...seeing some of the things that take place...It was scary, man."

Sam/Joe didn't go into specifics about what scared him or dirtied him up to such an alarming degree, except to say he'd asked the senator "some pretty direct questions" about the banking bailout and didn't like the answers. "They appalled me, absolutely," he said. "You know, I was angry. In fact, I wanted to get off the bus after I talked to him."

Given Sam's/Joe's weighty economic background (like failing to pay his taxes,) it's little wonder he took offense at McCain's approach to solving the nation's plunge into The Recession That Wasn't There. After careful analysis of both the financial crisis and Maverick's ideas on economic recovery, Sam/Joe was thoroughly disillusioned with his candidate.

He did, however, offer Beck a positive, in-depth analysis of Sarah Palin's qualifications. They clearly outdistanced John McCain's. Using his best policy wonk communications skills, Sam/Joe told Glenn Beck: "You know, it was been asked [sic] if I felt any presence when I was with John McCain or Barack Obama. You know, with Sarah Palin, I don't want to say I felt a presence, but she definitely had energy and she definitely went to work for the American people, and it disgusts me on how often [sic] they try to bash her…and, I mean, I wish people would listen to her and let them, and let her work for us."

Beck seemed mightily impressed with Sam's/Joe's command of the facts and assessment of the GOP candidates' strengths and weaknesses. So he asked for the Plumber's opinion on what might lie in store for the country if nothing changes in D.C.

"Well, I mean, you know, I'm not comparing anybody," Sam/Joe replied. "You know, I don't want to stir up a hornet's nest here, but, you know, when Adolf Hitler had come to power, one of the first things he did was take guns away. You know, we're a country that doesn't really listen to history…and we seem to, our country repeating the mistakes other countries have already made and they are bogged down in now and, you know, some of the things that our current elected President Obama is suggesting really does go down a socialist path…"

Sic, sic, sic.

We must appreciate the wisdom when the well-informed, student-of-history policy wonk warns us about history's tendency to repeat itself like a bowl full of greasy collard greens.

And then there's Sam Wurzelbacher/Joe the Plumber, a policy wonk wannabe who doesn't know the president-elect has made it clear he supports the second amendment. No

Sturmabteilung Brownshirt posse is going to descend on gun owners in some 21st century neo-Kristalnacht. No broken glass, no assault on your weapons of choice.

As for your "non-comparison" to Hitler, you're absolutely right, Sam/Joe. There is none. If you'd "listened to history," good buddy, you'd have known it is philosophically impossible for any president of the United States to be both Adolf Hitler and a socialist. Look up your ideologies.

For the record, Sam/Joe did not get off the bus when John McCain's positions on public policy proved unworthy of his support. He never said a word. Never spoke out on behalf of regular Americans and plumbers everywhere. He kept on riding, dirty and scared, right through election day.

Coal for Christmas: One Lump or Two?

Dec. 23, 2008

When it comes to candidates and elected officials, there's an old political saw: Republicans fall in line, Democrats fall in love.

It's not always true. Contrary to what conventional wisdom, Bill O'Reilly, Sean Hannity and Rush Limbaugh would have you believe, not every liberal voter loves all Democrats. Quite the contrary.

When Democratic Illinois Governor Rod Blagojevich was arrested in early December, his approval rating was lower than George W.'s. Illinois Obama supporters I know were thrilled when their governor, who's been under federal investigation for three years, got his comeuppance. I got several

"Woo-hoo — finally!" e-mails. One of the best messages was this simple quote: "Illinois, where our Governors make our license plates."

Blagojevich, who's done everything he could think of to sell Barack Obama's vacated senate seat (short of posting it on e-Bay), is not the first leader of the Land of Lincoln to get himself in trouble with the law. Not by a long shot. He's the 5th of the last eight Illinois governors to be charged with a felony. Which begs the question: Who's the lump of Christmas coal — the governors or the voters?

In government, we get (and keep) what we're willing to tolerate. Too often, what we fail to get is what we pay for. Factor in governors' mansions and perks, and gubernatorial salaries are right tidy little sums.

Governor Blagojevich is paid $155,600 a year for serving the people of Illinois (population nearly 13 million.) North Carolina's 8.9 million citizens pay Governor Mike Easley $130,629 annually. Georgia, with a population over four and a half million, forks out $135,281 to Governor Sonny Perdue. Here in South Carolina there are just under four and a half million of us paying Governor Mark Sanford $106,078.

Our Sanford, when compared to Rod Blagojevich, deserves a raise.

Up in Alaska, where Russia's Putin likes to rear his head over the horizon, Governor Sarah Palin got a 46% raise in 2006. Her predecessor, Frank Murkowski, earned $86,000 annually for serving the 670,053 folks who live and work in the far north. Palin began her tenure as governor two years ago with a salary of $125,000. That's a lot of money for a state with a population well under a million citizens. She makes substantially more than South Carolina's governor — who serves about six times as many people.

That's about to change. No, as far as I know, Governor Sanford is not getting a salary increase. But Sarah Palin just may be getting another hefty one. According to the Anchorage Daily News, Palin appointed a commission last year to "figure out how much the state should pay top officials." That's a mighty tough job when the economy is circling the drain, unemployment is on the rise and foreclosures are as common as bad weather. Ordinary folks in every state are having a hard time surviving the current economic downturn. But Palin's commission was clearly up to the task.

They've recommended salary increases for a number of top Alaskans. Chief among them? Governor Sarah. She should get, they say, another 20% raise. That would mean a cool $150,000 per year, a salary which would put Palin among the top ten highest paid governors in the nation. For serving a population larger than only Wyoming, Vermont and North Dakota. In a recession so deep and dark the light at the end of the tunnel looks suspiciously like and oncoming train.

Maybe she needs it. She didn't have nice enough clothes to run as McCain's veep. The GOP had to invest about $200,000 in her appearance for two month's worth of new duds and hair care. And maybe she deserves it. If you ignore the financial misery of middle- and working-class America.

And if you compare her to Illinois' Rod Blagojevich.

See the USA in your Chevrolet! Fat Chance.

Dec. 31, 2008

I made the final payment on my Chevrolet Cavalier in November.

The title to my finally-all-paid-for American made car sits on my desk.

Along with a lovely thank you note from GMAC (I always paid promptly) and a reimbursement check (it seems, in my enthusiasm to honor my debt to General Motors, I overpaid).

It's a right fancy looking check, too.

Lots of flourishes and curlicues, a big GMAC logo and not one, but two authorized signatures.

Impressive.

I'm worth it, being so loyal to General Motors for forty years and all. The amount of my refund? It's right there on the line: Pay Exactly *******0* Dollars and *57* Cents.

That's right. GMAC sent me a check for fifty-seven cents. They appreciate me.

They want to be of further service to this valued customer.

But they took my dealership.

They took my mechanic, one of several who'd taken very good care of my cars (and me) for decades.

Some overpaid fat cat in Detroit decided that my town, which has had a Chevy dealership for decades, no longer merited such a weensy one. After all, times are hard for GM.

Yes, We Did

We've had a Chevy dealership here for as long as I can remember. Longer. Local lore has it that Hursey Chevrolet, right here in Pageland, is where General George Patton replaced his own broken vehicle during WWII.

I'm as mad as any short-changed, hot flash suffering menopausal woman can possibly be.

I'm sending that 57 cent check right back to GM. And I'm taping 2 (two) shiny new pennies to the letter I'll be sending along with it. I want it clear I'm giving someone up there my two cents' worth. For the sake of my sanity — and the auto industry bail-out.

The letter (and the check, which cost more to cut and send than it was worth) will be going directly to the chief source of all my woes: Mr. G. Richard Wagoner. He's been GM's overpaid fat cat CEO since 2003. Long enough, it appears, to have finished off the job of running the General Motors Corporation right into the ground.

The UAW, he'll tell me is the real culprit in GM's financial woes.

Those assembly line guys, with their big, ugly union, have been making as much as thirty-something bucks an hour. And they've been turning out substandard autos to boot.

But they aren't the ones who designed the cars nobody wanted anymore.

They're not the ones who opted out of producing fuel efficient autos when we needed them.

They're not the ones who cut corners with cheaper and cheaper parts which GM knew were flawed when the vehicles rolled off the assembly line.

All they did was assemble what Wagoner and his ilk

deemed was "good enough" for America.

And what made the most profit for the fat cats.

Mr. Wagoner — or Richie Rich, as we call him at our house — made $10,191,153 in salary and perks in 2006.

Over ten million dollars for a single year.

When the proverbial horse puckey hit the fan in 2008 — with Richie begging for a bail-out — did he sacrifice for the company he loves?

Nah.

As GM tanked in calendar year 2007, Ole Richie took home $14,451,914 in salary and perks.

Fourteen million dollars and change. That's nearly four million more than he made in '06.

I think we've had about enough.

Enough corporate greed and the corporate looting of America.

The Wagoners of the big business world insist they're worth the mass-millions they skim off company profits.

Even when they're laying off "real Americans" by the thousands.

Or robbing me of my mechanic.

They work long hours, they say, and their expertise is critical to the nation. The same could be said for the President of the United States.

His salary and perks for a calendar year?

Factoring in $169,000 for an expense account, travel and entertainment, the POTUS makes $569,000 annually.

That's just over half a million dollars.

Maybe the president doesn't work as hard as an auto exec.

Maybe his expertise isn't worth the big bucks. I've been no fan of George W.'s expertise. He's done plenty of damage in eight years.

But he never took my mechanic when I needed one.

Lance, Inc.: The Heart of American Business
Jan. 6, 2009

Sometimes, at Christmas, It's a Wonderful Life. Somewhere the bell of conscience and character rings and a few corporate angels get their wings.

In Ashland, Ohio, the bankrupt Archway cookie factory closed without warning in early October. Nearly 300 employees were left jobless. Right before the holiday season. In the middle of a recession. Times are hard. For those former Archway employees, some of whom had spent as many as 30 years on the job, times were about to get harder. Much harder.

Early December brought Ashland, Ohio a Christmas surprise. Charlotte, North Carolina's Lance, Inc. bought the shuttered Archway plant, bringing jobs, renewed hope and the sweet aroma of cookies back to the small Midwestern town. Lance began the process of rehiring former Archway employees, promising to honor seniority for all of those who came back. The cookie factory on Claremont Avenue was up and running again.

The new owners could not guarantee there would be business enough to rehire all 278 former employees but would bring them back in waves, depending upon how sales opportunities unfold in an uncertain economy.

This story is enough to warm the heart of any sentimental lover of the Christmas season. Even one like me, who has little respect for what's become of corporate America in the last twenty years. In an era marred by Golden Parachutes for CEOs who've run major companies aground, by multi-million dollar bonuses awarded top echelon execs for laying off thousands of hardworking Americans, by the shameless outsourcing of jobs for corporate profit, what Lance chose to do is a breath of sweet, clean air. But there is more to the story.

While not every former employee was immediately rehired, Lance decided to make the holiday season a little brighter for every one of the 278 Archway full time employees who'd lost their jobs.

Times are hard. In the spirit of the Season of Love, Lance, Inc. gave each of them a $1,500 Visa gift card. Why would any for-profit company, in a recession, do such a thing? Lance's Vice President of Strategic Initiatives J. Mark Carter said, "… because it was the right thing to do."

Doing "the right thing" for nearly 300 ordinary, hardworking Americans cost Lance over $400,000.

You've gotta love a company like that.

And you've got to love them for the message inherent in such a generous act. Loyalty in business is a two-way street — or it should be. Too many American companies demand loyalty from their employees (and from consumers) without feeling any responsibility to return the favor. There's been precious little respect or concern from the top down. Lance offers us a model for human decency in business. If there is any heart at all left in corporate America, Lance has just indicated that the corporate body still has a pulse.

The Lance/Archway story has been a topic of inspired conversation at our home over the holidays: The "anti-big business as usual callousness;" the best of America in tough times. Our family will be doing what we can to support this kind of business ethic. We're investing in humane corporate policy. We're buying Lance.

Bad Business, Good Business and Monkey Business

Jan. 6, 2009

There's no doubt we're scraping the bottom of the bail-out barrel.

Big oil's been getting huge government subsidies for years while making record profits. That's a pre-emptive federal bail-out if ever there was one. Then we get the Fannie Maes and Freddie Macs, big banks, the Wall Street debacle; businesses which have been gambling with (and losing) our 401Ks and IRAs for profit at the very top of the food chain get their chunk of federal rescue money. The auto industry is next in line, execs flying into D.C. in corporate jet style for a handout. These guys have made millions of dollars while running the Big Three aground.

It's enough to make a hardworking, penny-pinching, bill juggling, real American lose all faith in the free market. Our savings are shrinking, our jobs are in jeopardy, our homes aren't worth what we paid for them.

Then Lance, Inc. comes along with a corporate con-science, feeling the pain of jobless Archway employees and doing something concrete to help them. We feel better. There is hope for us, and for good American business ethics, after all. As President-elect Obama has told us time and again, we are a better nation, a better people, than this. Hallelujah!

Not so fast. When I said we're scraping the bottom of the bail-out barrel, I wasn't kidding. I wasn't being hyperbolic. This is for real:

According to Hustler magazine's Larry Flynt and "Girls Gone Wild" video king Joe Francis, the porn industry is not recession proof. They're suffering the ill-effects of a bad economy.

"With all this economic misery and people losing all that money," Flynt says, "sex is the farthest thing from their mind. People are too depressed to be sexually active."

"Congress seems willing to help shore up our nation's most important businesses," Francis adds. "We feel we deserve the same consideration."

Flynt and Francis say they'd like the porn industry to get their fair share of the big bail-out. They'd like $5 billion in federal shoring-up-business-aid, please. Real Americans work in this industry, too, ya know. Filmmakers, actors, writers, technicians, distributors, retailers... They have some stats to back them up. The U.S. porn industry made about $12 billion (that we know of) in 2007, but video sales, they say, have been falling by 15% annually since 2005. And they have some mighty tough competition. There are internet websites, porn professionals complain, just giving away their product willy-nilly. Free of charge. To just anybody.

Imagine how GM, Ford and Chrysler would suffer if there were websites giving free rides to just anybody.

The truth is that this is more a Flynt/Francis publicity stunt than an actual appeal for our tax dollars. But there's a lesson in here somewhere about the looting of America by big business whose motives are suspect and whose reluctance to be held fully (and openly) accountable for every bail-out dollar is, well, pornographic. Any business can make the valid claim that real people will lose their jobs and everything they own without a piece of the bail-out pie.

Don't lose any sleep over the porn industry. They'll come out of the recession just fine. According to one porn shop retailer, video rentals are way up since the economy tanked. A nasty little X-rated video is cheaper than a girlfriend.

The Mindless, Starry-eyed Cult of Barack Obama

Jan. 20, 2008

There isn't one. There never was.

In the political parlance of President-elect Obama's competitors for the Oval Office, both Democratic and Republican, the notion of a new American cultism was born. The enormous grass-roots campaign for change, inspired by Barack Obama's vision for the nation, was quickly (and rather cynically) tweaked by his opponents, redefined as a gaggle of glassy-eyed geese who could not think for themselves.

It's hard to blame the opposition for their attempt to discount the importance of over two million American voters who connected online to support a candidate they believed in. Thousands and thousands of them became activists. They wrote, they manned phone banks, they canvassed, they set up tables at malls and public events to register voters. They were tireless. They were doggedly determined to change the face of American policy and politics.

But they never marched in lock-step on every issue.

I plugged into My.BarackObama.com at its inception in February of 2007. I liked the candidate. Despite my age, which found me knocking on the Senior Citizens' door, I still held to an idealistic vision of what the best of America was all about. The generosity. The genius of smart diplomacy. The each-one-reach-one ideal of lifting "The least of these…" out of poverty and despair. Tolerance. The democracy which honored disparate points of view rather than labeling them "unAmerican." Obama gave voice to those ideals.

But the compelling reason for signing on to the vast Obama network was, for me, a pragmatic exercise. This campaign was an historic one, by every imaginable standard. I wanted to see it unfold from the inside. I wanted to record it, write about it — for good or for ill; the good, the bad and the ugly. All of it. I thought I might vote for Candidate Obama, but in the early part of that February, I wasn't absolutely committed to any individual. I was committed to positive, progressive change.

Over the 22 months of the primary and campaign season — and since — I've been an observant member of large groups: the Obama Rapid Response Team, Writers for Obama, News Junkies for Obama, Moms for Obama and others too numerous to mention. I joined or monitored groups from other states: Texas, Illinois, Florida, California, Missouri, Pennsylvania. At the height of the campaign I was getting as many as a thousand e-mail messages a day. Policy position statements, pleas for action, alerts about misinformation in the media. It was both exhilarating and exhausting.

From day one, these ardent supporters of Barack Obama disagreed about policy. They argued, often with passion and eloquence, prioritizing gay rights, war and economic policy, single payer vs. a lesser version of universal healthcare. There were folks who leaned a little to the right, Independents, slightly-left-of-center folks and committed liberals.

They fought over individual issues and over decisions made by the Obama campaign staff.

They're still arguing. Some are furious that Obama chose very conservative evangelical Pastor Rick Warren to deliver the inaugural invocation. Some are outraged that cabinet picks have not been purely left-wing. Others fret, angry that Obama has not rushed to the bully pulpit demanding that Bush, Cheney, Rumsfeld et al., be prosecuted for abuse of office and/or war crimes. And for each of these arguments, there is an equally passionate response from among them for the other side of that argument.

There is no hypnotic hold on the vast Obama network. They are groups as diverse as are the individual voters among them. What they do share, without a doubt, is the core belief that this man is the right president for this time in American history.

Even when they disagree with some of the choices he makes.

The Inauguration of Hope, of Promise (and of an American Dream)

Jan. 27, 2009

"It is nearly impossible, in this small space, to cobble together the proper collection of nouns, verbs and conjunctions that might do justice to the scene at noon Tuesday at the slave-built Capitol, when Barack Obama places his left hand on the Great Emancipator's Bible, raises his right hand and recites the identical presidential oath that George Washington took 220 years ago...

"...let the word go forth that on this day and in this place we come together to celebrate the fact that the dream lives on and the hope is still alive. And, although it took a lot longer than it should have, on this day, January 20, 2009, America kept its promise."

— Jim Mills, The Hill

Jim Mills is no left-wing ideologue. He's a veteran D.C. journalist who's spent long years covering Capitol Hill. He's nothing if not a straight-shooter. And, if I had to speculate as to his political preferences, I'd tell you I suspect he's a centrist who leans just a tad toward traditional conservatism. Finding his remarkable post for The Hill in my inbox, early in the morning on Inauguration Day, underscored both the historical and emotional import of this chapter in the American story.

Hours later a message came from Carrie Rowell, a long-time friend and former editor of the Pageland Journal, whose career path took her to Capitol Hill to work in S.C. Congressman Butler Derrick's office over 20 years ago. She wrote: "...imagine what it must feel like to be African American and witness [this]."

It's not easy, as a white American who's never borne the yokes of slavery or racism or discrimination, to go there. But reading Jim's words and Carrie's moved me to try. It is an exercise all of us should undertake, an exercise — if we're honest — which would benefit every American.

According to the U.S. Census Bureau there are 300 million American citizens. Of that 300 million, 12.9% are African American. That's how vast the gap is between the number of white and black citizens of this nation. Now, let's play the game:

Imagine our being the 12.9% white minority in an all-black, rich, powerful country. Imagine being here only because at some time — six, seven, eight or more generations ago — our ancestors were kidnapped from their homelands, from their families and everything they knew and loved, were brought to this country to serve as a sub-human labor force. After the initial cost to powerful black slave owners (the price-per-new-slave), all of our beloved babies and grandbabies were born into free-labor slavery, abused, tortured, forced into submission as their own parents, siblings, wives, husbands and children were sold away from them.

Then, after "freedom," we were denied basic human rights. The right to live where we wanted to live, eat where we wanted to eat, use public restrooms and water fountains, attend the best schools. Despite the fact that we had served our country in every war and faithfully paid our taxes, we were denied equal rights, equal treatment under the law. We were denied the right to vote. Imagine that, when we stood tall or peacefully resisted the oppression of racism, we were abused by the authorities, condemned by the majority, threatened, lynched, burned alive, wrapped in chains and thrown in Southern rivers to drown.

YES, WE DID

Imagine that we knew this truth: Terrorism on American soil is not solely a 21st century import from the Middle East. It was born here, in our own land, as a response to our human desire to be free and equal.

Imagine political parties, after we won the vote, using us for the numbers they needed at the polls while turning a blind eye to our suffering and telling us to be patient. Be patient. Be patient.

Now imagine Inauguration Day 2009. The day we know we are fully, integrally true partners this democracy when one of our own becomes the leader of the free world. On his own terms. And because the "other-colored" majority was moved by ideals and issues and by conscience to vote for him. To vote for change — and more. This day is a sea-change; a day of hope, of a dream fulfilled. A promise kept.

That's how I imagine African Americans felt on January 20th. Acknowledged. Valued. Real. Visible. Central to the best nature and best interests of their country; ready to dig deep, to help renew and heal a suffering nation.

Inauguration Day was not about race; neither was Campaign 2008. But rising above the racial divide surely redefines America in powerfully positive terms. No matter the color of our skin, no matter our minority or majority status, we know there is a word for the renewed spirit of this country. It is greater than liberal or conservative, deeper than patriotic in a way that embraces all Americans, richer than the pride that comes with winning.

There is a word —

The word for the way we felt on Inauguration Day was *joy*.

Epilogue

American Pie:
Civil Discourse, Bipartisanship and the Stimulus Bill: A Bitter Taste of Things to Come?

From an interview with Felix Rohatyn in The New York Times Magazine, February 8, 2009:

NYT: "We should point out that you're the investment banker credited with solving New York's fiscal woes in 1975 and saving the city from bankruptcy."

Rohatyn: "The New York City crisis was less dangerous than the current situation. Maybe, for the first time in history, the U.S. is faced with doubts about its destiny. In less than 50 years, we have gone from the American Century to the American Crisis."

NYT: "What do you make of President Obama's $800-billion-plus stimulus package?"

Rohatyn: "I totally support Obama, but I would argue in favor of a greater amount of infrastructure investment and probably fewer tax cuts ..."

So, who is this guy? What makes him a qualified judge of an "invest federal money in an American economic recovery" bill the GOP condemns as "Democrat big spending" and a disaster in the making? In 1975, when New York City was three weeks from bankruptcy, Rohatyn was recruited to solve their looming economic collapse. He was a successful banker/financier back in the good old "There are regulations in place to keep your greed from overwhelming your business sense" days. Rohatyn became a central player in the plan to save his city. The plan, with a combination of restructuring, private and federal funding, worked. To make it work, all parties had to be on board. The city had to come first. Friction between factions, politics and personalities had to be set aside.

About that effort, Rohatyn says: "What we needed was for people who had never really worked together before — and some who had antagonistic relationships — to cooperate, quickly and on hugely difficult political and economic matters. [What] saved New York [was] sound financial structure, shared sacrifice and a remarkable collaboration among adversaries."

President Barack Obama has long spoken to the need for bipartisan cooperation to trump petty politics on the Hill. You know, the need to stifle that nasty, good vs. evil game-playing Congress is loath to give up. Ideologue partisans operate with an eye on the next election, which party can one-up the other power plays, and winning at any cost. Better to be the reigning power in full control of a pile of smoking rubble than a team player for a higher purpose that might get the other party re-elected in 2010 or 2012.

We have managed, in true, snarling, partisan American fashion, to go from the historic highs of Barack Obama's civil, inclusive transition, his honoring rival John McCain at a pre-inauguration dinner, his meeting with (and answering to) members of the conservative press (and conservative legislators) and his accommodating GOPolicy by including $288 billion in tax cuts in the stimulus bill … to a recycling of the same old vitriolic poison in Congress.

The GOP definition of bipartisan? My way or the highway! Maybe you won, but how dare you allow Democrats to author this bill? And, despite the fact that the Dubya and GOP-led tax cuts in the last eight years — the ones that were going to ensure prosperity for everyone — failed utterly to benefit anyone other than the few at the top of the economic food chain, most Republicans had only one serious contribution to make in the authoring of a stimulus package: Tax cuts and more tax cuts. More of the same disastrous financial policy that helped get us in the mess we're in now.

Okay. That's their best solution. There is something, always, to be said for the loyal opposition. But when that opposition sinks to more of the same old ugly speechifying and obstructionism, then bipartisanship is not the goal of the opposition. Loyal or otherwise.

Rep. Pete Sessions (R-TX), the chairman of the National Republican Congressional Committee, openly uses a Taliban analogy to encourage a do-or-die GOP opposition: "[The Taliban] went about systematically understanding how to disrupt and change a person's entire processes ... I simply said there is a model out there for insurgency ... [Republicans] need to get over the idea that they're participating in legislation and ought to start thinking of themselves as an insurgency instead."

Well, that's certainly a model approach to statesmanship in the best interests of this nation.

South Carolina's Lindsey Graham throws a hissy fit on the Senate floor, waving his copy of the stimulus bill in the air and wailing that, because he wasn't among the bipartisan group reviewing the bill and finding areas of compromise, he feels "left out." And, since he didn't feel appropriately included in the Republican/Democratic Group Compromise Party, the bill, he snapped, "stinks." America, he hissed, "is screwed." Such soaring rhetoric for the ages.

The Palmetto State's Jim DeMint, a paragon of civility, says the stimulus bill is "…one of the worst bills in the history of Congress." He offers an alternative. His solution? All tax cuts. George W. Economics Redux. Or else.

John McCain raves on about "generational theft" while the Iraq War he loves and "knows how to win" cost the taxpayer $12.5 billion a month in 2008 alone. The estimated $3 trillion we will owe for this war, at the end of the day, never created jobs in this country, never rebuilt a road or a bridge, never improved a school building or our tragically lacking educational opportunities in math and the sciences, never got us access to decent health care or saved a home or stopped the outsourcing of our jobs or cured the ills of U.S. businesses now closing their doors and declaring bankruptcy. Which begs the question: Who stole what from generations to come? And why? When it suits their purposes, the GOP can always quote Dick Cheney, who said, "Reagan proved that deficits don't matter." Generational debt is dandy. As long as it's Republican debt.

There is little evidence of any effort on the part of the Republican minority to meet President Obama even a quarter of the way here. We are left with what appears to be a hardening, far-right coalition with a mandated GOP group-think:

"We do not lose gracefully. Karl Rove promised us a 'permanent Republican majority' and we mean to have it. We must seize back the throne. To do this, we must destroy any alternative to uber-conservatism (the only base we have left). That means we take down this president by any means necessary. We block or neuter any notion he has or legislation he wants for stemming the tide of (our GOP-sponsored) recession or of effecting any real change in Washington or — God forbid — of achieving even a modicum of civil discourse, of rational bipartisan cooperation, even when the survival of this nation is at stake. Will American citizens suffer? Sure. But war is hell and they're only collateral damage in the partisan political war we have to win. If we can ensure that Obama fails (even if the country fails with him) it will have been worth the effort. We will have won the greater war. Four years from now we'll not only have regained control of Congress, we'll have taken back the White House as well.

"No progress for Barack Obama; not even progress which might salvage this nation.

"By the way — absent any leadership within party ranks, Rush Limbaugh will serve to lead us on this; he'll lead the way in getting out the 'Obama is a crazed socialist out to destroy America" meme. He'll deliver us our mindless angry masses as soon as he gets them all fired up again."

To recycle the favorite old GOP meme (as it applies to the newly reconstituted divide in Washington): This right wing group-think is lethally divisive while we are fighting two wars in the Middle East and an economic one at home. It is unpatriotic. It's unAmerican. It's a clear and present danger to our national security; all done for politics-as-usual and a deluded, grand strategy power grab.

In the face of this new version of the same old scorched-earth political warfare, President Obama remains steadily calm, unremittingly optimistic and intent on continuing his effort to bridge the Great D.C. Divide. His personal infrastructure project — that bridge — will likely be one he must build single-handedly. And the folks on the other side of the chasm don't seem to be concerned about bridges. They prefer their wars. Both foreign and domestic.

Acknowledgements

Always and in all ways there is a network involved in the writing process. They are the ones who ante up, who feed the kitty, and they deserve all the thanks any writer can give them:

My family, especially my husband of 41 years, who have had to live with George W. & Co. in the house for so long a time. I'm none too good at separating my working life from my home life. In the run-up to election '08, to one degree or another, every candidate for the Republican and Democratic nominations moved in with us, as well. It got mighty crowded around here. Those closest to me deserve credit for tolerating my passion for politics and my compulsion to write about the impact of public policy on the ordinary American. They've tolerated my absorption with Campaign 2008 and my tendency to ignore them all completely for twenty-two months (except for those daily lapses when I demanded they drop everything to read what I was writing.)

The folks online with www.My.BarackObama.com, a vast, well-informed, passionate group of Americans who became the nucleus of a stellar grassroots movement. I am especially indebted to Obama Rapid Response, Writers for Obama, News Junkies for Obama, Women for Obama and Moms for Obama. They shared their stories, their insight, their knowledge, their singular areas of expertise. Contrary to the MSM-fed misconception, Obama supporters were not (and are not) blind followers of a charismatic candidate. Their online discussions/debates on every issue were invaluable. I learned much and am gratified to have found new friends among them.

The Huffington Post, one of the leading online news sources, deserves both gratitude and praise for their bold foray into Hunter Thompson-style journalism during Campaign 2008. Huff gave voice, on the page, to writers/journalists whose creds did not merit space in the candidates' traveling show. OffThe-Bus was courageous and innovative. My thanks to Jay Rosen, Marc Cooper, Amanda Michel, Neil Nagraj and John Tomasic for creating and maintaining a terrific environment for the writer.

In this case, the last is not the least. Far from it. Wallace Mc-Bride has been my editor at the Progressive Journal for more than three years. He has given me total freedom to write what I wanted to write — the way I wanted to write it. In a deeply conservative Southern market this takes some serious fortitude. He has been first in the line of fire when my liberal outrage on the Op-Ed page incited equal outrage from conservative readers. If you ask me, he deserves a medal for grace under pressure. Wallace is the impetus behind this book. It was his idea, he's the editor and the cover design — which moved me to tears — is entirely his creation. His enthusiasm for this project, even in the face of a small mountain of columns and posts, has made a daunting task much easier for the writer. Oh. Maybe it's more than just his enthusiasm that's made this process easy for me. Maybe it's because he's the one doing most of the work here.

Thank you all.

— *Linda*

About the Author

Linda Hansen is a 61-year-old journalist, living and working in South Carolina, where she serves as the rather lonely voice of the Left. Writing political commentary from that POV seldom gets her invited to the annual pig pickin' but she is happy to report that, even in the Heart of Dixie, the political mood is beginning to change. She hasn't been called an "unAmerican Godless heathen who hates our troops" in months.

She attended both Columbia College and the University of South Carolina but never succeeded in finishing her degree (some silly criteria about having to sit through any classes other than every available writing class). Besides, she was busy having babies, keeping house and tending to a very Southern husband.

Linda is a columnist for The Progressive Journal, a weekly newspaper in Pageland, S.C. During Campaign 2008 she was an Op-Ed contributor to Barack the Youth Vote and Rock With Barack, despite her advanced age. She also served as a regular contributor to the Huffington Post for campaign season 2007-2008.

Neocons infuriate her. So does the notion that all Southerners, South Carolinians in particular, are dead from the neck up. She blames the MSM proclivity to tap the redneck witness pool for opinions. She hopes to change that dynamic.